Blend-It Books

Houghton Mifflin Harcourt

Houghton Mifflin Harcourt

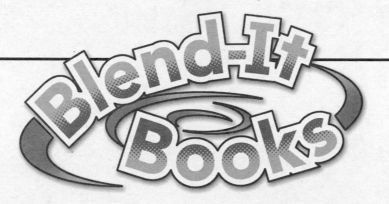

What is the purpose of the **Blend-It Books**?

The **Blend-It Books** provide engaging, highly decodable texts (75% or more decodable words) for independent blending and reading practice, to promote decoding automaticity and fluency. For each sound-spelling taught in Grade 1 of the Houghton Mifflin Harcourt *Journeys* program, two four-page books feature the skill within connected text. For sounds with multiple spellings, two sound-spellings are sometimes paired in the same books for comparison. For example, there are two books for the short *o* sound. For the long *o* sound, there are two books for the *o* and *o_e* spellings, and two more books for the *ow* and *oa* spellings taught at this grade.

In addition, the **Blend-It Books** provide practice for key structural analysis skills. For example, for the *-ed* inflection there are two books for *each* pronunciation: /ĕd/, /d/, and /t/. Later in the year, two more books feature *-ed*, this time using words with spelling changes (dropped final *e*, doubled final consonant) before the inflection.

The text for each book also includes a smaller number (25% or fewer) of high-frequency words taught previously in *Journeys*. Those words were drawn from research studies on the most commonly used words in English, and words were chosen only when they received high scores on multiple lists.

For reference, the back of each book lists all the decodable words, decoding skills, and high-frequency words featured in that selection. A summary list inside the back cover shows all the decoding skills and high-frequency words taught to date in *Journeys*.

How are the **Blend-It Books** organized?

The **Blend-It Books** are numbered sequentially and reflect the order of the decoding skills taught in each unit of *Journeys*. The chart on the following pages lists all the books for Grade 1.
Volume 1: Books 1–112 for the skills in Units 1–3
Volume 2: Books 113–200 for the skills in Units 4–6

When do I use the **Blend-It Books**?

• Users of *Journeys* will find references to corresponding **Blend-It Books** in the phonics lessons in the Teacher's Editions.
• The books are also an excellent resource any time a child needs extra practice reading words with a specific sound/spelling.

How can I use **Blend-It Books** to meet specific needs?

• Help children differentiate between two or more similar sound/spellings by reading and comparing books that feature them.
• Have English learners focus on sounds and spellings they find difficult in English by reading books chorally with an adult.
• Informally assess children's understanding of a new skill by having them read a book aloud to you.

What are the options for setting up the **Blend-It Books**?

• The books are available as blackline masters for copying, or in digital files that can be read onscreen or downloaded.
• Provide children with the books only as they need them, or set up the numbered books for children to access on their own all year.
• Make copies for children to read and color in class or take home, or prepare a laminated set for use at school.
• Set up a chart for children to track their own progress as they read.

This chart lists all the Grade 1 **Blend-It Books** (both volumes) and identifies books that correspond to the *Journeys* Sound/Spelling Cards.

Book	Skill	Sound/Spelling Cards	Book	Skill	Sound/Spelling Cards
Book 1	*m, s, t, c,* short *a*	Mouse, Seal, Tiger, Cat, Apple	Book 30	inflection *-s*	
Book 2	*m, s, t, c,* short *a*	Mouse, Seal, Tiger, Cat, Apple	Book 31	short *e*	Elephant
			Book 32	short *e*	Elephant
Book 3	consonant *n*	Noodles	Book 33	consonant *y*	Yo-yo
Book 4	consonant *n*	Noodles	Book 34	consonant *y*	Yo-yo
Book 5	consonant *d*	Duck	Book 35	consonant *w*	Worm
Book 6	consonant *d*	Duck	Book 36	consonant *w*	Worm
Book 7	consonant *p*	Pig	Book 37	consonant *k*	Kangaroo
Book 8	consonant *p*	Pig	Book 38	consonant *k*	Kangaroo
Book 9	consonant *f*	Fish	Book 39	consonant *v*	Volcano
Book 10	consonant *f*	Fish	Book 40	consonant *v*	Volcano
Book 11	short *i*	Igloo	Book 41	consonant *j*	Jump
Book 12	short *i*	Igloo	Book 42	consonant *j*	Jump
Book 13	consonant *r*	Rooster	Book 43	short *u*	Umbrella
Book 14	consonant *r*	Rooster	Book 44	short *u*	Umbrella
Book 15	consonant *h*	Horse	Book 45	/kw/ spelled *qu*	Queen
Book 16	consonant *h*	Horse	Book 46	/kw/ spelled *qu*	Queen
Book 17	/z/ spelled *s*	Zebra	Book 47	consonant *z*	Zebra
Book 18	/z/ spelled *s*	Zebra	Book 48	consonant *z*	Zebra
Book 19	consonant *b*	Bear	Book 49	final consonants *ll*	Lion
Book 20	consonant *b*	Bear	Book 50	final consonants *ll*	Lion
Book 21	consonant *g*	Goose	Book 51	final consonants *ss*	Seal
Book 22	consonant *g*	Goose	Book 52	final consonants *ss*	Seal
Book 23	short *o*	Ostrich	Book 53	consonants *ck*	Kangaroo
Book 24	short *o*	Ostrich	Book 54	consonants *ck*	Kangaroo
Book 25	consonant *l*	Lion	Book 55	final consonants *ff*	Fish
Book 26	consonant *l*	Lion	Book 56	final consonants *ff*	Fish
Book 27	consonant *x*	Fox	Book 57	final consonants *zz*	Zebra
Book 28	consonant *x*	Fox	Book 58	final consonants *zz*	Zebra
Book 29	inflection *-s*		Book 59	blends with *r*	
			Book 60	blends with *r*	

Book	Skill	Sound/Spelling Cards
Book 61	blends with *l*	
Book 62	blends with *l*	
Book 63	blends with *s*	
Book 64	blends with *s*	
Book 65	final blend *mp*	
Book 66	final blend *mp*	
Book 67	final blend *nt*	
Book 68	final blend *nt*	
Book 69	final blend *nd*	
Book 70	final blend *nd*	
Book 71	final blend *st*	
Book 72	final blend *st*	
Book 73	digraph *th*	Thumb
Book 74	digraph *th*	Thumb
Book 75	ending -*s*	
Book 76	ending -*s*	
Book 77	ending -*es*	
Book 78	ending -*es*	
Book 79	ending -*ed* /ĕd/	
Book 80	ending -*ed* /ĕd/	
Book 81	ending -*ed* /d/	Duck
Book 82	ending -*ed* /d/	Duck
Book 83	ending -*ed* /t/	Tiger
Book 84	ending -*ed* /t/	Tiger
Book 85	ending -*ing*	
Book 86	ending -*ing*	
Book 87	digraphs *ch, tch*	Chick
Book 88	digraphs *ch, tch*	Chick
Book 89	possessives with '*s*	
Book 90	possessives with '*s*	

Book	Skill	Sound/Spelling Cards
Book 91	digraph *sh*	Sheep
Book 92	digraph *sh*	Sheep
Book 93	digraph *wh*	Whale
Book 94	digraph *wh*	Whale
Book 95	digraph *ph*	Fish
Book 96	digraph *ph*	Fish
Book 97	contractions '*s, n't*	
Book 98	contractions '*s, n't*	
Book 99	long *a* (CVC*e*)	Acorn
Book 100	long *a* (CVC*e*)	Acorn
Book 101	soft *c* /s/	Seal
Book 102	soft *c* /s/	Seal
Book 103	/j/ spelled *g, dge*	Jump
Book 104	/j/ spelled *g, dge*	Jump
Book 105	long *i* (CVC*e*)	Ice Cream
Book 106	long *i* (CVC*e*)	Ice Cream
Book 107	digraphs *kn, gn*	Noodles
Book 108	digraphs *kn, gn*	Noodles
Book 109	digraph *wr*	Rooster
Book 110	digraph *wr*	Rooster
Book 111	digraph *mb*	Mouse
Book 112	digraph *mb*	Mouse
Book 113	long o (CV, CVC*e*)	Ocean
Book 114	long o (CV, CVC*e*)	Ocean
Book 115	long *u* (CVC*e*)	Uniform
Book 116	long *u* (CVC*e*)	Uniform
Book 117	long *e* (*e, ee*)	Eagle
Book 118	long *e* (*e, ee*)	Eagle
Book 119	long *e* (CVC*e, ea*)	Eagle
Book 120	long *e* (CVC*e, ea*)	Eagle

Book	Skill	Sound/Spelling Cards
Book 121	final consonants *ng*	Ring
Book 122	final consonants *ng*	Ring
Book 123	final consonants *nk*	
Book 124	final consonants *nk*	
Book 125	long *a* (*ai, ay*)	Acorn
Book 126	long *a* (*ai, ay*)	Acorn
Book 127	contractions *'ll, 'd*	
Book 128	contractions *'ll, 'd*	
Book 129	long *o* (*ow, oa*)	Ocean
Book 130	long *o* (*ow, oa*)	Ocean
Book 131	contractions *'ve, 're*	
Book 132	contractions *'ve, 're*	
Book 133	compound words	
Book 134	compound words	
Book 135	short *e* (*ea*)	Elephant
Book 136	short *e* (*ea*)	Elephant
Book 137	*r*-controlled *ar*	Artist
Book 138	*r*-controlled *ar*	Artist
Book 139	*r*-controlled *or, ore*	Orange
Book 140	*r*-controlled *or, ore*	Orange
Book 141	*r*-controlled *er, ir*	Bird
Book 142	*r*-controlled *er, ir*	Bird
Book 143	*r*-controlled *ur*	Bird
Book 144	*r*-controlled *ur*	Bird
Book 145	/o͞o/ spelled *oo*	Cook
Book 146	/o͞o/ spelled *oo*	Cook
Book 147	closed syllables (CVC)	
Book 148	closed syllables (CVC)	

Book	Skill	Sound/Spelling Cards
Book 149	/o͞o/ spelled *ou, ew*	Moon
Book 150	/o͞o/ spelled *ou, ew*	Moon
Book 151	/o͞o/ spelled *oo*	Moon
Book 152	/o͞o/ spelled *oo*	Moon
Book 153	/o͞o/ spelled *u, ue*	Moon
Book 154	/o͞o/ spelled *u, ue*	Moon
Book 155	/o͞o/ spelled *u_e* (CVC*e*)	Moon
Book 156	/o͞o/ spelled *u_e* (CVC*e*)	Moon
Book 157	/ou/ spelled *ou, ow*	Owl
Book 158	/ou/ spelled *ou, ow*	Owl
Book 159	/oi/ spelled *oy, oi*	Boy
Book 160	/oi/ spelled *oy, oi*	Boy
Book 161	/aw/ spelled *aw, au*	Saw
Book 162	/aw/ spelled *aw, au*	Saw
Book 163	ending -*ing*: drop *e*; double consonant	
Book 164	ending -*ing*: drop *e*; double consonant	
Book 165	ending -*ed*: drop *e*; double consonant	
Book 166	ending -*ed*: drop *e*; double consonant	
Book 167	long *e* spelled *y, ie*	Eagle
Book 168	long *e* spelled *y, ie*	Eagle
Book 169	endings -*es*, -*ed*: change *y* to *i*	
Book 170	endings -*es*, -*ed*: change *y* to *i*	
Book 171	ending -*er*	
Book 172	ending -*er*	

Book	Skill	Sound/Spelling Cards
Book 173	ending -est	
Book 174	ending -est	
Book 175	ending -er: drop e; double consonant	
Book 176	ending -er: drop e; double consonant	
Book 177	ending -est: drop e; double consonant	
Book 178	ending -est: drop e; double consonant	
Book 179	endings -er, -est: change y to i	
Book 180	endings -er, -est: change y to i	
Book 181	syllable _le	Table
Book 182	syllable _le	Table
Book 183	long i spelled ie, igh	Ice Cream
Book 184	long i spelled ie, igh	Ice Cream
Book 185	long i spelled y	Ice Cream
Book 186	long i spelled y	Ice Cream
Book 187	long i spelled y: change to i, add -es, -ed	
Book 188	long i spelled y: change to i, add -es, -ed	
Book 189	suffix -ful	
Book 190	suffix -ful	

Book	Skill	Sound/Spelling Cards
Book 191	suffix -ly	
Book 192	suffix -ly	
Book 193	suffix -y	
Book 194	suffix -y	
Book 195	open syllables (CV)	
Book 196	open syllables (CV)	
Book 197	prefix un-	
Book 198	prefix un-	
Book 199	prefix re-	
Book 200	prefix re-	

Go, Jo!

DECODABLE WORDS

Target Skill: long *o* (CV, CVC*e*)

cold	go	no
Cole	Jo	so

Previously Taught Skills

big	is	lake	wet
did	it	skating	with
in	jumping	top	

SKILLS APPLIED IN WORDS IN STORY: consonants *m, s, c, t*; consonant *n*; consonant *d*; consonant *p*; short *i*; consonant *r*; consonant *b*; consonant *g* (hard); short *o*; consonant *l*; short *e*; consonant *w*; consonant *k*; consonant *j*; short *u*; ending *-ing*; long *a* (CVC*e*); long *i* (CVC*e*); long *o* (CV, CVC*e*)

HIGH-FREQUENCY WORDS

me	the
said	to

Houghton Mifflin Harcourt

long *o* (CV, CVC*e*)

BOOK 113

Go, Jo!

High-Frequency Words Taught to Date

Grade 1

a	bring	find	he	long	our	some	was
after	brown	five	hear	look	out	starts	watch
all	call	fly	help	make	over	take	water
and	carry	for	her	many	own	the	we
animal	cold	four	here	me	pictures	their	what
are	come	friend	hold	my	play	they	where
around	do	full	how	never	pull	think	who
away	does	funny	I	new	put	those	why
be	down	give	into	no	read	three	with
because	draw	go	is	now	said	to	would
been	eat	goes	know	of	see	today	write
before	every	good	light	off	she	too	yellow
bird	eyes	green	like	one	show	two	you
blue	fall	grow	little	open	sing	very	
both	far	have	live	or	small	walk	

Decoding skills taught to date: consonants *m, s, c, t*; short *a*; consonant *n*; consonant *d*; consonant *p*; consonant *f*; short *i*; consonant *r*; consonant *h*; /z/ spelled *s*; consonant *b*; consonant *g*; short *o*; consonant *l*; consonant *x*; inflection *-s*; short *e*; consonant *y*; consonant *w*; consonant *k*; consonant *v*; consonant *j*; short *u*; /kw/ spelled *qu*; consonant *z*; final consonants *ll*; final consonants *ss*; consonants *ck*; final consonants *ff*; final consonants *zz*; blends with *r*; blends with *l*; blends with *s*; final blend *mp*; final blend *nt*; final blend *nd*; final blend *st*; digraph *th*; ending *-s*; ending *-es*; ending *-ed* /ed/; ending *-ed* /d/; ending *-ed* /t/; ending *-ing*; digraphs *ch, tch*; possessives with *'s*; digraph *sh*; digraph *wh*; digraph *ph*; contractions *'s, n't*; long *a* (CVC*e*); soft *c* /s/; /j/ spelled *g, dge*; long *i* (CVC*e*); digraphs *kn, gn*; digraph *wr*; digraph *mb*; long *o* (CV, CVC*e*)

Cole said, "Jo, go jumping
with me."
Jo did go!

4

Go, Jo!

Cole said, "Jo, go to the top
with me."
"No!" said Jo. "It is so big."

1

Cole said, "Jo, go skating with me."

"No!" said Jo. "It is so cold."

Cole said, "Jo, go in the lake with me."

"No!" said Jo. "It is so wet."

Po and Rose

DECODABLE WORDS

Target Skill: **long *o* (CV, CVC*e*)**

go	Po	slope
no	Rose	

Previously Taught Skills

and	dogs	in	not	slope
can	hats	let's	sleds	

SKILLS APPLIED IN WORDS IN STORY: consonants *m, s, c, t*; short *a*; consonant *n*; consonant *d*; consonant *p*; short *i*; consonant *r*; consonant *h*; /z/ spelled *s*; consonant *g* (hard); short *o*; consonant *l*; inflection *-s*; short *e*; blends with *l*; blends with *s*; final blend *nd*; ending *-s*; contraction *'s*; long *o* (CV, CVC*e*)

HIGH-FREQUENCY WORDS

a	know	we
I	said	where

© Houghton Mifflin Harcourt Publishing Company

long *o* (CV, CVC*e*)

BOOK 114

Po and Rose

High-Frequency Words Taught to Date

Grade 1

a	bring	find	he	long	our	some	was
after	brown	five	hear	look	out	starts	watch
all	call	fly	help	make	over	take	water
and	carry	for	her	many	own	the	we
animal	cold	four	here	me	pictures	their	what
are	come	friend	hold	my	play	they	where
around	do	full	how	never	pull	think	who
away	does	funny	I	new	put	those	why
be	down	give	into	no	read	three	with
because	draw	go	is	now	said	to	would
been	eat	goes	know	of	see	today	write
before	every	good	light	off	she	too	yellow
bird	eyes	green	like	one	show	two	you
blue	fall	grow	little	open	sing	very	
both	far	have	live	or	small	walk	

Decoding skills taught to date: consonants *m, s, c, t*; short *a*; consonant *n*; consonant *d*; consonant *p*; consonant *f*; short *i*; consonant *r*; consonant *h*; /z/ spelled *s*; consonant *b*; consonant *g*; short *o*; consonant *l*; consonant *x*; inflection *-s*; short *e*; consonant *y*; consonant *w*; consonant *k*; consonant *v*; consonant *j*; short *u*; /kw/ spelled *qu*; consonant *z*; final consonants *ll*; final consonants *ss*; consonants *ck*; final consonants *ff*; final consonants *zz*; blends with *r*; blends with *l*; blends with *s*; final blend *mp*; final blend *nt*; final blend *nd*; final blend *st*; digraph *th*; ending *-s*; ending *-es*; ending *ed* /ed/; ending *-ed* /d/; ending *-ed* /t/; ending *-ing*; digraphs *ch, tch*; possessives with *'s*; digraph *sh*; digraph *wh*; digraph *ph*; contractions *'s, n't*; long *a* (CVC*e*); soft *c* /s/; /j/ spelled *g, dge*; long *i* (CVC*e*); digraphs *kn, gn*; digraph *wr*; digraph *mb*; long *o* (CV, CVC*e*)

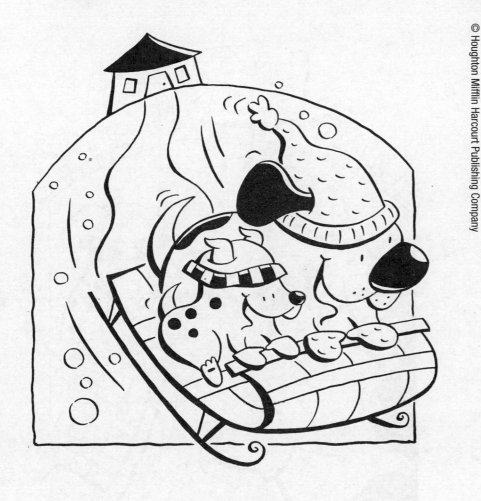

"Let's go, Po," said Rose.
"I know a slope where we can
go, go, go!"

4

Po and Rose

"Let's go, Rose!" said Po.
"No," said Rose. "No dogs!
We can not go in."

1

"Let's go, Rose!" said Po.
"No," said Rose. "No hats!
We can not go."

"Let's go, Rose!" said Po.
"No," said Rose. "No sleds!
We can not go."

I Use Huge Cubes

DECODABLE WORDS

Target Skill: long *u* (CVC*e*)

cube   huge

cubes   use

Previously Taught Skills

and	is	make	stack	up
can	like	next	stacking	will
fell	made	pile	this	with

SKILLS APPLIED IN WORDS IN STORY: consonants *m, s, c, t*; short *a*; consonant *n*; consonant *d*; consonant *p*; consonant *f*; short *i*; consonant *h*; /z/ spelled *s*; consonant *b*; consonant *l*; consonant *x*; short *e*; consonant *w*; consonant *k*; short *u*; final consonants *ll*; consonants *-ck*; blends with *s*; final blend *nd;* digraph *th*; ending *-s*; ending *-ing*; long *a* (CVC*e*); /j/ spelled *g*; long *i* (CVC*e*); long *u* (CVC*e*)

HIGH-FREQUENCY WORDS

a	I	to	what
do	my	too	

I Use Huge Cubes

High-Frequency Words Taught to Date

Grade 1

a	bring	find	he	long	our	some	was
after	brown	five	hear	look	out	starts	watch
all	call	fly	help	make	over	take	water
and	carry	for	her	many	own	the	we
animal	cold	four	here	me	pictures	their	what
are	come	friend	hold	my	play	they	where
around	do	full	how	never	pull	think	who
away	does	funny	I	new	put	those	why
be	down	give	into	no	read	three	with
because	draw	go	is	now	said	to	would
been	eat	goes	know	of	see	today	write
before	every	good	light	off	she	too	yellow
bird	eyes	green	like	one	show	two	you
blue	fall	grow	little	open	sing	very	
both	far	have	live	or	small	walk	

Decoding skills taught to date: consonants *m, s, c, t*; short *a*; consonant *n*; consonant *d*; consonant *p*; consonant *f*; short *i*; consonant *r*; consonant *h*; /z/ spelled *s*; consonant *b*; consonant *g*; short *o*; consonant *l*; consonant *x*; inflection *-s*; short *e*; consonant *y*; consonant *w*; consonant *k*; consonant *v*; consonant *j*; short *u*; /kw/ spelled *qu*; consonant *z*; final consonants *ll*; final consonants *ss*; consonants *ck*; final consonants *ff*; final consonants *zz*; blends with *r*; blends with *l*; blends with *s*; final blend *mp*; final blend *nt*; final blend *nd*; final blend *st*; digraph *th*; ending *-s*; ending *-es*; ending *ed* /ed/; ending *-ed* /d/; ending *-ed* /t/; ending *-ing*; digraphs *ch, tch*; possessives with *'s*; digraph *sh*; digraph *wh*; digraph *ph*; contractions *'s, n't*; long *a* (CVCe); soft *c* /s/; /j/ spelled *g, dge*; long *i* (CVCe); digraphs *kn, gn*; digraph *wr*; digraph *mb*; long *o* (CV, CVCe); long *u* (CVCe)

My huge, huge cube stack fell!
What will I do with my huge
cubes next?

4

I Use Huge Cubes

This is my huge cube pile.
I like stacking huge cubes.

1

I can use huge cubes to make
a huge, huge cube stack! I can
stack huge cubes up and up.

I made my cube stack too huge!

The Huge Mule

DECODABLE WORDS

Target Skill: **long *u* (CVC*e*)**

huge   mule

Previously Taught Skills

at	did	home	went
Cat's	Dog's	last	
Colt's	fit	not	

SKILLS APPLIED IN WORDS IN STORY: consonants *m, s, c, t*; short *a*; consonant *n*; consonant *d*; consonant *f*; short *i*; consonant *h*; consonant *g* (hard); short *o*; consonant *l*; short *e*; consonant *w*; final blend *nt*; final blend *st*; possessives with *'s*; /j/ spelled *g*; long *o* (CV, CVC*e*); long *u* (CVC*e*)

HIGH-FREQUENCY WORDS

Bird's   the   to

Houghton Mifflin Harcourt

long *u* (CVC*e*)

BOOK 116

The Huge Mule

High-Frequency Words Taught to Date

Grade 1

a	bring	find	he	long	our	some	was
after	brown	five	hear	look	out	starts	watch
all	call	fly	help	make	over	take	water
and	carry	for	her	many	own	the	we
animal	cold	four	here	me	pictures	their	what
are	come	friend	hold	my	play	they	where
around	do	full	how	never	pull	think	who
away	does	funny	I	new	put	those	why
be	down	give	into	no	read	three	with
because	draw	go	is	now	said	to	would
been	eat	goes	know	of	see	today	write
before	every	good	light	off	she	too	yellow
bird	eyes	green	like	one	show	two	you
blue	fall	grow	little	open	sing	very	
both	far	have	live	or	small	walk	

Decoding skills taught to date: consonants *m, s, c, t*; short *a*; consonant *n*; consonant *d*; consonant *p*; consonant *f*; short *i*; consonant *r*; consonant *h*; /z/ spelled *s*; consonant *b*; consonant *g*; short *o*, consonant *l*; consonant *x*, inflection *-s*; short *e*; consonant *y*; consonant *w*; consonant *k*; consonant *v*; consonant *j*; short *u*, /kw/ spelled *qu*; consonant *z*; final consonants *ll*; final consonants *ss*; consonants *ck*; final consonants *ff*; final consonants *zz*; blends with *r*; blends with *l*; blends with *s*; final blend *mp*; final blend *nt*; final blend *nd*; final blend *st*; digraph *th*; ending *-s*; ending *-es*; ending *ed* /ed/; ending *-ed* /d/; ending *-ed* /t/; ending *-ing*; digraphs *ch, tch*; possessives with *'s*; digraph *sh*; digraph *wh*; digraph *ph*; contractions *'s, n't*; long *a* (CVC*e*); soft *c* /s/; /j/ spelled *g, dge*; long *i* (CVC*e*); digraphs *kn, gn*; digraph *wr*; digraph *mb*; long *o* (CV, CVC*e*); long *u* (CVC*e*)

The huge mule went to
Colt's home. At last, the
huge mule did fit!

The Huge Mule

The huge mule went to Cat's
home. The huge mule did not
fit.

The huge mule went to
Dog's home. The huge mule
did not fit.

The huge mule went to
Bird's home. The huge mule
did not fit.

Meet the Animals

DECODABLE WORDS

Target Skill: long *e (e, ee)*

be	feet	Lee	she	three
cheep	green	meet	sheep	tree
deep	greens	see	sleeping	
feed	keeps	seeds	sweeping	

Previously Taught Skills

and	grass	mud	pigs
chicks	in	nice	pig's
damp	is	on	place
go	like	pig	this

SKILLS APPLIED IN WORDS IN STORY: consonants *m, s, c, t*; short *a*; consonant *n*; consonant *d*; consonant *p*; consonant *f*; short *i*; /z/ spelled *s*; consonant *g* (hard); short *o*; consonant *l*; inflection *-s*; consonant *k*; short *u*; final consonants *ss*; consonants *-ck*; blends with *r*; blends with *l*; blends with *s*; final blend *mp*; final blend *nd*; digraph *th*; ending *-s*; ending *-ing*; digraph *ch*; possessives with *'s*; digraph *sh*; long *a* (CVCe); soft *c* /s/; long *i* (CVCe); long *o* (CV); long *e (e, ee)*

HIGH-FREQUENCY WORDS

a	are	the
animals	by	to

Houghton Mifflin Harcourt.

Meet the Animals

High-Frequency Words Taught to Date

Grade 1

a	bring	eyes	grow	live	or	some	walk
about	brown	fall	have	long	our	starts	was
after	by	far	he	look	out	sure	watch
all	call	find	hear	make	over	take	water
and	car	five	help	many	own	the	we
animal	carry	fly	her	maybe	pictures	their	what
are	cold	for	here	me	play	there	where
around	come	four	hold	my	pull	they	who
away	could	friend	how	never	put	think	why
be	do	full	I	new	read	those	with
because	does	funny	into	no	said	three	would
been	don't	give	is	now	see	to	write
before	down	go	know	of	she	today	yellow
bird	draw	goes	light	off	show	too	you
blue	eat	good	like	one	sing	two	
both	every	green	little	open	small	very	

Decoding skills taught to date: consonants *m, s, c, t*; short *a*; consonant *n*; consonant *d*; consonant *p*; consonant *f*; short *i*; consonant *r*; consonant *h*; /z/ spelled *s*; consonant *b*; consonant *g*; short *o*; consonant *l*; consonant *x*; inflection *-s*; short *e*; consonant *y*; consonant *w*; consonant *k*; consonant *v*; consonant *j*; short *u*; /kw/ spelled *qu*; consonant *z*; final consonants *ll*; final consonants *ss*; consonants *ck*; final consonants *ff*; final consonants *zz*; blends with *r*; blends with *l*; blends with *s*; final blend *mp*; final blend *nt*; final blend *nd*; final blend *st*; digraph *th*; ending *-s*; ending *-es*; ending *-ed* /ed/; ending *-ed* /d/; ending *-ed* /t/; ending *-ing*; digraphs *ch, tch*; possessives with *'s*; digraph *sh*; digraph *wh*; digraph *ph*; contractions *'s, n't*; long *a* (CVC*e*); soft *c* /s/; /j/ spelled *g, dge*; long *i* (CVC*e*); digraphs *kn, gn*; digraph *wr*; digraph *mb*; long *o* (CV, CVC*e*); long *u* (CVC*e*); long *e* (*e, ee*)

The animals are sleeping.
Lee is sweeping. She keeps
the place nice.

Meet the Animals

Meet three chicks. Chicks go
"cheep, cheep, cheep!" Chicks
feed on seeds and greens.

See three sheep by a tree.
Sheep feed on green grass.

Meet a pig. Pigs like to be in mud. This pig's feet are deep in nice damp mud.

Beep, Beep, Beep!

DECODABLE WORDS

Target Skill: long *e (e, ee)*

be	green	screeched	Sneed	sweep
beep	he	she	Sneed's	we
Dee	jeep	sheep	speed	
Dee's	meet	sleeping	street	

Previously Taught Skills

came	his	late	not	up
glad	home	man	on	went
got	in	must	Sam	will

SKILLS APPLIED IN WORDS IN STORY: consonants *m, s, c, t*; short *a*; consonant *n*; consonant *d*; consonant *p*; short *i*; consonant *h*; /z/ spelled *s*; consonant *b*; consonant *g* (hard); short *o*; consonant *l*; short *e*; consonant *w*; consonant *j*; short *u*; final consonants *ll*; blends with *l*; blends with *s*; final blend *nt*; ending *-ed* /t/; ending *-ing*; possessives with *'s*; digraph *sh*; long *a* (CVCe); long *o* (CVCe); long *e* (e, ee)

HIGH-FREQUENCY WORDS

a	I	said	was
by	out	to	

Houghton Mifflin Harcourt

long *e (e, ee)*

BOOK 118

Beep, Beep, Beep!

GREEN STREET

High-Frequency Words Taught to Date

Grade 1

a	bring	eyes	grow	live	or	some	walk
about	brown	fall	have	long	our	starts	was
after	by	far	he	look	out	sure	watch
all	call	find	hear	make	over	take	water
and	car	five	help	many	own	the	we
animal	carry	fly	her	maybe	pictures	their	what
are	cold	for	here	me	play	there	where
around	come	four	hold	my	pull	they	who
away	could	friend	how	never	put	think	why
be	do	full	I	new	read	those	with
because	does	funny	into	no	said	three	would
been	don't	give	is	now	see	to	write
before	down	go	know	of	she	today	yellow
bird	draw	goes	light	off	show	too	you
blue	eat	good	like	one	sing	two	
both	every	green	little	open	small	very	

Decoding skills taught to date: consonants *m, s, c, t*; short *a*; consonant *n*; consonant *d*; consonant *p*; consonant *f*; short *i*; consonant *r*; consonant *h*; /z/ spelled *s*; consonant *b*; consonant *g*; short *o*; consonant *l*; consonant *x*; inflection *-s*; short *e*; consonant *y*; consonant *w*; consonant *k*; consonant *v*; consonant *j*; short *u*; /kw/ spelled *qu*; consonant *z*; final consonants *ll*; final consonants *ss*; consonants *ck*; final consonants *ff*; final consonants *zz*; blends with *r*; blends with *l*; blends with *s*; final blend *mp*; final blend *nt*; final blend *nd*; final blend *st*; digraph *th*; ending *-s*; ending *-es*; ending *-ed* /ed/; ending *-ed* /d/; ending *-ed* /t/; ending *-ing*; digraphs *ch, tch*; possessives with *'s*; digraph *sh*; digraph *wh*; digraph *ph*; contractions *'s, n't*; long *a* (CVC*e*); soft *c* /s/; /j/ spelled *g, dge*; long *i* (CVC*e*); digraphs *kn, gn*; digraph *wr*; digraph *mb*; long *o* (CV, CVC*e*); long *u* (CVC*e*); long *e* (*e, ee*)

Sam Sneed got to Dee Dee's home on Green Street.

Dee Dee was not glad. She said, "Sam Sneed! We must not speed on Green Street!"

Beep, Beep, Beep!

"I must meet Dee Dee! I will be late!" said Sam Sneed.

He screeched up Green Street in his jeep.

A man on Green Street came out to sweep. Sam Sneed's jeep went "Beep! Beep!"

A sheep was sleeping by Green Street. Sam Sneed's jeep went "Beep! Beep!"

Crete

DECODABLE WORDS

Target Skill: long *e* (CVC*e*, *ea*)

Crete	here	Jean's	sea	these
eat	Jean	reads	Steve	

Previously Taught Skills

and	in	lunch	past	went
Greek	is	made	so	
home	land	much	takes	
homes	liked	on	this	

SKILLS APPLIED IN WORDS IN STORY: consonants *m, s, c, t*; short *a*; consonant *n*; consonant *d*; consonant *p*; short *i*; consonant *r*; consonant *h*; /z/ spelled *s*; consonant *g* (hard); short *o*; consonant *l*; inflection -*s*; short *e*; consonant *w*; consonant *k*; consonant *j*; short *u*; blends with *r*; blends with *s*; final blend *nt*; final blend *nd;* final blend *st*; digraph *th*; ending -*s*; digraph *ch*; possessives with *'s*; long *a* (CVC*e*); long *o* (CV, CVC*e*); long *e* (ee); long *e* (CVC*e*, *ea*)

HIGH-FREQUENCY WORDS

a	are	picture	the	to
about	of	pictures	they	today

© Houghton Mifflin Harcourt Publishing Company

Crete

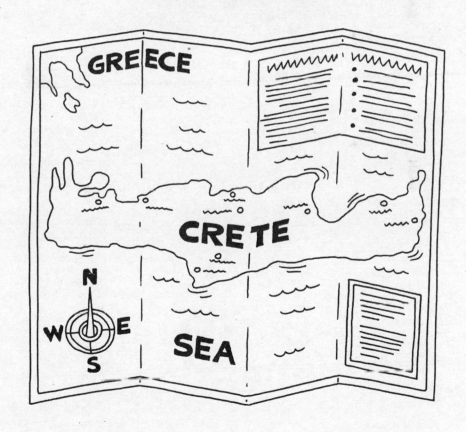

High-Frequency Words Taught to Date

Grade 1

a	bring	eyes	grow	live	or	some	walk
about	brown	fall	have	long	our	starts	was
after	by	far	he	look	out	sure	watch
all	call	find	hear	make	over	take	water
and	car	five	help	many	own	the	we
animal	carry	fly	her	maybe	pictures	their	what
are	cold	for	here	me	play	there	where
around	come	four	hold	my	pull	they	who
away	could	friend	how	never	put	think	why
be	do	full	I	new	read	those	with
because	does	funny	into	no	said	three	would
been	don't	give	is	now	see	to	write
before	down	go	know	of	she	today	yellow
bird	draw	goes	light	off	show	too	you
blue	eat	good	like	one	sing	two	
both	every	green	little	open	small	very	

Decoding skills taught to date: consonants *m, s, c, t*; short *a*; consonant *n*; consonant *d*; consonant *p*; consonant *f*; short *i*; consonant *r*; consonant *h*; /z/ spelled *s*; consonant *b*; consonant *g*; short *o*; consonant *l*; consonant *x*; inflection *-s*; short *e*; consonant *y*; consonant *w*; consonant *k*; consonant *v*; consonant *j*; short *u*; /kw/ spelled *qu*; consonant *z*; final consonants *ll*; final consonants *ss*; consonants *ck*; final consonants *ff*; final consonants *zz*; blends with *r*; blends with *l*; blends with *s*; final blend *mp*; final blend *nt*; final blend *nd*; final blend *st*; digraph *th*; ending *-s*; ending *-es*; ending *ed* /ed/; ending *-ed* /d/; ending *-ed* /t/; ending *-ing*; digraphs *ch, tch*; possessives with *'s*; digraph *sh*; digraph *wh*; digraph *ph*; contractions *'s, n't*; long *a* (CVC*e*); soft *c* /s/; /j/ spelled *g, dge*; long *i* (CVC*e*); digraphs *kn, gn*; digraph *wr*; digraph *mb*; long *o* (CV, CVC*e*); long *u* (CVC*e*); long *e* (*e, ee*); long *e* (CVC*e, ea*)

These are Steve and Jean's pictures. They liked Crete so much!

Crete

Steve and Jean went to Crete. Crete is a Greek land in the sea. Here, Steve and Jean eat lunch.

Steve reads about Crete today
and Crete in the past.
These are homes on Crete
today.

This is a home on Crete made
in the past.
Jean takes a picture of Steve.

Can Zeke Reach?

DECODABLE WORDS

Target Skill: long *e* (CVC*e*, *ea*)

reach	these	Zeke

Previously Taught Skills

can	cubes	Dad	no	them
cans	cups	ice	not	yes

SKILLS APPLIED IN WORDS IN STORY: consonants *m, s, c, t*; short *a*; consonant *n*; consonant *d*; consonant *p*; consonant *r*; /z/ spelled *s*; consonant *b*; short *o*; inflection *-s*; short *e*; consonant *y*; consonant *k*; short *u*; consonant *z*; digraph *th*; ending *-s*; digraph *ch*; soft *c* /s/; long *i* (CVC*e*); long *o* (CV); long *u* (CVC*e*); long *e* (CVC*e*, *ea*)

HIGH-FREQUENCY WORDS

I	said

© Houghton Mifflin Harcourt Publishing Company

long *e* (CVC*e*, *ea*)

BOOK 120

Can Zeke Reach?

High-Frequency Words Taught to Date

Grade 1

a	bring	eyes	grow	live	or	some	walk
about	brown	fall	have	long	our	starts	was
after	by	far	he	look	out	sure	watch
all	call	find	hear	make	over	take	water
and	car	five	help	many	own	the	we
animal	carry	fly	her	maybe	pictures	their	what
are	cold	for	here	me	play	there	where
around	come	four	hold	my	pull	they	who
away	could	friend	how	never	put	think	why
be	do	full	I	new	read	those	with
because	does	funny	into	no	said	three	would
been	don't	give	is	now	see	to	write
before	down	go	know	of	she	today	yellow
bird	draw	goes	light	off	show	too	you
blue	eat	good	like	one	sing	two	
both	every	green	little	open	small	very	

Decoding skills taught to date: consonants *m, s, c, t;* short *a;* consonant *n;* consonant *d;* consonant *p;* consonant *f;* short *i;* consonant *r;* consonant *h;* /z/ spelled *s;* consonant *b;* consonant *g;* short *o;* consonant *l;* consonant *x;* inflection *-s;* short *e;* consonant *y;* consonant *w;* consonant *k;* consonant *v;* consonant *j;* short *u;* /kw/ spelled *qu;* consonant *z;* final consonants *ll;* final consonants *ss;* consonants *ck;* final consonants *ff;* final consonants *zz;* blends with *r;* blends with *l;* blends with *s;* final blend *mp;* final blend *nt;* final blend *nd;* final blend *st;* digraph *th;* ending *-s;* ending *-es;* ending *-ed* /ed/; ending *-ed* /d/; ending *-ed* /t/; ending *-ing;* digraphs *ch, tch;* possessives with *'s;* digraph *sh;* digraph *wh;* digraph *ph;* contractions *'s, n't;* long *a* (CVC*e*); soft *c* /s/; /j/ spelled *g, dge;* long *i* (CVC*e*); digraphs *kn, gn;* digraph *wr;* digraph *mb;* long *o* (CV, CVC*e*); long *u* (CVC*e*); long *e* (*e, ee*); long *e* (CVC*e, ea*)

Dad said, "I can reach these
ice cubes, Zeke."

4

Can Zeke Reach?

Can Zeke reach these cups?
Yes, Zeke can reach them!

1

Can Zeke reach these cans?
Yes, Zeke can reach them!

Can Zeke reach these ice
cubes? No, Zeke can not
reach them.

A Big Gong

DECODABLE WORDS

Target Skill: **final consonants** *ng*

Bing	bring	King	sing
bong	gong	ring	songs

Previously Taught Skills

am	Dad	it	not	wake
bells	did	me	that	
big	is	Meg	up	

SKILLS APPLIED IN WORDS IN STORY: consonants *m, s, c, t*; short *a*; consonant *n*; consonant *d*; short *i*; consonant *r*; consonant *h*; /z/ spelled *s*; consonant *b*; consonant *g* (hard); short *o*; consonant *l*; inflection *-s*; short *e*; consonant *w*; consonant *k*; short *u*; final consonants *ll*; blends with *r*; digraph *th*; long *a* (CVCe); final consonants *ng*

HIGH-FREQUENCY WORDS

a	said
I	the

Houghton Mifflin Harcourt.

A Big Gong

High-Frequency Words Taught to Date

Grade 1

a	brown	far	hear	many	pictures	there	who
about	by	find	help	maybe	play	they	why
after	call	five	her	me	pull	think	with
all	car	fly	here	my	put	those	would
and	carry	for	hold	never	read	three	write
animal	cold	four	how	new	said	to	yellow
are	come	friend	I	no	see	today	you
around	could	full	into	now	she	too	
away	do	funny	is	of	show	two	
be	does	give	know	off	sing	very	
because	don't	go	light	one	small	walk	
been	down	goes	like	open	some	was	
before	draw	good	little	or	starts	watch	
bird	eat	green	live	our	sure	water	
blue	every	grow	long	out	take	we	
both	eyes	have	look	over	the	what	
bring	fall	he	make	own	their	where	

Decoding skills taught to date: consonants *m, s, c, t*; short *a*; consonant *n*; consonant *d*; consonant *p*; consonant *f*; short *i*; consonant *r*; consonant *h*; /z/ spelled *s*; consonant *b*; consonant *g* (hard); short *o*; consonant *l*; consonant *x*; inflection *-s*; short *e*; consonant *y*; consonant *w*; consonant *k*; consonant *v*; consonant *j*; short *u*; /kw/ spelled *qu*; consonant *z*; final consonants *ll*; final consonants *ss*; consonants *-ck*; final consonants *ff*; final consonants *zz*; blends with *r*; blends with *l*; blends with *s*; final blend *mp*; final blend *nt*; final blend *nd*; final blend *st*; digraph *th*; ending *-s*; ending *-es*; ending *-ed* /ed/; ending *-ed* /d/; ending *-ed* /t/; ending *-ing*; digraphs *ch, tch*; possessives with *'s*; digraph *sh*; digraph *wh*; digraph *ph*; contractions *'s, n't*; long *a* (CVC*e*); soft *c* /s/; /j/ spelled *g, dge*; long *i* (CVC*e*); digraphs *kn, gn*; digraph *wr*; digraph *mb*; long *o* (CV, CVC*e*); long *u* (CVC*e*); long *e* (*e, ee*); long *e* (CVC*e*, *ea*); final consonants *ng*

A Big Gong

BONG! BONG! BONG!
"I am up! I am up, Dad!"
said Meg.

"Wake up!" said King Bing.
Meg did not wake up.

"Ring bells! Sing songs!" said
King Bing. Meg did not wake up.

"That is it!" said King Bing.
"Bring me the big gong!"

Ring, Bang, Bong

DECODABLE WORDS

Target Skill: final consonants *ng*

bang	gang	gongs	Wang
bong	gong	ring	

Previously Taught Skills

chimes	drums	here	Miss	this
drum	go	is	these	we

SKILLS APPLIED IN WORDS IN STORY: consonants *m, s, c, t*; short *a*; consonant *n*; consonant *d*; short *i*; consonant *r*; consonant *h*; /z/ spelled *s*; consonant *b*; consonant *g* (hard); short *o*; inflection *-s*; consonant *w*; short *u*; final consonants *ss*; blends with *r*; digraph *th*; ending *-s*; digraph *ch*; long *i* (CVCe); long *o* (CV); long *e* (e); long *e* (CVCe); final consonants *ng*

HIGH-FREQUENCY WORDS

a	said
are	the

Ring, Bang, Bong

Houghton Mifflin Harcourt

High-Frequency Words Taught to Date

Grade 1

a	bring	eyes	grow	live	or	some	walk
about	brown	fall	have	long	our	starts	was
after	by	far	he	look	out	sure	watch
all	call	find	hear	make	over	take	water
and	car	five	help	many	own	the	we
animal	carry	fly	her	maybe	pictures	their	what
are	cold	for	here	me	play	there	where
around	come	four	hold	my	pull	they	who
away	could	friend	how	never	put	think	why
be	do	full	I	new	read	those	with
because	does	funny	into	no	said	three	would
been	don't	give	is	now	see	to	write
before	down	go	know	of	she	today	yellow
bird	draw	goes	light	off	show	too	you
blue	eat	good	like	one	sing	two	
both	every	green	little	open	small	very	

Decoding skills taught to date: consonants *m, s, c, t*; short *a*; consonant *n*; consonant *d*; consonant *p*; consonant *f*; short *i*; consonant *r*; consonant *h*; /z/ spelled *s*; consonant *b*; consonant *g*; short *o*; consonant *l*; consonant *x*; inflection -*s*; short *e*; consonant *y*; consonant *w*; consonant *k*; consonant *v*; consonant *j*; short *u*; /kw/ spelled *qu*; consonant *z*; final consonants *ll*; final consonants *ss*; consonants *ck*; final consonants *ff*; final consonants *zz*; blends with *r*; blends with *l*; blends with *s*; final blend *mp*; final blend *nt*; final blend *nd*; final blend *st*; digraph *th*; ending -*s*; ending -*es*; ending -*ed* /ed/; ending -*ed* /d/; ending -*ed* /t/; ending -*ing*; digraphs *ch, tch*; possessives with '*s*; digraph *sh*; digraph *wh*; digraph *ph*; contractions '*s, n't*; long *a* (CVC*e*); soft *c* /s/; /j/ spelled *g, dge*; long *i* (CVC*e*); digraphs *kn, gn*; digraph *wr*; digraph *mb*; long *o* (CV, CVC*e*); long *u* (CVC*e*); long *e* (*e, ee*); long *e* (CVC*e, ea*); final consonants *ng*

Ring, Bang, Bong

"Here we go, gang," said Miss Wang. "Ring the chimes! Bang the drum! Bong the gong!"

Miss Wang said, "These are chimes. Chimes ring."
Ring, ring, ring!

Miss Wang said, "This is a
drum. Drums bang."
Bang, bang, bang!

Miss Wang said, "This is a
gong. Gongs bong."
Bong, bong, bong!

Thanks, Frank!

DECODABLE WORDS

Target Skill: final consonants *nk*

blank	Hank	tank	thanks
Frank	ink	thank	trunk

Previously Taught Skills

and	gift	much	small	this
fish	got	nice	so	will
gave	left	page	then	

SKILLS APPLIED IN WORDS IN STORY: consonants *m, s, c, t*; short *a*; consonant *n*; consonant *p*; consonant *f*; short *i*; consonant *r*; consonant *h*; consonant *b*; consonant *g* (hard); short *o*; consonant *l*; short *e*; consonant *w*; consonant *k*; consonant *v*; short *u*; final consonants *ll*; blends with *r*; blends with *l*; blends with *s*; final blend *nd*; digraph *th*; ending -*s*; digraph *ch*; digraph *sh*; long *a* (CVCe); soft *c* /s/; /j/ spelled *g*; long *i* (CVCe); long *o* (CV); final consonants *nk*

HIGH-FREQUENCY WORDS

a	friend	said	you
for	I	to	your

© Houghton Mifflin Harcourt Publishing Company

Thanks, Frank!

High-Frequency Words Taught to Date

Grade 1

a	bring	eyes	grow	live	or	some	walk
about	brown	fall	have	long	our	starts	was
after	by	far	he	look	out	sure	watch
all	call	find	hear	make	over	take	water
and	car	five	help	many	own	the	we
animal	carry	fly	her	maybe	pictures	their	what
are	cold	for	here	me	play	there	where
around	come	four	hold	my	pull	they	who
away	could	friend	how	never	put	think	why
be	do	full	I	new	read	those	with
because	does	funny	into	no	said	three	would
been	don't	give	is	now	see	to	write
before	down	go	know	of	she	today	yellow
bird	draw	goes	light	off	show	too	you
blue	eat	good	like	one	sing	two	
both	every	green	little	open	small	very	

Decoding skills taught to date: consonants *m, s, c, t*; short *a*; consonant *n*; consonant *d*; consonant *p*; consonant *f*; short *i*; consonant *r*; consonant *h*; /z/ spelled *s*; consonant *b*; consonant *g*; short *o*; consonant *l*; consonant *x*; inflection *-s*; short *e*; consonant *y*; consonant *w*; consonant *k*; consonant *v*; consonant *j*; short *u*; /kw/ spelled *qu*; consonant *z*; final consonants *ll*; final consonants *ss*; consonants *ck*; final consonants *ff*; final consonants *zz*; blends with *r*; blends with *l*; blends with *s*; final blend *mp*; final blend *nt*; final blend *nd*; final blend *st*; digraph *th*; ending *-s*; ending *-es*; ending *-ed* /ed/; ending *-ed* /d/; ending *-ed* /t/; ending *-ing*; digraphs *ch, tch*; possessives with *'s*; digraph *sh*; digraph *wh*; digraph *ph*; contractions *'s, n't*; long *a* (CVC*e*); soft *c* /s/; /j/ spelled *g, dge*; long *i* (CVC*e*); digraphs *kn, gn*; digraph *wr*; digraph *mb*; long *o* (CV, CVC*e*); long *u* (CVC*e*); long *e* (*e, ee*); long *e* (CVC*e, ea*); final consonants *ng*; final consonants *nk*

Hank gave this page to Frank!

Thanks, Frank!

Frank gave Hank a nice fish tank.

"Thanks for this nice gift, Frank!" said Hank.

Frank gave Hank a small trunk.
"Thank you so much, Frank!" said
Hank.

Then Frank left. Hank got
ink and a blank page. "I will
thank Frank," said Hank.

Think, Link!

DECODABLE WORDS

Target Skill: **final consonants *nk***

Hank's	Link	tank	thinking
honk	Link's	think	

Previously Taught Skills

can	gas	he	not	went
fast	go	his	quick	
filled	got	in	rear	
from	had	need	this	

SKILLS APPLIED IN WORDS IN STORY: consonants *m, s, c, t*; short *a*; consonant *n*; consonant *d*; consonant *f*; short *i*; consonant *r*; consonant *h*; /z/ spelled *s*; consonant *g* (hard); short *o*; consonant *l*; inflection *-s*; short *e*; consonant *w*; consonant *k*; /kw/ spelled *qu*; consonants *-ck*; blends with *r*; final blend *nt*; final blend *st*; digraph *th*; ending *-s*; ending *-ed* /d/; ending *-ing*; possessives with *'s*; long *o* (CV); long *e* (*e, ee*); long *e* (*ea*); final consonants *nk*

HIGH-FREQUENCY WORDS

a	cars	said	to
car	I	the	would

Houghton Mifflin Harcourt.

Think, Link!

High-Frequency Words Taught to Date

Grade 1

a	bring	eyes	grow	live	or	some	walk
about	brown	fall	have	long	our	starts	was
after	by	far	he	look	out	sure	watch
all	call	find	hear	make	over	take	water
and	car	five	help	many	own	the	we
animal	carry	fly	her	maybe	pictures	their	what
are	cold	for	here	me	play	there	where
around	come	four	hold	my	pull	they	who
away	could	friend	how	never	put	think	why
be	do	full	I	new	read	those	with
because	does	funny	into	no	said	three	would
been	don't	give	is	now	see	to	write
before	down	go	know	of	she	today	yellow
bird	draw	goes	light	off	show	too	you
blue	eat	good	like	one	sing	two	
both	every	green	little	open	small	very	

Decoding skills taught to date: consonants *m, s, c, t*; short *a*; consonant *n*; consonant *d*; consonant *p*; consonant *f*; short *i*; consonant *r*; consonant *h*; /z/ spelled *s*; consonant *b*; consonant *g*; short *o*; consonant *l*; consonant *x*; inflection *-s*; short *e*; consonant *y*; consonant *w*; consonant *k*; consonant *v*; consonant *j*; short *u*; /kw/ spelled *qu*; consonant *z*; final consonants *ll*; final consonants *ss*; consonants *ck*; final consonants *ff*; final consonants *zz*; blends with *r*; blends with *l*; blends with *s*; final blend *mp*; final blend *nt*; final blend *nd*; final blend *st*; digraph *th*; ending *-s*; ending *-es*; ending *-ed* /ed/; ending *-ed* /d/; ending *-ed* /t/; ending *-ing*; digraphs *ch, tch*; possessives with *'s*; digraph *sh*; digraph *wh*; digraph *ph*; contractions *'s, n't*; long *a* (CVCe); soft *c* /s/; /j/ spelled *g, dge*; long *i* (CVCe); digraphs *kn, gn*; digraph *wr*; digraph *mb*; long *o* (CV, CVCe); long *u* (CVCe); long *e* (*e, ee*); long *e* (CVCe, *ea*); final consonants *ng*; final consonants *nk*

Think, Link!

Quick thinking, Link!

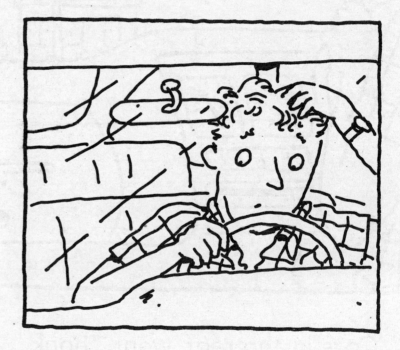

Link's car would not go. "Not this!" said Link.

4

1

Cars in the rear went "honk, honk, honk." Link had to think fast.

"I think I need gas in the tank!" said Link.

Link got a gas can from Hank's Gas. He filled his tank.

Snail's Mail Trail

DECODABLE WORDS

Target Skill: long *a* (*ai*, *ay*)

day	mail	Snail	strain	wailed
fail	Quail	Snail's	trail	way
gray	rain	stayed		

Previously Taught Skills

and	go	is	on	went
did	got	it	steep	wet
fell	had	nice	take	
glad	he	not	up	

SKILLS APPLIED IN WORDS IN STORY: consonants *m*, *s*, *c*, *t*; short *a*; consonant *n*; consonant *d*; consonant *f*; short *i*; consonant *r*; consonant *h*; /z/ spelled *s*; consonant *g* (hard); short *o*; consonant *l*; short *e*; consonant *y*; consonant *w*; consonant *k*; short *u*; /kw/ spelled *qu*; final consonants *ll*; blends with *r*; blends with *l*; blends with *s*; final blend *nt*; final blend *nd*; ending -*ed* /d/; possessives with *'s*; long *a* (CVC*e*); soft *c* /s/; long *i* (CVC*e*); long *o* (CV); long *e* (*e*, *ee*); long *a* (*ai*, *ay*)

HIGH-FREQUENCY WORDS

a	some	to
now	the	was

Houghton Mifflin Harcourt.

long *a* (*ai*, *ay*)

BOOK 125

Snail's Mail Trail

High-Frequency Words Taught to Date

Grade 1

a	by	first	he	maybe	pull	these	who
about	call	five	help	me	put	they	why
after	car	fly	here	my	read	think	with
all	carry	food	her	never	right	those	would
and	cold	for	hold	new	said	three	write
animal	come	four	how	no	see	to	yellow
are	could	friend	I	now	she	today	you
around	do	full	into	of	show	too	your
away	does	funny	is	off	sing	two	
be	don't	give	know	one	small	under	
because	down	green	light	open	some	very	
been	draw	go	like	or	sometimes	walk	
before	eat	goes	little	our	starts	was	
bird	every	good	live	out	sure	watch	
blue	eyes	ground	long	over	take	water	
both	fall	grow	look	own	their	we	
bring	far	have	make	pictures	the	what	
brown	find	hear	many	play	there	where	

Decoding skills taught to date: consonants *m*, *s*, *c*, *t*; short *a*; consonant *n*; consonant *d*; consonant *p*; consonant *f*; short *i*; consonant *r*; consonant *h*; /z/ spelled *s*; consonant *b*; consonant *g* (hard); short *o*; consonant *l*; consonant *x*; inflection -*s*; short *e*; consonant *y*; consonant *w*; consonant *k*; consonant *v*; consonant *j*; short *u*; /kw/ spelled *qu*; consonant *z*; final consonants *ll*; final consonants *ss*; consonants -*ck*; final consonants *ff*; final consonants *zz*; blends with *r*; blends with *l*; blends with *s*; final blend *mp*; final blend *nt*; final blend *nd*; final blend *st*; digraph *th*; ending -*s*; ending -*es*; ending -*ed* /ed/; ending -*ed* /d/; ending -*ed* /t/; ending -*ing*; digraphs *ch*, *tch*; possessives with '*s*; digraph *sh*; digraph *wh*; digraph *ph*; contractions '*s*, *n't*, long *a* (CVC*e*); soft *c* /s/; /j/ spelled *g*, *dge*; long *i* (CVC*e*); digraphs *kn*, *gn*; digraph *wr*; digraph *mb*; long *o* (CV, CVC*e*); long *u* (CVC*e*); long *e* (*e*, *ee*); long *e* (CVC*e*, *ea*); final consonants *ng*; final consonants *nk*; long *a* (*ai*, *ay*)

Snail stayed on the trail. He did not fail. Snail got the mail to Quail.

Snail's Mail Trail

Snail had some mail to take to Quail. He was glad it was a nice day.

Snail went up the Mail Trail. It was a steep way to go. Snail had to strain.

Rain fell on the Mail Trail. "Rain, rain, rain!" wailed Snail. "The day is now gray and wet!"

Ray's Clay Pot

DECODABLE WORDS

Target Skill: **long *a* (*ai*, *ay*)**

clay	laid	paints	play	Ray's
day	lays	plain	Ray	

Previously Taught Skills

and	is	on	side	time
as	it	pot	spins	wheel
at	last	pots	takes	will
bake	long	run	that	
he	lots	sells	then	
his	makes	shape	this	

SKILLS APPLIED IN WORDS IN STORY: consonants *m, s, t; c*; short *a*; consonant *n*; consonant *d*; consonant *p*; short *i*; consonant *r*; consonant *h*; /z/ spelled *s*; short *o*; consonant *l*; inflection –*s*; short *e*; consonant *y*; consonant *w*; short *u*; final consonants *ll*; blends with *l*; blends with *s*; final blend *nt*; final blend *nd*; final blend *st*; digraph *th*; ending –*s*; possessives with *'s*; digraph *sh*; digraph *wh*; long *a* (CVCe); long *i* (CVCe); long *e* (*e, ee*); final consonants *ng*; long *a* (*ai, ay*)

HIGH-FREQUENCY WORDS

a	animals	by	new	the
all	are	for	of	they

© Houghton Mifflin Harcourt Publishing Company

Ray's Clay Pot

High-Frequency Words Taught to Date

Grade 1

a	by	first	he	maybe	pull	these	who
about	call	five	help	me	put	they	why
after	car	fly	her	my	read	think	with
all	carry	food	here	never	right	those	would
and	cold	for	hold	new	said	three	write
animal	come	four	how	no	see	to	yellow
are	could	friend	I	now	she	today	you
around	do	full	into	of	show	too	your
away	does	funny	is	off	sing	two	
be	don't	give	know	one	small	under	
because	down	green	light	open	some	very	
been	draw	go	like	or	sometimes	walk	
before	eat	goes	little	our	starts	was	
bird	every	good	live	out	sure	watch	
blue	eyes	ground	long	over	take	water	
both	fall	grow	look	own	their	we	
bring	far	have	make	pictures	the	what	
brown	find	hear	many	play	there	where	

Decoding skills taught to date: consonants *m*, *s*, *c*, *t*; short *a*; consonant *n*; consonant *d*; consonant *p*; consonant *f*; short *i*; consonant *r*; consonant *h*; /z/ spelled *s*; consonant *b*; consonant *g* (hard); short *o*; consonant *l*; consonant *x*; inflection *-s*; short *e*; consonant *y*; consonant *w*; consonant *k*; consonant *v*; consonant *j*; short *u*; /kw/ spelled *qu*; consonant *z*; final consonants *ll*; final consonants *ss*; consonants *-ck*; final consonants *ff*; final consonants *zz*; blends with *r*; blends with *l*; blends with *s*; final blend *mp*; final blend *nt*; final blend *nd*; final blend *st*; digraph *th*; ending *-s*; ending *-es*; ending *-ed* /ed/; ending *-ed* /d/; ending *-ed* /t/; ending *-ing*; digraphs *ch*, *tch*; possessives with *'s*; digraph *sh*; digraph *wh*; digraph *ph*; contractions *'s*, *n't*; long *a* (CVC*e*); soft *c* /s/; /j/ spelled *g*, *dge*; long *i* (CVC*e*); digraphs *kn*, *gn*; digraph *wr*; digraph *mb*; long *o* (CV, CVC*e*); long *u* (CVC*e*); long *e* (*e*, *ee*); long *e* (CVC*e*, *ea*); final consonants *ng*; final consonants *nk*; long *a* (*ai*, *ay*)

At last Ray will bake his clay pot. The pots are laid side by side. They bake for a long time.

Ray sells lots of pots. Then he makes new pots.

4

Ray's Clay Pot

This is Ray. Ray makes clay pots.

1

Ray lays clay on a wheel. The clay spins as it takes shape. It is a pot!

Ray paints animals that run and play on his plain clay pot. Ray paints all day.

It's a Snake!

DECODABLE WORDS

Target Skill: contractions *'ll, 'd*

it'd	it'll	you'd	you'll

Previously Taught Skills

at	go	let's	slide	stretch
but	if	not	smell	that
can	in	run	smells	well
can't	it	see	snake	when
den	its	shed	snakes	
fast	it's	skin	so	

SKILLS APPLIED IN WORDS IN STORY: consonants *m, s, t, c*; short *a*; consonant *n*; consonant *d*; short *i*; consonant *r*; /z/ spelled *s*; consonant *b*; consonant *g* (hard); short *o*; consonant *l*; inflection *-s*; short *e*; consonant *y*; consonant *w*; consonant *k*; short *u*; final consonants *ll*; blends with *r*; blends with *l*; blends with *s*; digraph *th*; ending *-s*; digraph *tch*; possessives with *'s*; digraph *sh*; digraph *wh*; contractions *'s, n't*; long *a* (CVCe); long *i* (CVCe); long *o* (CV); long *e* (*ee*); contractions *'ll, 'd*

HIGH-FREQUENCY WORDS

a	away	look
animals	grows	you

Houghton Mifflin Harcourt

It's a Snake!

High-Frequency Words Taught to Date

Grade 1

a	brown	far	grow	long	out	starts	walk
about	by	find	have	look	over	sure	was
after	call	first	he	make	own	take	watch
all	car	five	hear	many	pictures	their	water
and	carry	fly	help	maybe	play	the	we
animal	cold	food	her	me	pull	there	what
are	come	for	here	my	put	these	where
around	could	four	hold	never	read	they	who
away	do	friend	how	new	right	think	why
be	does	full	I	no	said	those	with
because	don't	funny	into	now	see	three	would
been	down	give	is	of	she	to	write
before	draw	green	know	off	show	today	yellow
bird	eat	go	light	one	sing	too	you
blue	every	goes	like	open	small	two	your
both	eyes	good	little	or	some	under	
bring	fall	ground	live	our	sometimes	very	

Decoding skills taught to date: consonants *m, s, c, t*; short *a*; consonant *n*; consonant *d*; consonant *p*; consonant *f*; short *i*; consonant *r*; consonant *h*; /z/ spelled *s*; consonant *b*; consonant *g* (hard); short *o*; consonant *l*; consonant *x*; inflection *-s*; short *e*; consonant *y*; consonant *w*; consonant *k*; consonant *v*; consonant *j*; short *u*; /kw/ spelled *qu*; consonant *z*; final consonants *ll*; final consonants *ss*; consonants *-ck*; final consonants *ff*; final consonants *zz*; blends with *r*; blends with *l*; blends with *s*; final blend *mp*; final blend *nt*; final blend *nd*; final blend *st*; digraph *th*; ending *-s*; ending *-es*; ending *-ed* /ed/; ending *-ed* /d/; ending *-ed* /t/; ending *-ing*; digraphs *ch, tch*; possessives with *'s*; digraph *sh*; digraph *wh*; digraph *ph*; contractions *'s, n't*; long *a* (CVC*e*); soft *c* /s/; /j/ spelled *g, dge*; long *i* (CVC*e*); digraphs *kn, gn*; digraph *wr*; digraph *mb*; long *o* (CV, CVC*e*); long *u* (CVC*e*); long *e* (*e, ee*); long *e* (CVC*e*, *ea*); final consonants *ng*; final consonants *nk*; long *a* (*ai, ay*); contractions *'ll, 'd*

It's a Snake!

Let's look at a snake. You'll
see that it's in a den.

Snakes can't run. Snakes slide.
If a snake smells you, it'll slide
away. It'd go fast so you'd not
see it go.

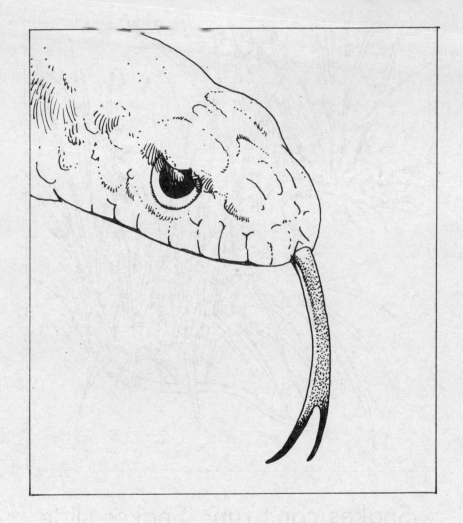

Snake skin can't stretch. When a snake grows, it'll shed its skin.

A snake can't see well, but it can smell well. It can smell animals.

2

3

Don't Walk

DECODABLE WORDS

Target Skill: contractions *'ll, 'd*

it'd	she'll	we'd	we'll	you'll

Previously Taught Skills

be	him	no	spot	us
but	home	not	take	we
can't	isn't	on	tell	when
cross	it	pet	tells	with
dogs	it's	play	that	yet
don't	like	safe	this	

SKILLS APPLIED IN WORDS IN STORY: consonants *m, s, t, c*; short *a*; consonant *n*; consonant *d*; consonant *p*; consonant *f*; short *i*; consonant *r*; consonant *h*; /z/ spelled *s*; consonant *b*; consonant *g* (hard); short *o*; consonant *l*; inflection *-s*; short *e*; consonant *y*; consonant *w*; consonant *k*; short *u*; final consonants *ll*; final consonants *ss*; blends with *r*; blends with *l*; blends with *s*; digraph *th*; ending *-s*; digraph *sh*; digraph *wh*; contractions *'s, n't*; long *a* (CVC*e*); long *i* (CVC*e*); long *o* (CV, CVC*e*); long *e* (*e*); long *a* (*ay*); contractions *'ll, 'd*

HIGH-FREQUENCY WORDS

animals	bird	our	to	walk

Don't Walk

High-Frequency Words Taught to Date

Grade 1

a	brown	far	grow	long	out	starts	walk
about	by	find	have	look	over	sure	was
after	call	first	he	make	own	take	watch
all	car	five	hear	many	pictures	their	water
and	carry	fly	help	maybe	play	the	we
animal	cold	food	her	me	pull	there	what
are	come	for	here	my	put	these	where
around	could	four	hold	never	read	they	who
away	do	friend	how	new	right	think	why
be	does	full	I	no	said	those	with
because	don't	funny	into	now	see	three	would
been	down	give	is	of	she	to	write
before	draw	green	know	off	show	today	yellow
bird	eat	go	light	one	sing	too	you
blue	every	goes	like	open	small	two	your
both	eyes	good	little	or	some	under	
bring	fall	ground	live	our	sometimes	very	

Decoding skills taught to date: consonants *m, s, c, t*; short *a*; consonant *n*; consonant *d*; consonant *p*; consonant *f*; short *i*; consonant *r*; consonant *h*; /z/ spelled *s*; consonant *b*; consonant *g* (hard); short *o*; consonant *l*; consonant *x*; inflection *-s*; short *e*; consonant *y*; consonant *w*; consonant *k*; consonant *v*; consonant *j*; short *u*; /kw/ spelled *qu*; consonant *z*; final consonants *ll*; final consonants *ss*; consonants *-ck*; final consonants *ff*; final consonants *zz*; blends with *r*; blends with *l*; blends with *s*; final blend *mp*; final blend *nt*; final blend *nd*; final blend *st*; digraph *th*; ending *-s*; ending *-es*; ending *-ed* /ed/; ending *-ed* /d/; ending *-ed* /t/; ending *-ing*; digraphs *ch, tch*; possessives with *'s*; digraph *sh*; digraph *wh*; digraph *ph*; contractions *'s, n't*; long *a* (CVC*e*); soft *c* /s/; /j/ spelled *g, dge*; long *i* (CVC*e*); digraphs *kn, gn*; digraph *wr*; digraph *mb*; long *o* (CV, CVC*e*); long *u* (CVC*e*); long *e* (*e, ee*); long *e* (CVC*e, ea*); final consonants *ng*; final consonants *nk*; long *a* (*ai, ay*); contractions *'ll, 'd*

You'll be safe to play with us
on this spot. It's our home!

Don't Walk

"Don't Walk" tells us that it
isn't safe to cross yet. She'll tell
us when it's safe.

"Don't Pet Animals" tells us that we can't pet this bird. We'd like to pet it, but it'd not be safe.

"No Dogs" tells us that dogs can't walk on this spot. We'll take him home.

A Snow Map

DECODABLE WORDS

Target Skill: long *o* (*ow, oa*)

blow	coats	shows	snow
coat	know	slow	

Previously Taught Skills

Chen	has	Lee	that	when
dog's	hills	let	then	will
fast	home	map	us	wind
get	it	on	we	

SKILLS APPLIED IN WORDS IN STORY: consonants *m, s, t, c*; short *a*; consonant *n*, consonant *d*, consonant *p*, consonant *f*; short *i*; consonant *h*; /z/ spelled *s*; consonant *g* (hard); short *o*; consonant *l*; short *e*; consonant *w*; short *u*; final consonants *ll*; consonants *-ck*; final blends *nd, st*; digraph *th*; ending *-s*; digraph *ch*; possessives with *'s*; digraph *wh*; digraph *kn*; long *o* (CV, CVCe); long *e* (*e, ee*); long *o* (*ow, oa*)

HIGH-FREQUENCY WORDS

a	now	over	the	where
fall	our	soon	too	

Houghton Mifflin Harcourt

A Snow Map

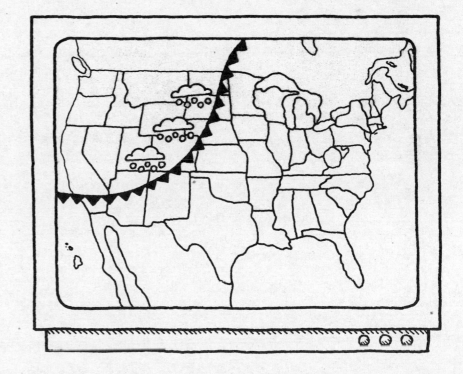

High-Frequency Words Taught to Date

Grade 1

a	by	find	have	look	own	sure	was
about	call	first	he	make	paper	take	watch
after	car	five	hear	many	pictures	talk	water
all	carry	fly	help	maybe	play	their	we
and	cold	food	her	me	pull	the	were
animal	come	for	here	my	put	there	what
are	could	four	hold	never	read	these	where
around	do	friend	how	new	right	they	who
away	does	full	I	no	said	think	why
be	done	funny	into	now	see	those	with
because	don't	give	is	of	she	three	work
been	down	great	know	off	show	to	would
before	draw	green	laugh	one	sing	today	write
bird	eat	go	light	open	small	too	yellow
blue	every	goes	like	or	some	two	you
both	eyes	good	little	our	sometimes	under	your
bring	fall	ground	live	out	soon	very	
brown	far	grow	long	over	starts	walk	

Decoding skills taught to date: consonants *m, s,* c, *t*; short *a*; consonant *n*; consonant *d*; consonant *p*; consonant *f*; short *i*; consonant *r*; consonant *h*; /z/ spelled *s*; consonant *b*; consonant *g* (hard); short *o*; consonant *l*; consonant *x*; inflection *-s*; short *e*; consonant *y*; consonant *w*; consonant *k*; consonant *v*; consonant *j*; short *u*; /kw/ spelled *qu*; consonant *z*; final consonants *ll*; final consonants *ss*; consonants *-ck*; final consonants *ff*; final consonants *zz*; blends with *r*; blends with *l*; blends with *s*; final blend *mp*; final blend *nt*; final blend *nd*; final blend *st*; digraph *th*; ending *-s*; ending *-es*; ending *-ed* /ed/; ending *-ed* /d/; ending *-ed* /t/; ending *-ing*; digraphs *ch, tch*; possessives with *'s*; digraph *sh*; digraph *wh*; digraph *ph*; contractions *'s, n't*; long *a* (CVC*e*); soft *c* /s/; /j/ spelled *g, dge*; long *i* (CVC*e*); digraphs *kn, gn*; digraph *wr*; digraph *mb*; long *o* (CV, CVC*e*); long *u* (CVC*e*); long *e* (*e, ee*); long *e* (CVC*e, ea*); final consonants *ng*; final consonants *nk*; long *a* (*ai, ay*); contractions *'ll, 'd*; long *o* (*ow, oa*)

Now we know when the snow will fall. We will get our coats. We will get our dog's coat, too. Let it snow, snow, snow!

4

A Snow Map

Lee Chen has a map that shows where it will snow.

1

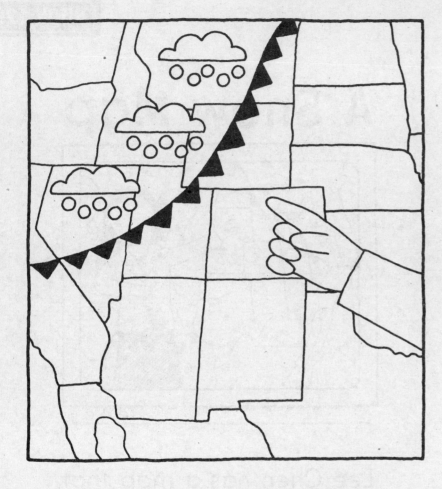

Lee Chen shows us that a slow wind will blow the snow over the hills.

© Houghton Mifflin Harcourt Publishing Company

Then Lee Chen shows us that the wind will blow fast. Soon the snow will fall on our home.

Our Goat

DECODABLE WORDS

Target Skill: long o (ow, oa)

coach	goat	own	soap
coat	oats	show	

Previously Taught Skills

and	day	in	run	tub
be	feed	is	scrub	we
big	fun	leap	set	which
brush	he	lots	then	will
can	his	prize	tricks	wins

SKILLS APPLIED IN WORDS IN STORY: consonants s, t, c, short a; consonant n; consonant d; consonant p; consonant f; short i; consonant r; consonant h; /z/ spelled s; consonant b; consonant g (hard); short o; consonant l; inflection -s; short e; consonant w; short u; consonant z; final consonants ll; consonants -ck; blends with r; blends with s; final blend nd; digraph th; ending -s; digraph ch; digraph sh; digraph wh; long i (CVCe); long e (e, ea, ee); long a (ay); long o (ow, oa)

HIGH-FREQUENCY WORDS

a	every	of	the
do	for	our	

Houghton Mifflin Harcourt.

Our Goat

High-Frequency Words Taught to Date

Grade 1

a	by	find	have	look	own	sure	was
about	call	first	he	make	paper	take	watch
after	car	five	hear	many	pictures	talk	water
all	carry	fly	help	maybe	play	their	we
and	cold	food	her	me	pull	the	were
animal	come	for	here	my	put	there	what
are	could	four	hold	never	read	these	where
around	do	friend	how	new	right	they	who
away	does	full	I	no	said	think	why
be	done	funny	into	now	see	those	with
because	don't	give	is	of	she	three	work
been	down	great	know	off	show	to	would
before	draw	green	laugh	one	sing	today	write
bird	eat	go	light	open	small	too	yellow
blue	every	goes	like	or	some	two	you
both	eyes	good	little	our	sometimes	under	your
bring	fall	ground	live	out	soon	very	
brown	far	grow	long	over	starts	walk	

Decoding skills taught to date: consonants *m, s, c, t*; short *a*; consonant *n*; consonant *d*; consonant *p*; consonant *f*; short *i*; consonant *r*; consonant *h*; /z/ spelled *s*; consonant *b*; consonant *g* (hard); short *o*; consonant *l*; consonant *x*; inflection *-s*; short *e*; consonant *y*; consonant *w*; consonant *k*; consonant *v*; consonant *j*; short *u*; /kw/ spelled *qu*; consonant *z*; final consonants *ll*; final consonants *ss*; consonants *-ck*; final consonants *ff*; final consonants *zz*; blends with *r*; blends with *l*; blends with *s*; final blend *mp*; final blend *nt*; final blend *nd*; final blend *st*; digraph *th*; ending *-s*; ending *-es*; ending *-ed* /ed/; ending *-ed* /d/; ending *-ed* /t/; ending *-ing*; digraphs *ch, tch*; possessives with *'s*; digraph *sh*; digraph *wh*; digraph *ph*; contractions *'s, n't*; long *a* (CVC*e*); soft *c* /s/; /j/ spelled *g, dge*; long *i* (CVC*e*); digraphs *kn, gn*; digraph *wr*; digraph *mb*; long *o* (CV, CVC*e*); long *u* (CVC*e*); long *e* (*e, ee*); long *e* (CVC*e, ea*); final consonants *ng*; final consonants *nk*; long *a* (*ai, ay*); contractions *'ll, 'd*; long *o* (*ow, oa*)

Which goat wins the big prize in the goat show? Our own goat wins!

4

Our Goat

We own a goat. We feed our goat lots of oats.

1

We coach our goat every day. He can run and leap. He can do fun tricks.

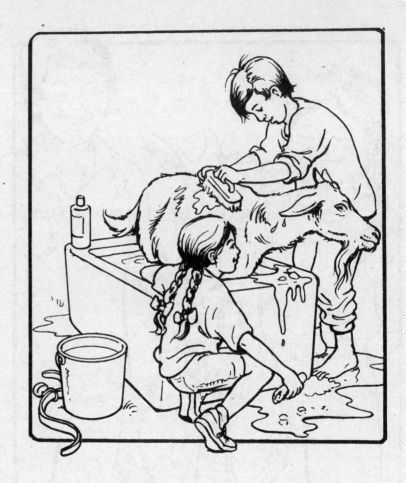

Our goat is in the tub of soap. We scrub our goat. We brush his coat. Then he will be set for the goat show.

Pop! Pop! Pop!

DECODABLE WORDS

Target Skill: contractions *'ve, 're*

we're	we've	you're	you've	

Previously Taught Skills

and	got	make	Red	waiting
Ben	has	much	snack	will
big	in	no	so	yelled
but	it	not	stop	
drop	Jen	pop	Ted	
eat	let's	pot	this	
going	made	put	us	

SKILLS APPLIED IN WORDS IN STORY: consonants *m, s, t, c*; short *a*; consonant *n*; consonant *d*; consonant *p*; short *i*; consonant *r*; consonant *h*; /z/ spelled *s*; consonant *b*; consonant *g* (hard); short *o*; consonant *l*; short *e*; consonant *y*; consonant *w*; consonant *k*; consonant *v*; consonant *j*; short *u*; final consonants *ll*; consonants -*ck*; blends with *r*; blends with *s*; final blend *nd*; digraph *th*; ending -*ed* /d/; ending -*ing*; digraph *ch*; contraction *'s*; long *a* (CVCe); long *o* (CV); long *e* (ea); long *a* (ai); contractions *'ve, 're*

HIGH-FREQUENCY WORDS

a	for	I	said	to
come	help	our	the	too

Pop! Pop! Pop!

High-Frequency Words Taught to Date

Grade 1

a	by	find	have	look	own	sure	was
about	call	first	he	make	paper	take	watch
after	car	five	hear	many	pictures	talk	water
all	carry	fly	help	maybe	play	the	we
and	cold	food	her	me	pull	their	were
animal	come	for	here	my	put	there	what
are	could	four	hold	never	read	these	where
around	do	friend	how	new	right	they	who
away	does	full	I	no	said	think	why
be	done	funny	into	now	see	those	with
because	don't	give	is	of	she	three	work
been	down	green	know	off	show	to	would
before	draw	go	laugh	one	sing	today	write
bird	eat	goes	light	open	small	too	yellow
blue	every	good	like	or	some	two	you
both	eyes	great	little	our	sometimes	under	your
bring	fall	ground	live	out	soon	very	
brown	far	grow	long	over	starts	walk	

Decoding skills taught to date: consonants *m, s, c, t;* short *a;* consonant *n;* consonant *d;* consonant *p;* consonant *f;* short *i;* consonant *r;* consonant *h;* /z/ spelled *s;* consonant *b;* consonant *g* (hard); short *o;* consonant *l;* consonant *x;* inflection *-s;* short *e;* consonant *y;* consonant *w;* consonant *k;* consonant *v;* consonant *j;* short *u;* /kw/ spelled *qu;* consonant *z;* final consonants *ll;* final consonants *ss;* consonants *-ck;* final consonants *ff;* final consonants *zz;* blends with *r;* blends with *l;* blends with *s;* final blend *mp;* final blend *nt;* final blend *nd;* final blend *st;* digraph *th;* ending *-s;* ending *-es;* ending *-ed* /ed/; ending *-ed* /d/; ending *-ed* /t/; ending *-ing;* digraphs *ch, tch;* possessives with *'s;* digraph *sh;* digraph *wh;* digraph *ph;* contractions *'s, n't;* long *a* (CVC*e*); soft *c* /s/; /j/ spelled *g, dge;* long *i* (CVC*e*); digraphs *kn, gn;* digraph *wr;* digraph *mb;* long *o* (CV, CVC*e*); long *u* (CVC*e*); long *e* (*e, ee*); long *e* (CVC*e, ea*); final consonants *ng;* final consonants *nk;* long *a* (*ai, ay*); contractions *'ll, 'd;* long *o* (*ow, oa*); contractions *'ve, 're*

"Come in, Ben," said Red
and Jen and Ted. "We've made
a big snack. You're going to
help us eat it!"

© Houghton Mifflin Harcourt Publishing Company

Pop! Pop! Pop!

"We've got a pot," said Jen.
"Let's make a snack."

"We're waiting for our snack.
But the pot has no pop. So I will
drop this in," said Ted.

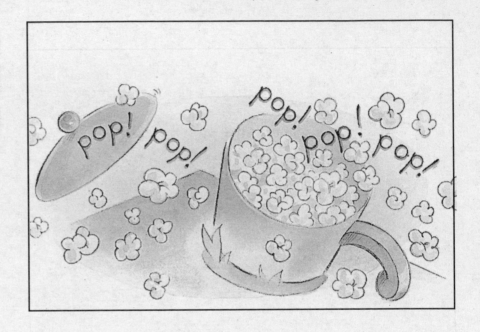

Pop! Pop! Pop! Pop!
"You've put too much in the
pot!" yelled Red. "It will not
stop!"

What Is It?

DECODABLE WORDS

Target Skill: contractions *'ve, 're*

I've	we're	we've	you're

Previously Taught Skills

an	can't	it	show	waiting
asked	cat	it's	tail	will
be	got	leg	that	wrong
big	huffed	Mel	then	yelled
but	in	must	tree	
Cam	is	see	us	

SKILLS APPLIED IN WORDS IN STORY: consonants *m, s, t, c*; short *a*; consonant *n*; short *i*; consonant *h*; /z/ spelled *s*; consonant *m*; consonant *l*; consonant *b*; consonant *g* (hard); short *o*; short *e*; consonant *y*; consonant *k*; consonant *v*; short *u*; final consonants *ll*; final consonants *ff*; blends with *r*; blends with *s*; final blend *st*; digraph *th*; ending *-ed* /d/; ending *-ed* /t/; ending *-ing*; contractions *'s, n't*; long *o* (CV); long *e* (*e, ee*); long *a* (*ai*); contractions *'ll, 'd*; long *o* (*ow*); contractions *'ve, 're*

HIGH-FREQUENCY WORDS

a	friend	looked	said	what
animal	I	new	small	

Houghton Mifflin Harcourt

What Is It?

High-Frequency Words Taught to Date

Grade 1

a	by	find	have	look	own	sure	was
about	call	first	he	make	paper	take	watch
after	car	five	hear	many	pictures	talk	water
all	carry	fly	help	maybe	play	their	we
and	cold	food	her	me	pull	the	were
animal	come	for	here	my	put	there	what
are	could	four	hold	never	read	these	where
around	do	friend	how	new	right	they	who
away	does	full	I	no	said	think	why
be	done	funny	into	now	see	those	with
because	don't	give	is	of	she	three	work
been	down	great	know	off	show	to	would
before	draw	green	laugh	one	sing	today	write
bird	eat	go	light	open	small	too	yellow
blue	every	goes	like	or	some	two	you
both	eyes	good	little	our	sometimes	under	your
bring	fall	ground	live	out	soon	very	
brown	far	grow	long	over	starts	walk	

Decoding skills taught to date: consonants *m, s, c, t*; short *a*; consonant *n*; consonant *d*; consonant *p*; consonant *f*; short *i*; consonant *r*; consonant *h*; /z/ spelled *s*; consonant *b*; consonant *g* (hard); short *o*; consonant *l*; consonant *x*; inflection *-s*; short *e*; consonant *y*; consonant *w*; consonant *k*; consonant *v*; consonant *j*; short *u*; /kw/ spelled *qu*; consonant *z*; final consonants *ll*; final consonants *ss*; consonants *-ck*; final consonants *ff*; final consonants *zz*; blends with *r*; blends with *l*; blends with *s*; final blend *mp*; final blend *nt*; final blend *nd*; final blend *st*; digraph *th*; ending *-s*; ending *-es*; ending *-ed* /ed/; ending *-ed* /d/; ending *-ed* /t/; ending *-ing*; digraphs *ch, tch*; possessives with '*s*; digraph *sh*; digraph *wh*; digraph *ph*; contractions '*s*, *n't*; long *a* (CVC*e*); soft *c* /s/; /j/ spelled *g, dge*; long *i* (CVC*e*); digraphs *kn, gn*; digraph *wr*; digraph *mb*; long *o* (CV, CVC*e*); long *u* (CVC*e*); long *e* (*e, ee*); long *e* (CVC*e*, *ea*); final consonants *ng*; final consonants *nk*; long *a* (*ai, ay*); contractions '*ll*, '*d*; long *o* (*ow, oa*); contractions '*ve*, '*re*

What Is It?

"It's a cat!" yelled Cam.
"We've got a new friend,"
said Mel.

"An animal is in that tree,"
said Mel.
"What is it?" asked Cam.

"I've looked. But I can't see it.
It must be big," said Mel.
    "You're wrong," huffed Cam.
"It's small."
    "Then we're waiting. It will
show us what it is," said Mel.

"It's a tail!" yelled Cam.
"It's a leg!" yelled Mel.

© Houghton Mifflin Harcourt Publishing Company

Jean's Painting

DECODABLE WORDS

Target Skill: compound words

classmates   outside   paintbrush   sunshine

Previously Taught Skills

and	in	nice	red	tree
at	it	on	seem	trees
big	Jean	paint	showed	up
branch	Jean's	painting	sketch	was
can	leaves	pasted	take	will
Clay	lots	peek	that	with
Dave	make	peeked	then	you've
day	Miss	picked	these	
go	next	real	this	

SKILLS APPLIED IN WORDS IN STORY: consonants *m, s, t,* c, short *a*; consonant *n*, consonant *d*; consonant *p*; short *i*; consonant *r*; consonant *g* (hard); short *o*; consonant *l*; short *e*; consonant *w*; consonant *k*; consonant *v*; short *u*; final consonants *ss*; consonants -*ck*; blends with *r*; blends with *l*; blends with *s*; final blend *nt*; final blend *nd*; final blend *st*; digraph *th*; ending -*s*; ending -*ed* /ed/; ending -*ed* /d/; ending -*ed* /t/; ending -*ing*; digraph *tch*; possessives with '*s*; digraph *sh*; long *a* (CVCe); soft *c* /s/; long *i* (CVCe); long *o* (CV); long *e* (*e, ee*); long *e* (*ea, e_e*); long *a* (*ai, ay*); long *o* (*ow*); compound words

HIGH-FREQUENCY WORDS

a	I	out	to	what
have	look	said	used	yellow
her	of	the	were	you

 Houghton Mifflin Harcourt.

Jean's Painting

High-Frequency Words Taught to Date

Grade 1

a	car	fly	here	my	read	think	where
about	carry	food	hold	never	right	those	who
after	cold	for	how	new	said	three	why
all	come	four	I	no	see	to	with
and	could	friend	into	now	she	today	work
animal	do	full	is	of	show	too	would
are	does	funny	know	off	sing	try	write
around	done	give	laugh	old	small	two	yellow
away	don't	great	light	one	some	under	you
be	door	green	like	open	sometimes	use	your
because	down	go	little	or	soon	very	
been	draw	goes	live	our	starts	walk	
before	eat	good	long	out	sure	want	
bird	every	ground	look	over	take	was	
blue	eyes	grow	make	own	talk	wash	
both	fall	have	many	paper	their	watch	
bring	far	he	maybe	pictures	the	water	
brown	find	hear	me	play	there	we	
by	first	help	more	pull	these	were	
call	five	her	mother	put	they	what	

Decoding skills taught to date: consonants *m*, *s*, *c*, *t*; short *a*; consonant *r*; consonant *d*; consonant *p*; consonant *f*; short *i*; consonant *r*; consonant *h*; /z/ spelled *s*; consonant *b*; consonant *g* (hard); short *o*; consonant *l*; consonant *x*; inflection -*s*; short *e*; consonant *y*; consonant *w*; consonant *k*; consonant *v*; consonant *j*; short *u*; /kw/ spelled *qu*; consonant *z*; final consonants *ll*; final consonants *ss*; consonants -*ck*; final consonants *ff*; final consonants *zz*; blends with *r*; blends with *l*; blends with *s*; final blend *mp*; final blend *nt*; final blend *nd*; final blend *st*; digraph *th*; ending -*s*; ending -*es*; ending -*ed* /ed/; ending -*ed* /d/; ending -*ed* /t/; ending -*ing*; digraphs *ch*, *tch*; possessives with *'s*; digraph *sh*; digraph *wh*; digraph *ph*; contractions *'s*, *n't*; long *a* (CVC*e*); soft *c* /s/; /j/ spelled *g*, *dge*; long *i* (CVC*e*); digraphs *kn*, *gn*; digraph *wr*; digraph *mb*; long *o* (CV, CVC*e*); long *u* (CVC*e*); long *e* (*e*, *ee*); long *e* (CVC*e*, *ea*); final consonants *ng*; final consonants *nk*; long *a* (*ai*, *ay*); contractions *'ll*, *'d*; long *o* (*ow*, *oa*); contractions *'ve*, *'re*; compound words

Jean's Painting

Jean peeked outside. It was a nice day with lots of sunshine. Outside, the leaves on the trees were red and yellow.

Jean showed her classmates the painting. "I picked up real leaves," Jean said. "Then I used a paintbrush to paint this tree branch. Next, I pasted leaves on the branch."

Miss Clay said, "Go out and take a peek! Then in painting class, you can sketch and paint what you've seen."

"Look at these nice, big leaves," said Dave.

"I will sketch and paint," said Jean. "And then I will make leaves that seem real!"

Rainbow

DECODABLE WORDS

Target Skill: compound words

inside	rainbow	sunshine	weekend

Previously Taught Skills

Ben	in	must	Sam	wish
best	is	no	see	with
can	it	play	stay	yelled
games	it's	playing	stop	
go	let's	rain	this	
grass	like	rained	time	
has	long	sad	we	

SKILLS APPLIED IN WORDS IN STORY: consonants *m, s, t, c*; short *a*; consonant *n*; consonant *d*; consonant *p*; short *i*; consonant *r*; /z/ spelled *s*; consonant *b*; consonant *g* (hard); short *o*; consonant *l*; inflection *-s*; consonant *y*; consonant *w*; consonant *k*; final consonants *ll*; final consonants *ss*; blends with *r*; blends with *l*; blends with *s*; final blend *nd*; final blend *st*; digraph *th*; ending *-ed* /d/; ending *-ing*; digraph *sh*; contraction *'s*; long *a* (CVC*e*); long *i* (CVC*e*); long *o* (CV); long *e* (*e, ee*); final consonants *ng*; long *a* (*ai, ay*); compound words

HIGH-FREQUENCY WORDS

a	look	the
I	said	would

© Houghton Mifflin Harcourt Publishing Company

Rainbow

High-Frequency Words Taught to Date

Grade 1

a	call	first	hear	maybe	paper	talk	was
about	car	five	help	me	pictures	their	wash
after	carry	fly	her	more	play	the	watch
all	cold	food	here	mother	pull	there	water
and	come	for	hold	my	put	these	we
animal	could	four	how	never	read	they	were
are	do	friend	I	new	right	think	what
around	does	full	into	no	said	those	where
away	done	funny	is	now	see	three	who
be	don't	give	know	of	she	to	why
because	door	great	laugh	off	show	today	with
been	down	green	light	old	sing	too	work
before	draw	go	like	one	small	try	would
bird	eat	goes	little	open	some	two	write
blue	every	good	live	or	sometimes	under	yellow
both	eyes	ground	long	our	soon	use	you
bring	fall	grow	look	out	starts	very	your
brown	far	have	make	over	sure	walk	
by	find	he	many	own	take	want	

Decoding skills taught to date: consonants *m, s, c, t;* short *a;* consonant *n;* consonant *d;* consonant *p;* consonant *f;* short *i;* consonant *r;* consonant *h;* /z/ spelled *s;* consonant *b;* consonant *g* (hard); short *o;* consonant *l;* consonant *x;* inflection *-s;* short *e;* consonant *y;* consonant *w;* consonant *k;* consonant *v;* consonant *j;* short *u;* /kw/ spelled *qu;* consonant *z;* final consonants *ll;* final consonants *ss;* consonants *-ck;* final consonants *ff;* final consonants *zz;* blends with *r,* blends with *l,* blends with *s;* final blend *mp;* final blend *nt;* final blend *nd;* final blend *st;* digraph *th;* ending *-s;* ending *-es;* ending *-ed* /ed/; ending *-ed* /d/; ending *-ed* /t/; ending *-ing;* digraphs *ch, tch;* possessives with *'s;* digraph *sh;* digraph *wh;* digraph *ph;* contractions *'s, n't;* long *a* (CVCe); soft *c* /s/; /j/ spelled *g, dge;* long *i* (CVCe); digraphs *kn, gn;* digraph *wr;* digraph *mb;* long *o* (CV, CVCe); long *u* (CVCe); long *e* (e, ee); long *e* (CVCe, ea); final consonants *ng;* final consonants *nk;* long *a* (ai, ay); contractions *'ll, 'd;* long *o* (ow, oa); contractions *'ve, 're;* compound words

Rainbow

"It's a rainbow!" yelled Sam.
"We can play in the sunshine with a rainbow," said Sam.

"It has rained a long time," said sad Ben.
"I wish it would stop. This is the weekend," said sad Sam.

"We must stay inside," said Ben. "We can play games."

"No. We like playing in the grass best," said Sam.

"Look! No rain. Let's go!" yelled Ben.

We Ate Bread

DECODABLE WORDS

Target Skill: short e (ea)

bread breakfast read

Previously Taught Skills

and	eat	meat	then	went
at	fed	needed	this	will
ate	it	next	time	with
beans	jam	on	toast	
buns	loaf	slice	top	
cheese	lunch	sliced	us	
day	made	step	we	

SKILLS APPLIED IN WORDS IN STORY: *m, s, c, t*; short *a*; consonant *n*; consonant *d*; consonant *p*; consonant *f*; short *i*; consonant *r*; /z/ spelled *s*; consonant *b*; short *o*; consonant *l*; consonant *x*; inflection -*s*; short *e*; consonant *y*; consonant *w*; consonant *k*; consonant *j*; short *u*; final consonants *ll*; consonants -*ck*; blends with *r*; blends with *s*; final blend *nt*; final blend *nd*; final blend *st*; digraph *th*; ending -*s*; ending -*ed* /ed/; digraph *ch*; long *a* (CVC*e*); soft *c* /s/; long *i* (CVC*e*); long *e* (*e, ee*); long *e* (*ea*); long *a* (*ay*); long *o* (*oa*); compound words; short *e* (*ea*)

HIGH-FREQUENCY WORDS

a	first	of	the
all	for	one	what
by	little	put	worked

© Houghton Mifflin Harcourt Publishing Company

We Ate Bread

Houghton Mifflin Harcourt

High-Frequency Words Taught to Date

Grade 1

a	car	fly	here	my	read	think	where
about	carry	food	hold	never	right	those	who
after	cold	for	how	new	said	three	why
all	come	four	I	no	see	to	with
and	could	friend	into	now	she	today	work
animal	do	full	is	of	show	too	would
are	does	funny	know	off	sing	try	write
around	done	give	laugh	old	small	two	yellow
away	don't	great	light	one	some	under	you
be	door	green	like	open	sometimes	use	your
because	down	go	little	or	soon	very	
been	draw	goes	live	our	starts	walk	
before	eat	good	long	out	sure	want	
bird	every	ground	look	over	take	was	
blue	eyes	grow	make	own	talk	wash	
both	fall	have	many	paper	their	watch	
bring	far	he	maybe	pictures	the	water	
brown	find	hear	me	play	there	we	
by	first	help	more	pull	these	were	
call	five	her	mother	put	they	what	

Decoding skills taught to date: consonants *m, s, c, t*; short *a*; consonant *n*; consonant *d*; consonant *p*; consonant *f*; short *i*; consonant *r*; consonant *h*; /z/ spelled *s*; consonant *b*; consonant *g* (hard); short *o*; consonant *l*; consonant *x*; inflection *-s*; short *e*; consonant *y*; consonant *w*; consonant *k*; consonant *v*; consonant *j*; short *u*; /kw/ spelled *qu*; consonant *z*; final consonants *ll*; final consonants *ss*; consonants *-ck*; final consonants *ff*; final consonants *zz*; blends with *r*; blends with *l*; blends with *s*; final blend *mp*; final blend *nt*; final blend *nd*; final blend *st*; digraph *th*; ending *-s*; ending *-es*; ending *-ed* /ed/; ending *-ed* /d/; ending *-ed* /t/; ending *-ing*; digraphs *ch*, *tch*; possessives with *'s*; digraph *sh*; digraph *wh*; digraph *ph*; contractions *'s, n't*; long *a* (CVC*e*); soft *c* /s/; /j/ spelled *g*, *dge*; long *i* (CVC*e*); digraphs *kn*, *gn*; digraph *wr*; digraph *mb*; long *o* (CV, CVC*e*); long *u* (CVC*e*); long *e* (*e*, *ee*); long *e* (CVC*e*, *ea*); final consonants *ng*; final consonants *nk*; long *a* (*ai, ay*); contractions *'ll, 'd*; long *o* (*ow, oa*); contractions *'ve, 're*; compound words; short *e* (*ea*)

We made bread for the next
day. First we read what we
needed. Then we worked step
by step.

We will eat bread for breakfast!

4

We Ate Bread

We ate bread for breakfast.
This loaf fed us all. We made
toast with the bread and ate it
with jam.

1

We ate bread at lunch. We sliced the bread. We put cheese on one slice. Then a slice of bread went on top!

We ate bread with meat and beans. This time we ate little buns of bread.

What Jet Meant

DECODABLE WORDS

Target Skill: short *e* (*ea*)

breath	head	meant

Previously Taught Skills

and	dug	just	sniffed	we
but	fast	keep	spotted	went
called	fox	next	swam	will
came	he	no	that	with
can	his	play	think	
Dad	hold	pond	this	
dashed	hole	ran	time	
den	in	sad	up	
ducks	Jet	skunk	walking	

SKILLS APPLIED IN WORDS IN STORY: consonants *m, s, t, c*; short *a*; consonant *n*; consonant *d*; consonant *p*; consonant *f*; short *i*; consonant *r*; consonant *h*; /z/ spelled *s*; consonant *b*; consonant *g* (hard); short *o*; consonant *l*; consonant *x*; inflection *-s*; short *e*; consonant *y*; consonant *w*; consonant *k*; consonant *j*; short *u*; final consonants *ll*; final consonants *ff*; consonants *-ck*; blends with *l*; blends with *s*; final blend *nt*; final blend *nd*; final blend *st*; digraph *th*; ending *-s*; ending *-ed* /ed/; ending *-ed* /d/; ending *-ed* /t/; ending *-ing*; digraph *sh*; long *a* (CVCe); long *i* (CVCe); long *o* (CV, CVCe); long *e* (*e, ee*); long *e* (*ea*); ending *nk*; long *a* (*ay*); short *e* (*ea*)

HIGH-FREQUENCY WORDS

a	I	put	to
after	looked	said	what
away	out	the	

© Houghton Mifflin Harcourt Publishing Company

What Jet Meant

High-Frequency Words Taught to Date

Grade 1

a	call	first	hear	maybe	paper	talk	was
about	car	five	help	me	pictures	their	wash
after	carry	fly	her	more	play	the	watch
all	cold	food	here	mother	pull	there	water
and	come	for	hold	my	put	these	we
animal	could	four	how	never	read	they	were
are	do	friend	I	new	right	think	what
around	does	full	into	no	said	those	where
away	done	funny	is	now	see	three	who
be	don't	give	know	of	she	to	why
because	door	great	laugh	off	show	today	with
been	down	green	light	old	sing	too	work
before	draw	go	like	one	small	try	would
bird	eat	goes	little	open	some	two	write
blue	every	good	live	or	sometimes	under	yellow
both	eyes	ground	long	our	soon	use	you
bring	fall	grow	look	out	starts	very	your
brown	far	have	make	over	sure	walk	
by	find	he	many	own	take	want	

Decoding skills taught to date: consonants *m, s, c, t*; short *a*; consonant *n*; consonant *d*; consonant *p*; consonant *f*; short *i*; consonant *r*; consonant *h*; /z/ spelled *s*; consonant *b*; consonant *g* (hard); short *o*; consonant *l*; consonant *x*; inflection *-s*; short *e*; consonant *y*; consonant *w*; consonant *k*; consonant *v*; consonant *j*; short *u*; /kw/ spelled *qu*; consonant *z*; final consonants *ll*; final consonants *ss*; consonants *-ck*; final consonants *ff*; final consonants *zz*; blends with *r*; blends with *l*; blends with *s*; final blend *mp*; final blend *nt*; final blend *nd*; final blend *st*; digraph *th*; ending *-s*; ending *-es*; ending *-ed* /ed/; ending *-ed* /d/; ending *-ed* /t/; ending *-ing*; digraphs *ch, tch*; possessives with *'s*; digraph *sh*; digraph *wh*; digraph *ph*; contractions *'s, n't*; long *a* (CVC*e*); soft *c* /s/; /j/ spelled *g, dge*; long *i* (CVC*e*); digraphs *kn, gn*; digraph *wr*; digraph *mb*; long *o* (CV, CVC*e*); long *u* (CVC*e*); long *e* (*e, ee*); long *e* (CVC*e, ea*); final consonants *ng*; final consonants *nk*; long *a* (*ai, ay*); contractions *'ll, 'd*; long *o* (*ow, oa*); contractions *'ve, 're*; compound words; short *e* (*ea*)

Jet sniffed in a hole. "No, Jet, no!" Dad called. "A skunk dug that hole!"

This time Jet ran. And Dad and I ran!

4

What Jet Meant

Dad and I went walking with Jet. We came to the pond. Jet dashed in.

"Dad!" I called. "Will Jet put his head in? Can he hold his breath?"

"Jet will keep his head up," Dad said.

1

Jet swam after ducks. The
ducks swam away fast. Jet
looked sad.

"I think Jet just meant to
play, but the ducks swam away,"
Dad said.

Next Jet spotted a den.
He put his head in, and a fox ran
out! Jet looked sad.

"I think Jet just meant to play,
but the fox ran," Dad said.

At the Market

DECODABLE WORDS

Target Skill: *r*-controlled *ar*

Barb	cart	far	market	tart
car	Clark	jars	parks	

Previously Taught Skills

and	home	jam	she
at	in	meat	then
back	into	not	
drive	is	plums	
get	it	sees	

SKILLS APPLIED IN WORDS IN STORY: consonants *m, s, t, c*; short *a*; consonant *n*; consonant *d*; consonant *p*; consonant *f*; short *i*; consonant *r*; consonant *h*; /z/ spelled *s*; consonant *b*; consonant *g* (hard); short *o*; consonant *l*; inflection -*s*; short *e*; consonant *y*; consonant *k*; consonant *v*; consonant *j*; short *u*; consonants -*ck*; blends with *r*; blends with *l*; digraph *th*; ending -*s*; digraph *sh*; long *i* (CVCe); long *o* (CVCe); long *e* (*e, ee*); long *e* (*ea*); compound words; *r*-controlled *ar*

HIGH-FREQUENCY WORDS

a	the
of	they
puts	to
some	too

Houghton Mifflin Harcourt

r-controlled *ar*

BOOK 137

At the Market

High-Frequency Words Taught to Date

Grade 1

a	carry	food	how	new	right	think	who
about	cold	for	I	night	said	those	why
after	come	four	into	no	see	three	window
all	could	friend	is	noise	shall	to	with
and	do	full	know	now	she	today	work
animal	does	funny	laugh	of	show	too	world
are	done	give	light	off	sing	try	would
around	don't	go	like	old	small	two	write
away	door	goes	little	one	some	under	yellow
be	down	good	live	open	sometimes	use	you
because	draw	great	long	or	soon	very	your
been	eat	green	look	our	starts	walk	
before	every	ground	loudly	out	story	want	
bird	eyes	grow	make	over	sure	was	
blue	fall	have	many	own	take	wash	
both	far	he	maybe	paper	talk	watch	
bring	few	hear	me	picture	the	water	
brown	find	help	more	play	their	we	
by	first	her	mother	pull	there	were	
call	five	here	my	put	these	what	
car	fly	hold	never	read	they	where	

Decoding skills taught to date: consonants *m, s, c, t*; short *a*; consonant *n*; consonant *d*; consonant *p*; consonant *f*; short *i*; consonant *r*; consonant *h*; /z/ spelled *s*; consonant *b*; consonant *g* (hard); short *o*; consonant *l*; consonant *x*; inflection *-s*; short *e*; consonant *y*; consonant *w*; consonant *k*; consonant *v*; consonant *j*; short *u*; /kw/ spelled *qu*; consonant *z*; final consonants *lf*; final consonants *ss*; consonants *-ck*; final consonants *ff*; final consonants *zz*; blends with *r*; blends with *l*; blends with *s*; final blend *mp*; final blend *nt*; final blend *nd*; final blend *st*; digraph *th*; ending *-s*; ending *-es*; ending *-ed* /ed/; ending *-ed* /d/; ending *-ed* /t/; ending *-ing*; digraphs *ch, tch*; possessives with *'s*; digraph *sh*; digraph *wh*; digraph *ph*; contractions *'s, n't*; long *a* (CVC*e*); soft *c* /s/; /j/ spelled *g, dge*; long *i* (CVC*e*); digraphs *kn, gn*; digraph *wr*; digraph *mb*; long *o* (CV, CVC*e*); long *u* (CVC*e*); long *e* (*e, ee*); long *e* (CVC*e, ea*); final consonants *ng*; final consonants *nk*; long *a* (*ai, ay*); contractions *'ll, 'd*; long *o* (*ow, oa*); contractions *'ve, 're*; compound words; short *e* (*ea*); *r*-controlled *ar*

Clark puts the jars, meat, plums, and tart into the car. Then Barb and Clark drive back home.

At the Market

Barb and Clark drive to the market. It is not too far.

At the market, Barb parks the car. She and Clark get a cart.

Clark puts meat, a tart, and plums in the cart. Barb sees some jars of jam.

Sharks

DECODABLE WORDS

Target Skill: *r-controlled ar*

are	far	large	sharks
dark	hard	shark	sharp

Previously Taught Skills

be	fast	in	sea
can	feet	is	swim
catch	fish	it	teeth
deep	grow	long	use
dogfish	huge	most	whale

SKILLS APPLIED IN WORDS IN STORY: consonants *m, s, t, c*; short *a*; consonant *n*; consonant *d*; consonant *p*; consonant *f*; short *i*; consonant *r*; consonant *h*; /z/ spelled *s*; consonant *b*; consonant *g* (hard); short *o*; consonant *l*; consonant *w*; consonant *k*; blends with *r*; blends with *s*; digraph *th*; ending -*s*; digraph *tch*; digraph *sh*; digraph *wh*; long *a* (CVCe); /j/ spelled *g*; long *o* (CV); long *u* (CVCe); long *e* (*e, ee*); long *e* (*ea*); final consonants *ng*; long *o* (*ow*); compound words; *r*-controlled *ar*

HIGH-FREQUENCY WORDS

a	or	their
blue	small	to
live	the	

Houghton Mifflin Harcourt.

r-controlled ar

BOOK 138

Sharks

High-Frequency Words Taught to Date

Grade 1

a	carry	food	how	new	right	think	who
about	cold	for	I	night	said	those	why
after	come	four	into	no	see	three	window
all	could	friend	is	noise	shall	to	with
and	do	full	know	now	she	today	work
animal	does	funny	laugh	of	show	too	world
are	done	give	light	off	sing	try	would
around	don't	go	like	old	small	two	write
away	door	goes	little	one	some	under	yellow
be	down	good	live	open	sometimes	use	you
because	draw	great	long	or	soon	very	your
been	eat	green	look	our	starts	walk	
before	every	ground	loudly	out	story	want	
bird	eyes	grow	make	over	sure	was	
blue	fall	have	many	own	take	wash	
both	far	he	maybe	paper	talk	watch	
bring	few	hear	me	picture	the	water	
brown	find	help	more	play	their	we	
by	first	her	mother	pull	there	were	
call	five	here	my	put	these	what	
car	fly	hold	never	read	they	where	

Decoding skills taught to date: consonants *m, s, c, t;* short *a;* consonant *n;* consonant *d;* consonant *p;* consonant *f;* short *i;* consonant *r;* consonant *h;* /z/ spelled *s;* consonant *b;* consonant *g* (hard); short *o;* consonant *l;* consonant *x;* inflection *-s;* short *e;* consonant *y;* consonant *w;* consonant *k;* consonant *v;* consonant *j;* short *u;* /kw/ spelled *qu;* consonant *z;* final consonants *ll;* final consonants *ss;* consonants *-ck;* final consonants *ff;* final consonants *zz;* blends with *r;* blends with *l;* blends with *s;* final blend *mp;* final blend *nt;* final blend *nd;* final blend *st;* digraph *th;* ending *-s;* ending *-es;* ending *-ed* /ed/; ending *-ed* /d/; ending *-ed* /t/; ending *-ing;* digraphs *ch, tch;* possessives with *'s;* digraph *sh;* digraph *wh;* digraph *ph;* contractions *'s, n't;* long *a* (CVC*e*); soft *c* /s/; /j/ spelled *g, dge;* long *i* (CVC*e*); digraphs *kn, gn;* digraph *wr;* digraph *mb;* long *o* (CV, CVC*e*); long *u* (CVC*e*); long *e* (*e, ee*); long *e* (CVC*e, ea*); final consonants *ng;* final consonants *nk;* long *a* (*ai, ay*); contractions *'ll, 'd;* long *o* (*ow, oa*); contractions *'ve, 're;* compound words; short *e* (*ea*); *r*-controlled *ar*

The whale shark can grow to be 40 feet long. It is huge!

Sharks

Sharks are fish. Most sharks live in the deep, dark sea.

Sharks can swim fast. Sharks can swim far. Sharks use their sharp, hard teeth to catch fish.

Sharks can be large or small. A dogfish is a small shark. A blue shark is a large shark.

Storm at Sea

DECODABLE WORDS

Target Skill: *r-controlled or, ore*

chore	horns	port	short
cords	more	ports	storm
forth	north	shore	

Previously Taught Skills

and	docks	in	put	ships
at	find	is	rain	time
blow	from	it	reach	wind
can	go	keep	safe	
dock	hard	men	sea	

SKILLS APPLIED IN WORDS IN STORY: consonants *m, s, c, t*, short *a*; consonant *n*; consonant *d*; consonant *p*; consonant *f*; short *i*; consonant *b*; consonant *r*; consonant *h*; /z/ spelled *s*; short *o*; consonant *w*; consonant *l*; inflection *-s*; consonant *w*; consonant *k*; short *u*; consonants *-ck*; blends with *r*; blends with *l*; blends with *s*; final blend *nd*; digraph *th*; ending *-s*; digraph *ch*; digraph *sh*; long *a* (CVC*e*); long *i* (CVC*e*); long *o* (CV); long *e* (ee); long *e* (ea); long *a* (ai); long *o* (ow); *r*-controlled *ar*; *r*-controlled *or, ore*

HIGH-FREQUENCY WORDS

a	soon	there
around	the	to

Storm at Sea

Houghton Mifflin Harcourt.

High-Frequency Words Taught to Date

Grade 1

a	car	five	her	more	picture	talk	wash
about	carry	fly	here	mother	play	the	watch
after	cold	food	hold	my	pull	their	water
all	come	for	how	never	put	there	we
and	could	four	I	new	read	these	were
animal	do	friend	into	night	right	they	what
are	does	full	is	no	said	think	where
around	done	funny	know	noise	see	those	who
away	don't	give	laugh	now	shall	three	why
be	door	go	light	of	she	to	window
because	down	goes	like	off	show	today	with
been	draw	good	little	old	sing	too	work
before	eat	great	live	one	small	try	world
bird	every	green	long	open	some	two	would
blue	eyes	ground	look	or	sometimes	under	write
both	fall	grow	loudly	our	soon	use	yellow
bring	far	have	make	out	starts	very	you
brown	few	he	many	over	story	walk	your
by	find	hear	maybe	own	sure	want	
call	first	help	me	paper	take	was	

Decoding skills taught to date: consonants *m, s, c, t*; short *a*; consonant *n*; consonant *d*; consonant *p*; consonant *f*; short *i*; consonant *r*; consonant *h*; /z/ spelled *s*; consonant *b*; consonant *g* (hard); short *o*; consonant *l*; consonant *x*; inflection *-s*; short *e*; consonant *y*; consonant *w*; consonant *k*; consonant *v*; consonant *j*; short *u*; /kw/ spelled *qu*; consonant *z*; final consonants *ll*; final consonants *ss*; consonants *-ck*; final consonants *ff*; final consonants *zz*; blends with *r*; blends with *l*; blends with *s*; final blend *mp*; final blend *nt*; final blend *nd*; final blend *st*; digraph *th*; ending *-s*; ending *-es*; ending *-ed* /ed/; ending *-ed* /d/; ending *-ed* /t/; ending *-ing*; digraphs *ch, tch*; possessives with *'s*; digraph *sh*; digraph *wh*; digraph *ph*; contractions *'s, n't*; long *a* (CVCe); soft *c* /s/; /j/ spelled *g, dge*; long *i* (CVCe); digraphs *kn, gn*; digraph *wr*; digraph *mb*; long *o* (CV, CVCe); long *u* (CVCe); long *e* (e, ee); long *e* (CVCe, ea); final consonants *ng*; final consonants *nk*; long *a* (ai, ay); contractions *'ll, 'd*; long *o* (ow, oa); contractions *'ve, 're*; compound words; short *e* (ea); r-controlled *ar*; r-controlled *or, ore*

Storm at Sea

It is a short storm. Soon, ships can go forth from the port at shore.

There is a storm at sea. Ships blow horns. It is time to reach shore!

4

1

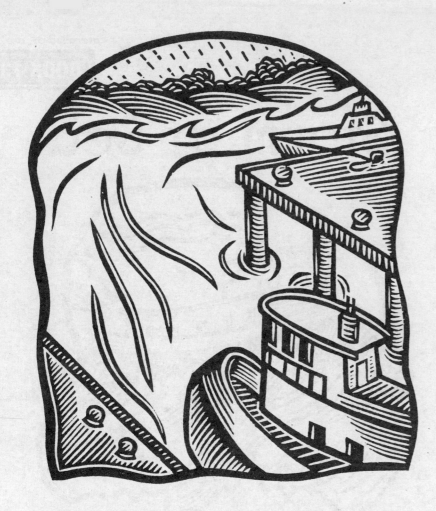

More wind and rain blow in
from the north. Ships can find
safe ports at shore.

Men put cords around a dock.
More cords keep ships safe! It is
a hard chore to put cords around
docks in a storm.

Al's Shorts

DECODABLE WORDS

Target Skill: *r-*controlled *or*, *ore*

for	score	shorts	store	wore
more	shore	sports	tore	

Previously Taught Skills

Al	at	his	played
Al's	dad	need	went
and	got	old	with

SKILLS APPLIED IN WORDS IN STORY: consonants *m, s, c, t*, short *a*; consonant *n*; consonant *d*; consonant *p*; consonant *f*; short *i*; consonant *b*; consonant *r*; consonant *h*; /z/ spelled *s*; short *o*; consonant *w*; consonant *l*; consonant *w*; consonant *k*; short *u*; blends with *l*; blends with *s*; digraph *th*; digraph *sh*; possessives with *'s*; ending *-s*; long *a* (*ay*); long *e* (*ēe*)

HIGH-FREQUENCY WORDS

I	said	they
new	the	to

Houghton Mifflin Harcourt

*r-*controlled *or*, *ore*

BOOK 140

Al's Shorts

High-Frequency Words Taught to Date

Grade 1

a	car	five	her	more	picture	their	water
about	carry	fly	here	mother	play	there	we
after	cold	food	hold	my	pull	these	were
all	come	for	how	never	put	they	what
and	could	four	I	new	read	think	where
animal	do	friend	into	night	right	those	who
are	does	full	is	no	said	three	why
around	done	funny	know	noise	see	to	with
away	don't	give	laugh	now	she	today	work
be	door	go	light	of	show	too	would
because	down	goes	like	off	sing	try	write
been	draw	good	little	old	small	two	yellow
before	eat	great	live	one	some	under	you
bird	every	green	long	open	sometimes	use	your
blue	eyes	ground	look	or	soon	very	
both	fall	grow	loudly	our	starts	walk	
bring	far	have	make	out	sure	want	
brown	few	he	many	over	take	was	
by	find	hear	maybe	own	talk	wash	
call	first	help	me	paper	the	watch	

Decoding skills taught to date: consonants *m, s, c, t;* short *a;* consonant *n;* consonant *d;* consonant *p;* consonant *f;* short *i;* consonant *r;* consonant *h;* /z/ spelled *s;* consonant *b;* consonant *g* (hard); short *o;* consonant *l;* consonant *x;* inflection *-s;* short *e;* consonant *y;* consonant *w;* consonant *k;* consonant *v;* consonant *j;* short *u;* /kw/ spelled *qu;* consonant *z;* final consonants *ll;* final consonants *ss;* consonants *-ck;* final consonants *ff;* final consonants *zz;* blends with *r;* blends with *l;* blends with *s;* final blend *mp;* final blend *nt;* final blend *nd;* final blend *st;* digraph *th;* ending *-s;* ending *-es;* ending *-ed* /ed/; ending *-ed* /d/; ending *-ed* /t/; ending *-ing;* digraphs *ch, tch;* possessives with *'s;* digraph *sh;* digraph *wh;* digraph *ph;* contractions *'s, n't;* long *a* (CVC*e*); soft *c* /s/; /j/ spelled *g, dge;* long *i* (CVC*e*); digraphs *kn, gn;* digraph *wr;* digraph *mb;* long *o* (CV, CVC*e*); long *u* (CVC*e*); long *e* (*e, ee*); long *e* (CVC*e, ea*); final consonants *ng;* final consonants *nk;* long *a* (*ai, ay*); contractions *'ll, 'd;* long *o* (*ow, oa*); contractions *'ve, 're;* compound words; short *e* (*ea*); r-controlled *ar;* r-controlled *or, ore*

Al and Dad went to the Shorts Store for new shorts. They got more shorts for Al!

4

Al's Shorts

Al wore his old shorts to the shore.

1

Al played sports with Dad at the shore. Score!

Al tore his old shorts. "I need new shorts," said Al.

Herb the Clerk

DECODABLE WORDS

Target Skill: *r-controlled er, ir*

clerk	fern	Gert	shirt	squirt
dirt	ferns	Herb	sir	

Previously Taught Skills

adds	his	plants	shop
big	in	pots	thank
grow	is	says	then
has	keeps	sells	works

SKILLS APPLIED IN WORDS IN STORY: consonants *m, s, c, t,* short *a;* consonant *n;* consonant *d;* consonant *p;* consonant *f;* short *i;* consonant *r;* consonant *h;* /z/ spelled *s;* consonant *b;* consonant *g* (hard); short *o;* short *e;* consonant *l;* short *e;* consonant *w;* consonant *k;* /kw/ spelled *qu;* final consonants *ll;* blends with *r;* blends with *l;* blends with *s;* final blend *nt;* digraph *th;* ending *-s;* digraph *sh;* long *e* (*ee*); final consonants *nk;* *r*-controlled *er, ir*

HIGH-FREQUENCY WORDS

a	of	to
all	small	water
friend	the	you

Houghton Mifflin Harcourt.

Herb the Clerk

High-Frequency Words Taught to Date

Grade 1

a	car	fly	hold	never	right	those	why
about	carry	follow	how	new	said	three	window
after	cold	food	I	night	see	to	with
all	come	for	into	no	shall	today	work
and	could	four	is	noise	she	too	world
animal	do	friend	know	now	show	try	would
are	does	full	laugh	of	sing	two	write
around	done	funny	learning	off	small	under	years
away	don't	give	light	old	some	until	yellow
baby	door	go	like	one	sometimes	use	you
be	down	goes	little	open	soon	very	young
because	draw	good	live	or	starts	walk	your
been	eat	great	long	our	story	want	
before	eight	green	look	out	sure	was	
begins	every	ground	loudly	over	take	wash	
bird	eyes	grow	make	own	talk	watch	
blue	fall	have	many	paper	the	water	
both	far	he	maybe	pictures	their	we	
bring	few	hear	me	play	there	were	
brown	find	help	more	pull	these	what	
by	first	her	mother	put	they	where	
call	five	here	my	read	think	who	

Decoding skills taught to date: consonants *m, s, c, t*; short *a*; consonant *n*; consonant *d*; consonant *p*; consonant *f*; short *i*; consonant *r*; consonant *h*; /z/ spelled *s*; consonant *b*; consonant *g* (hard); short *o*; consonant *l*; consonant *x*; inflection *-s*; short *e*; consonant *y*; consonant *w*; consonant *k*; consonant *v*; consonant *j*; short *u*; /kw/ spelled *qu*; consonant *z*; final consonants *ll*; final consonants *ss*; consonants *-ck*; final consonants *ff*; final consonants *zz*; blends with *r*; blends with *l*; blends with *s*; final blend *mp*; final blend *nt*; final blend *nd*; final blend *st*; digraph *th*; ending *-s*; ending *-es*; ending *-ed* /ed/; ending *-ed* /d/; ending *-ed* /t/; ending *-ing*; digraphs *ch, tch*; possessives with *'s*; digraph *sh*; digraph *wh*; digraph *ph*; contractions *'s, n't*; long *a* (CVC*e*); soft *c* /s/; /j/ spelled *g, dge*; long *i* (CVC*e*); digraphs *kn, gn*; digraph *wr*; digraph *mb*; long *o* (CV, CVC*e*); long *u* (CVC*e*); long *e* (*e, ee*); long *e* (CVC*e, ea*); final consonants *ng*; final consonants *nk*; long *a* (*ai, ay*); contractions *'ll, 'd*; long *o* (*ow, oa*); contractions *'ve, 're*; compound words; short *e* (*ea*); *r*-controlled *ar*; *r*-controlled *or, ore*; *r*-controlled *er, ir*

Herb has big ferns. Herb has small ferns. Herb keeps all his ferns in pots of dirt.

Herb the Clerk

Herb is a clerk. Herb works in a fern shop. His shirt says Herb.

Herb plants ferns in dirt.
Then, Herb sells ferns to his
friend Gert. "Thank you, sir!"
says Gert.

Ferns grow in dirt. Herb adds
a squirt of water to the dirt.

Kirk Chirps

DECODABLE WORDS

Target Skill: *r-controlled er, ir*

bird	chirping	first	perch
birds	chirps	Kirk	verse
chirp	fir	other	

Previously Taught Skills

are	his	on	up
day	in	other	wake
each	is	to	when
gets	lives	tree	with

SKILLS APPLIED IN WORDS IN STORY: consonants *s, t, c*; consonant *n*; consonant *d*; consonant *p*; consonant *f*; short *i*; consonant *r*; consonant *h*; /z/ spelled *s*; consonant *b*; consonant *g* (hard); short *o*; consonant *l*; short *e*; consonant *w*; consonant *k*; consonant *v*; blends with *r*; blends with *s*; digraph *th*; ending *-s*; ending *-ing*; digraph *ch*; digraph *wh*; long *a* (CVCe); long *e* (ee); long *e* (ea); long *a* (ay); *r*-controlled *er, ir*

HIGH-FREQUENCY WORDS

a	all	the	to

© Houghton Mifflin Harcourt Publishing Company

Kirk Chirps

High-Frequency Words Taught to Date

Grade 1

a	call	first	help	me	picture	the	watch
about	car	five	her	more	play	their	water
after	carry	fly	here	mother	pull	there	we
all	cold	follow	hold	my	put	these	were
and	come	food	how	never	read	they	what
animal	could	for	I	new	right	think	where
are	do	four	into	night	said	those	who
around	does	friend	is	no	see	three	why
away	done	full	know	noise	shall	to	window
baby	don't	funny	laugh	now	she	today	with
be	door	give	learning	of	show	too	work
because	down	go	light	off	sing	try	world
been	draw	goes	like	old	small	two	would
before	eat	good	little	one	some	under	write
begins	eight	great	live	open	sometimes	until	yellow
bird	every	green	long	or	soon	use	years
blue	eyes	ground	look	our	starts	very	you
both	fall	grow	loudly	out	story	walk	young
bring	far	have	make	over	sure	want	your
brown	few	he	many	own	take	was	
by	find	hear	maybe	paper	talk	wash	

Decoding skills taught to date: consonants *m, s, c, t*; short *a*; consonant *n*; consonant *d*; consonant *p*; consonant *f*; short *i*; consonant *r*; consonant *h*; /z/ spelled *s*; consonant *b*; consonant *g* (hard); short *o*; consonant *l*; consonant *x*; inflection *-s*; short *e*; consonant *y*; consonant *w*; consonant *k*; consonant *v*; consonant *j*; short *u*; /kw/ spelled *qu*; consonant *z*; final consonants *ll*; final consonants *ss*; consonants *-ck*; final consonants *ff*; final consonants *zz*; blends with *r*; blends with *l*; blends with *s*; final blend *mp*; final blend *nt*; final blend *nd*; final blend *st*; digraph *th*; ending *-s*; ending *-es*; ending *-ed* /ed/; ending *-ed* /d/; ending *-ed* /t/; ending *-ing*; digraphs *ch, tch*; possessives with *'s*; digraph *sh*; digraph *wh*; digraph *ph*; contractions *'s, n't*; long *a* (CVC*e*); soft *c* /s/; /j/ spelled *g, dge*; long *i* (CVC*e*); digraphs *kn, gn*; digraph *wr*; digraph *mb*; long *o* (CV, CVC*e*); long *u* (CVC*e*); long *e* (*e, ee*); long *e* (CVC*e, ea*); final consonants *ng*; final consonants *nk*; long *a* (*ai, ay*); contractions *'ll, 'd*; long *o* (*ow, oa*); contractions *'ve, 're*; compound words; short *e* (*ea*); r-controlled *ar*; r-controlled *or, ore*; r-controlled *er, ir*

Kirk Chirps

Kirk is a bird. Kirk lives on his perch in a fir tree.

All the birds in the fir tree are chirping a verse with Kirk. "Chirp, chirp, chirp!"

Each day Kirk gets on his perch. Kirk is the first bird to chirp. Kirk chirps a verse. "Chirp, chirp, chirp!"

When Kirk chirps on his perch, the other birds in the fir tree wake up.

The Fur Burr

DECODABLE WORDS

Target Skill: *r-controlled ur*

burr	fur	Kurt's	purr
burrs	hurt	lurk	Zurk
curls	Kurt	lurks	

Previously Taught Skills

but	ferns	in	makes	stern
can	get	it	on	up
cat	gets	lap	plant	will
comes	has	lets	plants	
face	her	likes	pull	

SKILLS APPLIED IN WORDS IN STORY: consonants *m, s, t, c*; short *a*; consonant *n*; consonant *p*; consonant *f*; short *i*; consonant *r*; consonant *h*; /z/ spelled *s*; consonant *b*; consonant *g* (hard); short *o*; consonant *l*; short *e*; consonant *w*; consonant *k*; short *u*; consonant *z*; final consonants *ll*; blends with *s*; blends with *l*; final blend *nt*; ending -*s*; possessives with *'s*; long *a* (CVCe); soft *c* /s/; long *i* (CVCe); *r*-controlled *er*; *r*-controlled *ur*

HIGH-FREQUENCY WORDS

a	I	one	the	your
by	of	out	to	

Houghton Mifflin Harcourt.

r-controlled ur

BOOK 143

The Fur Burr

High-Frequency Words Taught to Date

Grade 1

a	call	first	help	me	picture	the	watch
about	car	five	her	more	play	their	water
after	carry	fly	here	mother	pull	there	we
all	cold	follow	hold	my	put	these	were
and	come	food	how	never	read	they	what
animal	could	for	I	new	right	think	where
are	do	four	into	night	said	those	who
around	does	friend	is	no	see	three	why
away	done	full	know	noise	shall	to	window
baby	don't	funny	laugh	now	she	today	with
be	door	give	learning	of	show	too	work
because	down	go	light	off	sing	try	world
been	draw	goes	like	old	small	two	would
before	eat	good	little	one	some	under	write
begins	eight	great	live	open	sometimes	until	years
bird	every	green	long	or	soon	use	yellow
blue	eyes	ground	look	our	starts	very	you
both	fall	grow	loudly	out	story	walk	young
bring	far	have	make	over	sure	want	your
brown	few	he	many	own	take	was	
by	find	hear	maybe	paper	talk	wash	

Decoding skills taught to date: consonants *m, s, c, t*; short *a*; consonant *n*; consonant *d*; consonant *p*; consonant *f*; short *i*; consonant *r*; consonant *h*; /z/ spelled *s*; consonant *b*; consonant *g* (hard); short *o*; consonant *l*; consonant *x*; inflection *-s*; short *e*; consonant *y*; consonant *w*; consonant *k*; consonant *v*; consonant *j*; short *u*; /kw/ spelled *qu*; consonant *z*; final consonants *ll*; final consonants *ss*; consonants *-ck*; final consonants *ff*; consonants *zz*; blends with *r*; blends with *l*; blends with *s*; final blend *mp*; final blend *nt*; final blend *nd*; final blend *st*; digraph *th*; ending *-s*; ending *-es*; ending *-ed* /ed/; ending *-ed* /d/; ending *-ed* /t/; ending *-ing*; digraphs *ch, tch*; possessives with *'s*; digraph *sh*; digraph *wh*; digraph *ph*; contractions *'s, n't*; long *a* (CVCe); soft *c* /s/; /j/ spelled *g, dge*; long *i* (CVCe); digraphs *kn, gn*; digraph *wr*; digraph *mb*; long *o* (CV, CVCe); long *u* (CVCe); long *e* (*e, ee*); long *e* (CVCe, *ea*); final consonants *ng*; final consonants *nk*; long *a* (*ai, ay*); contractions *'ll, 'd*; long *o* (*ow, oa*); contractions *'ve, 're*; compound words; short *e* (*ea*); r-controlled *ar*; r-controlled *or, ore*; r-controlled *er, ir*; r-controlled *ur*

The Fur Burr

The burr comes out of her fur. Zurk Cat curls up on Kurt's lap. Purr, purr, purr.

Zurk Cat likes to lurk in the plants. Zurk Cat lurks by the ferns.

4

1

One plant has burrs. Zurk Cat gets a burr in her fur.

Kurt makes a stern face. "I will pull the burr out of your fur, but it can hurt." Zurk Cat lets Kurt get the burr.

Spur the Herd!

DECODABLE WORDS

Target Skill: *r-controlled ur*

hurls	spur	turn	turns

Previously Taught Skills

and	gate	hold	on	stern
be	get	home	plain	takes
big	gets	horse	rope	
can	has	is	same	
from	her	kind	shut	
Gert	herd	must	steer	

SKILLS APPLIED IN WORDS IN STORY: consonants *m, s, c, t*, short *a*; consonant *n*; consonant *d*; consonant *p*; consonant *f*; short *i*; consonant *r*; consonant *h*; /z/ spelled *s*; consonant *b*; consonant *g* (hard); short *o*; consonant *l*; short *e*; consonant *k*; short *u*; blends with *r*; blends with *l*; blends with *s*; final blend *nd*; final blend *st*; ending *-s*; digraph *sh*; long *a* (CVC*e*); long *i* (CVC*e*); long *o* (CV, CVC*e*); long *e* (*e, ee*); long *a* (*ai*); r-controlled *or*; r-controlled *er*; r-controlled *ur*

HIGH-FREQUENCY WORDS

a	many	the
animal	of	to

Spur the Herd!

Houghton Mifflin Harcourt.

High-Frequency Words Taught to Date

Grade 1

a	call	first	help	me	picture	their	water
about	car	five	her	more	play	there	we
after	carry	fly	here	mother	pull	these	were
all	cold	follow	hold	my	put	they	what
and	come	food	how	never	read	think	where
animal	could	for	I	new	right	those	who
are	do	four	into	night	said	three	why
around	does	friend	is	no	see	to	window
away	done	full	know	noise	she	today	with
baby	don't	funny	laugh	now	show	too	work
be	door	give	learning	of	sing	try	world
because	down	go	light	off	small	two	would
been	draw	goes	like	old	some	under	write
begins	eat	good	little	one	sometimes	until	years
before	eight	great	live	open	soon	use	yellow
bird	every	green	long	or	starts	very	you
blue	eyes	ground	look	our	story	walk	young
both	fall	grow	loudly	out	sure	want	your
bring	far	have	make	over	take	was	
brown	few	he	many	own	talk	wash	
by	find	hear	maybe	paper	the	watch	

Decoding skills taught to date: consonants *m, s, c, t*; short *a*; consonant *n*; consonant *d*; consonant *p*; consonant *f*; short *i*; consonant *r*; consonant *h*; /z/ spelled *s*; consonant *b*; consonant *g* (hard); short *o*; consonant *l*; consonant *x*; inflection *-s*; short *e*; consonant *y*; consonant *w*; consonant *k*; consonant *v*; consonant *j*; short *u*; /kw/ spelled *qu*; consonant *z*; final consonants *ll*; final consonants *ss*; consonants *-ck*; final consonants *ff*; final consonants *zz*; blends with *r*; blends with *l*; blends with *s*; final blend *mp*; final blend *nt*; final blend *nd*; final blend *st*; digraph *th*; ending *-s*; ending *-es*; ending *-ed* /ed/; ending *-ed* /d/; ending *-ed* /t/; ending *-ing*; digraphs *ch, tch*; possessives with *'s*; digraph *sh*; digraph *wh*; digraph *ph*; contractions *'s, n't*; long *a* (CVC*e*); soft *c* /s/; /j/ spelled *g, dge*; long *i* (CVC*e*); digraphs *kn, gn*; digraph *wr*; digraph *mb*; long *o* (CV, CVC*e*); long *u* (CVC*e*); long *e* (*e, ee*); long *e* (CVC*e, ea*); final consonants *ng*; final consonants *nk*; long *a* (*ai, ay*); contractions *'ll, 'd*; long *o* (*ow, oa*); contractions *'ve, 're*; compound words; short *e* (*ea*); *r*-controlled *ar*; *r*-controlled *or, ore*; *r*-controlled *er, ir*; *r*-controlled *ur*

Stern Gert gets the herd
home! Stern Gert turns to shut
the gate.

4

Spur the Herd!

Gert has a herd of steer
to spur. A herd is many of the
same kind of animal.

1

Gert must get the herd home
from the plain. Gert takes her
horse. The herd is big. Gert can
spur the herd.

© Houghton Mifflin Harcourt Publishing Company

Gert must be stern and hold
on. Gert can turn the herd.
Stern Gert hurls her rope.

Pam Is a Good Cook

DECODABLE WORDS

Target Skill: /o͝o/ spelled *oo*

cook	looked	wood
cooked	nook	
good	stood	
hook	took	

Previously Taught Skills

and	her	Pam
at	hot	she
back	in	slid
bite	is	smelled
bread	it	takes
from	last	then
got	likes	time
hat	long	was

SKILLS APPLIED IN WORDS IN STORY: consonants *m, s, t, c*; short *a*; consonant *n*; consonant *d*; short *i*; consonant *r*; /z/ spelled *s*; consonant *b*; consonant *g* (hard); short *o*; consonant *l*; short *e*; consonant *w*; consonant *k*; final consonants *ll*; consonants *-ck*; blends with *r*; blends with *s*; final blend *nd*; final blend *st*; diagraph *th*; ending *-ed* /d/; ending *-s*; digraph *sh*; long *a* (CVCe); long *i* (CVCe); long *e* (e); final consonants *ng*; short *e* (ea); r-controlled *er*; /o͝o/ spelled *oo*

HIGH-FREQUENCY WORDS

a	the	to

Houghton Mifflin Harcourt

Pam Is a Good Cook

High-Frequency Words Taught to Date

Grade 1

a	bring	find	her	more	pull	they	where
about	brown	first	here	mother	put	think	who
after	by	five	hold	my	read	those	why
again	call	fly	house	never	right	three	window
all	car	follow	how	new	said	to	with
along	carry	food	I	night	see	today	work
and	cold	for	in	no	shall	together	world
animal	come	four	into	noise	she	too	would
any	could	friend	is	nothing	show	try	write
are	do	full	kind	now	sing	two	years
around	does	funny	know	of	small	under	yellow
away	done	girl	laugh	off	so	until	you
baby	don't	give	learning	old	some	use	young
be	door	go	light	one	sometimes	very	your
bear	down	goes	like	open	soon	walk	
because	draw	good	little	or	starts	want	
been	eat	great	live	our	story	was	
before	eight	green	long	out	sure	wash	
began	every	ground	look	over	take	watch	
begins	eyes	grow	loudly	own	talk	water	
bird	fall	have	make	paper	the	we	
blue	far	he	many	pictures	their	wear	
both	father	hear	maybe	play	there	were	
boy	few	help	me	pretty	these	what	

Decoding skills taught to date: consonants *m, s, c, t;* short *a;* consonant *n;* consonant *d;* consonant *p;* consonant *f;* short *i;* consonant *r;* consonant *h;* /z/ spelled *s;* consonant *b;* consonant *g* (hard); short *o;* consonant *l;* consonant *x;* inflection *-s;* short *e;* consonant *y;* consonant *w;* consonant *k;* consonant *v;* consonant *j;* short *u;* /kw/ spelled *qu;* consonant *z;* final consonants *ll;* final consonants *ss;* consonants *-ck;* final consonants *ff;* final consonants *zz;* blends with *r;* blends with *l;* blends with *s;* final blend *mp;* final blend *nt;* final blend *nd;* final blend *st;* digraph *th;* ending *-s;* ending *-es;* ending *-ed* /ed/; ending *-ed* /d/; ending *-ed* /t/; ending *-ing;* digraphs *ch, tch;* possessives with *'s;* digraph *sh;* digraph *wh;* digraph *ph;* contractions *'s, n't;* long *a* (CVC*e*); soft *c* /s/; /j/ spelled *g, dge;* long *i* (CVC*e*); digraphs *kn, gn;* digraph *wr;* digraph *mb;* long *o* (CV, CVC*e*); long *u* (CVC*e*); long *e* (*e, ee*); long *e* (CVC*e, ea*); final consonants *ng;* final consonants *nk;* long *a* (*ai, ay*); contractions *'ll, 'd;* long *o* (*ow, oa*); contractions *'ve, 're;* compound words; short *e* (*ea*); *r*-controlled *ar;* *r*-controlled *or, ore;* *r*-controlled *er, ir;* *r*-controlled *ur;* /ŏŏ/ spelled *oo*

At last the bread was cooked.
It looked and smelled good!
Pam took a bite. The bread was
good. Pam is a good cook!

4

Pam Is a Good Cook

Pam likes to cook. She took
her hat from the hook.

1

Pam slid wood in the nook.
Then the cook stood back.

The nook got hot. Pam slid
bread in the hot nook. Bread
takes a long time to cook.

Let's Look at Books

DECODABLE WORDS

Target Skill: /ŏŏ/ spelled *oo*

book	cookbook	took
books	good	
Brooks	look	

Previously Taught Skills

at	got	it's	not
Ben	Hal	Jen	read
can	has	let's	she
did	her	lets	this
dog	is	lots	us
find	it	Miss	

SKILLS APPLIED IN WORDS IN STORY: consonants *m, s, t, c*; short *a*; consonant *n*; consonant *d*; consonant *f*; short *i*; consonant *r*; consonant *h*; /z/ spelled *s*; consonant *b*; consonant *g* (hard); short *o*; inflection -*s*; consonant *l*; short *e*; consonant *k*; consonant *j*; short *u*; final consonants *ss*; final blend *nd*; digraph *th*; digraph *sh*; contraction *'s*; long *e* (*e*); long *e* (*ea*); compound words; *r*-controlled *er*; /ŏŏ/ spelled *oo*

HIGH-FREQUENCY WORDS

a	she
I	the
of	

Houghton Mifflin Harcourt.

Let's Look at Books

High-Frequency Words Taught to Date

Grade 1

a	bring	few	hear	many	paper	talk	watched
about	brown	find	help	maybe	picture	the	water
after	by	first	her	me	play	their	we
again	call	five	here	more	pretty	there	wear
all	car	fly	hold	mother	pull	these	were
along	carry	follow	house	my	put	they	what
and	cold	food	how	never	read	think	where
animal	come	for	I	new	right	those	who
any	could	four	in	night	said	three	why
around	do	friend	into	no	see	to	window
away	does	full	is	noise	shall	today	with
baby	done	funny	kind	nothing	she	together	work
be	don't	girl	know	now	show	too	world
bear	door	give	laugh	of	sing	try	would
because	down	go	learning	off	small	two	write
been	draw	goes	light	old	so	under	years
before	eat	good	like	one	some	until	yellow
began	eight	great	little	open	sometimes	use	you
begins	every	green	live	or	soon	very	young
bird	eyes	ground	long	our	start	walk	your
blue	fall	grow	look	out	story	want	
both	far	have	loudly	over	sure	was	
boy	father	he	make	own	take	wash	

Decoding skills taught to date: consonants *m, s, c, t;* short *a;* consonant *n;* consonant *d;* consonant *p;* consonant *f;* short *i;* consonant *r;* consonant *h;* /z/ spelled *s;* consonant *b;* consonant *g* (hard); short *o;* consonant *l;* consonant *x;* inflection *-s;* short *e;* consonant *y;* consonant *w;* consonant *k;* consonant *v;* consonant *j;* short *u;* /kw/ spelled *qu;* consonant *z;* final consonants *ll;* final consonants *ss;* consonants *-ck;* final consonants *ff;* final consonants *zz;* blends with *r;* blends with *l;* blends with *s;* final blend *mp;* final blend *nt;* final blend *nd;* final blend *st;* digraph *th;* ending *-s;* ending *-es;* ending *-ed* /ed/; ending *-ed* /d/; ending *-ed* /t/; ending *-ing;* digraphs *ch, tch;* possessives with *'s;* digraph *sh;* digraph *wh;* digraph *ph;* contractions *'s, n't;* long *a* (CVC*e*); soft *c* /s/; /j/ spelled *g, dge;* long *i* (CVC*e*); digraphs *kn, gn;* digraph *wr;* digraph *mb;* long *o* (CV, CVC*e*); long *u* (CVC*e*); long *e* (*e, ee*); long *e* (CVC*e, ea*); final consonants *ng;* final consonants *nk;* long *a* (*ai, ay*); contractions *'ll, 'd;* long *o* (*ow, oa*); contractions *'ve, 're;* compound words; short *e* (*ea*); *r*-controlled *ar, r*-controlled *or, ore;* *r*-controlled *er, ir;* *r*-controlled *ur;* /o͞o/ spelled *oo*

Let's Look at Books

Ben took a look at the book.
Ben said, "Look! I can read
this book. It is a good book!"

Miss Brooks has lots of books.
She lets us look at her books.

Hal got a cookbook. Jen got a dog book. Ben did not find a book.

© Houghton Mifflin Harcourt Publishing Company

Miss Brooks said, "Look at this book, Ben. It's a good book." Ben took the book.

The Sisters

DECODABLE WORDS

Target Skill: **closed syllables (CVC)**

forgot	picnic	public	sisters	sunset
garden	pocket	rabbits	sudden	

Previously Taught Skills

and	her	missed	spend
are	home	Mom	time
back	in	Mom's	treat
can	is	not	was
days	Jo	park	we
for	June	run	
from	like	see	
gives	look	soon	

SKILLS APPLIED IN WORDS IN STORY: consonants *m*, *s*, *c*, *t*; short *a*; consonant *n*; consonant *d*; consonant *p*; short *i*; consonant *r*; consonant *h*; /z/ spelled *s*; consonant *b*; consonant *g* (go); short *o*; consonant *l*; inflection -*s*; short *e*; consonant *w*; consonant *k*; blends with *r*; blends with *s*; final blend *nd*; ending -*s*; final consonants *ss*; final consonants -*ck*; ending -*ed* /t/; possessives with '*s*; contractions with '*s*; long *a* (CVC*e*); long *i* (CVC*e*); long *o* (CV); long *u* (CVC*e*); long *e* (e); long *e* (ea); compound words; *r*-controlled *ar*; *r*-controlled *or*; /o͞o/ spelled *oo*; closed syllables (CVC)

HIGH-FREQUENCY WORDS

a	said	they	today
few	the	to	

Houghton Mifflin Harcourt.

The Sisters

High-Frequency Words Taught to Date

Grade 1

a	brown	father	hear	maybe	play	the	water
about	by	few	help	me	pretty	their	we
after	call	find	her	more	pull	there	wear
again	car	first	here	mother	put	these	were
all	carry	five	hold	my	read	they	what
along	cold	fly	house	never	ready	think	where
and	come	follow	how	new	right	those	who
animal	could	food	I	night	said	three	why
any	country	for	in	no	see	to	window
around	covers	four	into	noise	shall	today	with
away	do	friend	is	nothing	she	together	work
baby	does	full	kind(s)	now	show	too	world
be	done	funny	know	of	sing	try	would
bear	don't	girl	laugh	off	small	two	write
because	door	give	learning	old	so	under	years
been	down	go	light	one	soil	until	yellow
before	draw	goes	like	open	some	use	you
began	earth	good	little	or	sometimes	very	young
begins	eat	great	live	our	soon	walk	your
bird	eight	green	long	out	start	want	
blue	every	ground	look	over	story	warms	
both	eyes	grow	loudly	own	sure	was	
boy	fall	have	make	paper	take	wash	
bring	far	he	many	picture	talk	watched	

Decoding skills taught to date: consonants *m, s, c, t*; short *a*; consonant *n*; consonant *d*; consonant *p*; consonant *f*; short *i*; consonant *r*; consonant *h*; /z/ spelled *s*; consonant *b*; consonant *g* (hard); short *o*; consonant *l*; consonant *x*; inflection *-s*; short *e*; consonant *y*; consonant *w*; consonant *k*; consonant *v*; consonant *j*; short *u*; /kw/ spelled *qu*; consonant *z*; final consonants *ll*; final consonants *ss*; consonants *-ck*; final consonants *ff*; final consonants *zz*; blends with *r*; blends with *l*; blends with *s*; final blend *mp*; final blend *nt*; final blend *nd*; final blend *st*; digraph *th*; ending *-s*; ending *-es*; ending *-ed* /ed/; ending *-ed* /d/; ending *-ed* /t/; ending *-ing*; digraphs *ch, tch*; possessives with *'s*; digraph *sh*; digraph *wh*; digraph *ph*; contractions *'s, n't*; long *a* (CVC*e*); soft *c* /s/; /j/ spelled *g, dge*; long *i* (CVC*e*); digraphs *kn, gn*; digraph *wr*; digraph *mb*; long *o* (CV, CVC*e*); long *u* (CVC*e*); long *e* (*e, ee*); long e (CVC*e, ea*); final consonants *ng*; final consonants *nk*; long *a* (*ai, ay*); contractions *'ll, 'd*; long *o* (*ow, oa*); contractions *'ve, 're*; compound words; short *e* (*ea*); *r*-controlled *ar*; *r*-controlled *or, ore*; *r*-controlled *er*, ir; *r*-controlled ur; /o͝o/ spelled *oo*; closed syllables (CVC)

The sisters run back home. Mom is in her garden.

"Mom, we missed the picnic," said June.

Mom gives the sisters a treat from her pocket.

"The picnic was not today," said Mom. "The picnic is in a few days!"

4

The Sisters

Jo and June are sisters. They spend time in Mom's garden. June said, "We forgot the picnic, Jo!"

1

© Houghton Mifflin Harcourt Publishing Company

Jo and June run like rabbits to the picnic. They run to the public park.

Jo and June look and look for the picnic. Soon they can see the sunset. Jo and June missed the picnic!

The Hunt Game

DECODABLE WORDS

Target Skill: **closed syllables (CVC)**

basket	cobweb	napkin	puppet
button	mitten	pencil	sunset

Previously Taught Skills

and	fit	is	lots	she
asked	for	it	make	thing
at	game	last	me	things
big	get	let	Mom	this
can	got	let's	off	use
crossed	hunt	list	on	we
Dad	in	looked	play	will

SKILLS APPLIED IN WORDS IN STORY: consonants *m, s, t, c*; short *a*; consonant *n*; consonant *d*; consonant *p*; consonant *f*; short *i*; consonant *r*; consonant *h*; /z/ spelled *s*; consonant *g* (hard); short *o*; consonant *l*; inflection *-s*; short *e*; consonant *w*; short *u*; final consonants *ll*; final consonants *ss*; final consonants *ff*; blends with *r*; blends with *l*; final blends *nt*; final blends *nd*; final blends *st*; digraph *th*; ending *-s*; ending *-ed* /t/; digraph *sh*; long *a* (CVCe); contraction *'s*; long *e* (e); long *u* (CVCe); final consonants *ng*; compound words; *r*-controlled *or*; /o͞o/ spelled *oo*; closed syllables (CVC)

HIGH-FREQUENCY WORDS

a	I	picture	said
how	of	put	the

Houghton Mifflin Harcourt.

The Hunt Game

High-Frequency Words Taught to Date

Grade 1

a	bring	far	have	many	own	talk	wash
about	brown	father	he	maybe	paper	their	watch
after	by	few	hear	me	pictures	the	water
again	call	find	help	more	play	there	we
all	car	first	her	mother	pull	these	were
along	carry	five	here	my	put	they	what
and	cold	fly	hold	never	read	think	where
animal	come	follow	house	new	right	those	who
are	could	food	how	night	said	three	why
around	do	for	I	no	see	to	window
away	does	four	into	noise	shall	today	with
baby	done	friend	is	nothing	she	together	work
be	don't	full	know	now	show	too	world
because	door	funny	laugh	of	sing	try	would
been	down	give	light	off	small	two	write
before	draw	great	like	old	some	under	years
began	earning	green	little	one	sometimes	use	yellow
begins	eat	go	live	open	soon	until	you
bird	eight	goes	long	or	starts	very	young
blue	every	good	look	our	story	want	your
both	eyes	ground	loudly	out	sure	walk	
boy	fall	grow	make	over	take	was	

Decoding skills taught to date: consonants *m, s, c, t*; short *a*; consonant *n*; consonant *d*; consonant *p*; consonant *f*; short *i*; consonant *r*; consonant *h*; /z/ spelled *s*; consonant *b*; consonant *g* (hard); short *o*; consonant *l*; consonant *x*; inflection -*s*; short *e*; consonant *y*; consonant *w*; consonant *k*; consonant *v*; consonant *j*; short *u*; /kw/ spelled *qu*; consonant *z*; final consonants *ll*; final consonants *ss*; consonants -*ck*; final consonants *ff*; final consonants *zz*; blends with *r*; blends with *l*; blends with *s*; final blend *mp*; final blend *nt*; final blend *nd*; final blend *st*; digraph *th*; ending -*s*; ending -*es*; ending -*ed* /ed/; ending -*ed* /d/; ending -*ed* /t/; ending -*ing*; digraphs *ch, tch*; possessives with *'s*; digraph *sh*; digraph *wh*; digraph *ph*; contractions *'s, n't*; long *a* (CVC*e*); soft *c* /s/; /j/ spelled *g, dge*; long *i* (CVC*e*); digraphs *kn, gn*; digraph *wr*; digraph *mb*; long *o* (CV, CVC*e*); long *u* (CVC*e*); long *e* (*e, ee*); long *e* (CVC*e, ea*); final consonants *ng*; final consonants *nk*; long *a* (*ai, ay*); contractions *'ll, 'd*; long *o* (*ow, oa*); contractions *'ve, 're*; compound words; short *e* (*ea*); *r*-controlled *ar*; *r*-controlled *or, ore*; *r*-controlled *er, ir*; *r*-controlled *ur*; /o͞o/ spelled *oo*; closed syllables (CVC)

Mom looked at the list. "The last thing is a sunset," she said.

"Let me get it," I said. "I can make a picture."

The Hunt Game

"Let's play this game," said Mom. "We hunt for things on this list."

"We put things we get in this big basket," said Dad.

We got the napkin and the
mitten. We got a puppet and
a big button.

"How can we get this cobweb
in the basket?" I asked.

"We use this pencil and make
a picture," said Dad. "It will fit
in this basket."

We crossed off lots of things
on the list.

2

3

You Can Make Soup

DECODABLE WORDS

Target Skill: /o͞o/ spelled *ou*, *ew*

group	soup	you
new	stew	

Previously Taught Skills

and	get	may	shake
big	it	meat	spices
can	like	place	then
cook	look	pot	with
fill	make	rice	

SKILLS APPLIED IN WORDS IN STORY: consonants *m*, *s*, *t*, *c*; short *a*; consonant *n*; consonant *d*; consonant *p*; consonant *f*; short *i*; consonant *r*; consonant *h*; consonant *b*; consonant *g* (hard); short *o*; consonant *l*; short *e*; consonant *y*; consonant *w*; consonant *k*; final consonants *ll*; blends with *r*; blends with *l*; blends with *s*; final blend *nd*; digraph *th*; digraph *sh*; long *a* (CVCe); soft *c* /s/; long *i* (CVCe); long *e* (ea); long *a* (ay); r-controlled *or*; /o͞o/ spelled *oo*; /o͞o/ spelled *ou*, *ew*

HIGH-FREQUENCY WORDS

a	the
also	to
into	water

You Can Make Soup

Houghton Mifflin Harcourt.

High-Frequency Words Taught to Date

Grade 1

a	boy	eyes	grow	loudly	over	sure	was
about	bring	fall	have	make	own	take	wash
after	brown	far	he	many	paper	talk	watch
again	by	father	hear	maybe	pictures	the	water
all	call	few	help	me	play	their	we
almost	car	find	her	more	pull	there	were
along	carry	first	here	mother	put	these	what
and	cold	five	hold	my	read	they	where
animal	come	fly	house	never	ready	think	who
are	could	follow	how	new	right	those	why
around	country	food	I	night	said	three	window
away	covers	for	into	no	see	to	with
baby	do	four	is	noise	shall	today	work
be	does	friend	kinds	nothing	she	together	world
bear	done	full	know	now	show	too	would
because	don't	funny	laugh	of	sing	try	write
been	door	give	learning	off	small	two	years
before	down	go	light	old	soil	under	yellow
began	draw	goes	like	one	some	until	you
begins	earth	good	little	open	sometimes	use	young
bird	eat	great	live	or	soon	very	your
blue	eight	green	long	our	starts	walk	
both	every	ground	look	out	story	warms	

Decoding skills taught to date: consonants *m, s, c, t*; short *a*; consonant *n*; consonant *d*; consonant *p*; consonant *f*; short *i*; consonant *r*; consonant *h*; /z/ spelled *s*; consonant *b*; consonant *g* (hard); short *o*; consonant *l*; consonant *x*; inflection *-s*; short *e*; consonant *y*; consonant *w*; consonant *k*; consonant *v*; consonant *j*; short *u*; /kw/ spelled *qu*; consonant *z*; final consonants *ll*; final consonants *ss*; consonants *-ck*; final consonants *ff*; final consonants *zz*; blends with *r*; blends with *l*; blends with *s*; final blend *mp*; final blend *nt*; final blend *nd*; final blend *st*; digraph *th*; ending *-s*; ending *-es*; ending *-ed* /ed/; ending *-ed* /d/; ending *-ed* /t/; ending *-ing*; digraphs *ch, tch*; possessives with *'s*; digraph *sh*; digraph *wh*; digraph *ph*; contractions *'s, n't*; long *a* (CVC*e*); soft *c* /s/; /j/ spelled *g, dge*; long *i* (CVC*e*); digraphs *kn, gn*; digraph *wr*; digraph *mb*; long *o* (CV, CVC*e*); long *u* (CVC*e*); long *e* (*e, ee*); long *e* (CVC*e, ea*); final consonants *ng*; final consonants *nk*; long *a* (*ai, ay*); contractions *'ll, 'd*; long *o* (*ow, oa*); contractions *'ve, 're*; compound words; short *e* (*ea*); *r*-controlled *ar*; *r*-controlled *or, ore*; *r*-controlled *er*, ir; *r*-controlled *ur*; /o͞o/ spelled *oo*; closed syllables (CVC); /o͞o/ spelled *ou, ew*

You Can Make Soup

To make new soup, you get rice, meat, spices, and a big soup pot.

You may shake spices into the soup.

You can also make soup for a group!

You place the meat and rice into the big soup pot.

You fill the soup pot with water. Then you cook the soup. It may look like stew.

Dew in the Yew Tree

DECODABLE WORDS

Target Skill: /o͞o/ spelled *ou*, *ew*

Dew	knew	mewed	you
Drew	Lou	new	
group	mew	yew	

Previously Taught Skills

and	got	she
called	had	thank
can	his	tree
cat	in	up
did	know	wait
get	not	

SKILLS APPLIED IN WORDS IN STORY: consonants *m, s, c, t*; short *a*; consonant *n*; consonant *d*; consonant *p*; short *i*; consonant *r*; consonant *h*; /z/ spelled *s*; consonant *g* (hard); short *o*; consonant *l*; short *e*; consonant *y*; consonant *w*; consonant *k*; short *u*; final consonants *ll*; blends with *r*; digraph *th*; ending *-ed* /d/; digraph *sh*; digraph *kn*; long *e* (*e, ee*); final consonants *nk*; long *a* (*ai*); long *o* (*ow*); /o͞o/ spelled *ou*, *ew*

HIGH-FREQUENCY WORDS

a	said
do	the
down	to
how	what

Houghton Mifflin Harcourt.

Dew in the Yew Tree

High-Frequency Words Taught to Date

Grade 1

a	boy	eyes	grow	loudly	over	sure	was
about	bring	fall	have	make	own	take	wash
after	brown	far	he	many	paper	talk	watch
again	by	father	hear	maybe	pictures	the	water
all	call	few	help	me	play	their	we
almost	car	find	her	more	pull	there	were
along	carry	first	here	mother	put	these	what
and	cold	five	hold	my	read	they	where
animal	come	fly	house	never	ready	think	who
are	could	follow	how	new	right	those	why
around	country	food	I	night	said	three	window
away	covers	for	into	no	see	to	with
baby	do	four	is	noise	shall	today	work
be	does	friend	kinds	nothing	she	together	world
bear	done	full	know	now	show	too	would
because	don't	funny	laugh	of	sing	try	write
been	door	give	learning	off	small	two	years
before	down	go	light	old	soil	under	yellow
began	draw	goes	like	one	some	until	you
begins	earth	good	little	open	sometimes	use	young
bird	eat	great	live	or	soon	very	your
blue	eight	green	long	our	starts	walk	
both	every	ground	look	out	story	warms	

Decoding skills taught to date: consonants *m, s, c, t;* short *a;* consonant *n;* consonant *d;* consonant *p;* consonant *f;* short *i;* consonant *r;* consonant *h;* /z/ spelled *s;* consonant *b;* consonant *g* (hard); short *o;* consonant *l;* consonant *x;* inflection *-s;* short *e;* consonant *y;* consonant *w;* consonant *k;* consonant *v;* consonant *j;* short *u;* /kw/ spelled *qu;* consonant *z;* final consonants *ll;* final consonants *ss;* consonants *-ck;* final consonants *ff;* final consonants *zz;* blends with *r;* blends with *l;* blends with *s;* final blend *mp;* final blend *nt;* final blend *nd;* final blend *st;* digraph *th;* ending *-s;* ending *-es;* ending *-ed* /ed/; ending *-ed* /d/; ending *-ed* /t/; ending *-ing;* digraphs *ch, tch;* possessives with *'s;* digraph *sh;* digraph *wh;* digraph *ph;* contractions *'s, n't;* long *a* (CVC*e*); soft *c* /s/; /j/ spelled *g, dge;* long *i* (CVC*e*); digraphs *kn, gn;* digraph *wr;* digraph *mb;* long *o* (CV, CVC*e*); long *u* (CVC*e*); long *e* (*e, ee*); long *e* (CVC*e, ea*); final consonants *ng;* final consonants *nk;* long *a* (*ai, ay*); contractions *'ll, 'd;* long *o* (*ow, oa*); contractions *'ve, 're;* compound words; short *e* (*ea*); *r*-controlled *ar; r*-controlled *or, ore; r*-controlled *er,* ir*; r*-controlled *ur;* /o͞o/ spelled *oo;* closed syllables (CVC); /o͞o/ spelled *ou, ew*

Drew and his group got Dew.

"Thank you," said Lou.

"Mew, mew, mew," mewed
Dew.

Dew in the Yew Tree

Lou had a new cat, Dew.

Dew mewed.

"Mew, mew, mew."

Dew knew how to get up the yew tree. Dew did not know how to get down. Dew mewed. "Mew, mew, mew." What can Lou do?

"Wait!" called Lou. She knew what to do.

"Mew, mew, mew," mewed Dew.

Animals Eat Food, Too!

DECODABLE WORDS

Target Skill: /o͞o/ spelled *oo*

cool	loon	raccoon	too
food	pool	roots	

Previously Taught Skills

are	dives	get	its	own
bird	eat	hog	kind	this
brings	fish	is	likes	we
digs	for	it	mom	

SKILLS APPLIED IN WORDS IN STORY: consonants *m, s, t, c*; short *a*; consonant *n*; consonant *d*; consonant *p*; consonant *f*; short *i*; consonant *r*; consonant *h*; /z/ spelled *s*; consonant *b*; consonant *g* (hard); short *o*; consonant *l*; inflection -*s*; short *e*; consonant *w*; consonant *k*; consonant *v*; final blend *nd*; digraph *th*; ending -*s*; digraph *sh*; long *i* (CVC*e*); long *e* (*e, ee*); long *e* (*ea*); long *o* (*ow*); *r*-controlled *ir*; /o͞o/ spelled *oo*

HIGH-FREQUENCY WORDS

a	baby	little	to
animals	into	of	

Houghton Mifflin Harcourt.

Animals Eat Food, Too!

High-Frequency Words Taught to Date

Grade 1

a	brown	father	help	more	put	they	where
about	by	few	her	mother	read	think	who
after	call	find	here	my	ready	those	why
again	car	first	hold	never	right	three	window
all	carry	five	house	new	said	to	with
almost	cold	fly	how	night	see	today	work
along	come	follow	I	no	shall	together	world
and	could	food	into	noise	she	too	would
animal	country	for	is	nothing	show	try	write
are	covers	four	kinds	now	sing	two	years
around	do	friend	know	of	small	under	yellow
away	does	full	laugh	off	soil	until	you
baby	done	funny	learning	old	some	use	young
be	don't	give	light	one	sometimes	very	your
because	door	go	like	open	soon	walk	
been	down	goes	little	or	starts	want	
before	draw	good	live	our	story	warms	
began	earth	great	long	out	sure	was	
begins	eat	green	look	over	take	wash	
bird	eight	ground	loudly	own	talk	watch	
blue	every	grow	make	paper	the	water	
both	eyes	have	many	pictures	their	we	
boy	fall	he	maybe	play	there	were	
bring	far	hear	me	pull	these	what	

Decoding skills taught to date: consonants *m*, *s*, *c*, *t*; short *a*; consonant *n*; consonant *d*; consonant *p*; consonant *f*; short *i*; consonant *r*; consonant *h*; /z/ spelled *s*; consonant *b*; consonant *g* (hard); short *o*; consonant *l*; consonant *x*; inflection -*s*; short *e*; consonant *y*; consonant *w*; consonant *k*; consonant *v*; consonant *j*; short *u*; /kw/ spelled *qu*; consonant *z*; final consonants *ll*; final consonants *ss*; consonants -*ck*; final consonants *ff*; final consonants *zz*; blends with *r*; blends with *l*; blends with *s*; final blend *mp*; final blend *nt*; final blend *nd*; final blend *st*; digraph *th*; ending -*s*; ending -*es*; ending -*ed* /ed/; ending -*ed* /d/; ending -*ed* /t/; ending -*ing*; digraphs *ch*, *tch*; possessives with '*s*; digraph *sh*; digraph *wh*; digraph *ph*; contractions '*s*, *n't*; long *a* (CVC*e*); soft *c* /s/; /j/ spelled *g*, *dge*; long *i* (CVC*e*); digraphs *kn*, *gn*; digraph *wr*; digraph *mb*; long *o* (CV, CVC*e*); long *u* (CVC*e*); long *e* (*e*, *ee*); long *e* (CVC*e*, *ea*); final consonants *ng*; final consonants *nk*; long *a* (*ai*, *ay*); contractions '*ll*, '*d*; long *o* (*ow*, *oa*); contractions '*ve*, '*re*; compound words; short *e* (*ea*); r-controlled *ar*; r-controlled *or*, *ore*; r-controlled *er*, *ir*; r-controlled *ur*; /o͞o/ spelled *oo*; closed syllables (CVC); /o͞o/ spelled *ou*, *ew*; /o͞o/ spelled *oo*

This baby raccoon is too little
to get its own food. Its mom
brings it food.

4

Animals Eat Food, Too!

We eat food. Animals eat
food, too!

1

© Houghton Mifflin Harcourt Publishing Company

A loon is a kind of bird. This loon dives into a cool pool. Fish are food for a loon.

This hog digs for roots. It likes to eat roots. Roots are food for this hog.

2

3

Joon's Big Blooms

DECODABLE WORDS

Target Skill: /o͞o/ spelled *oo*

bloom	food	noon	scoop
blooms	Joon	room	too
drooping	Joon's	roots	tools

Previously Taught Skills

and	drops	Hee	need	them
are	fix	his	pot	then
at	gets	in	puts	
big	grows	lots	sets	
dirt	he	must	sun	

SKILLS APPLIED IN WORDS IN STORY: consonants *m, s, c, t*; short *a*; consonant *n*; consonant *d*; consonant *p*; consonant *t*; short *i*; consonant *h*; /z/ spelled *s*; consonant *b*; consonant *g* (hard); short *o*; consonant *l*; consonant *x*; inflection *-s*; short *e*; consonant *w*; consonant *j*; short *u*; blends with *r*; blends with *l*; blends with *s*; final blend *nd*; digraph *th*; ending *-s*; ending *-ing*; possessives with *'s*; long *e* (*e, ee*); long *o* (*ow*); r-controlled *ir*; /o͞o/ spelled *oo*

HIGH-FREQUENCY WORDS

a	of	they
gives	the	

Houghton Mifflin Harcourt

/o͞o/ spelled *oo*

BOOK 152

Joon's Big Blooms

High-Frequency Words Taught to Date

Grade 1

a	bring	far	hear	me	pull	these	what
about	brown	father	help	more	put	they	where
after	by	few	her	mother	read	think	who
again	call	find	here	my	ready	those	why
all	car	first	hold	never	right	three	window
almost	carry	five	house	new	said	to	with
along	cold	fly	how	night	see	today	work
and	come	follow	I	no	shall	together	world
animal	could	food	into	noise	she	too	would
are	country	for	is	nothing	show	try	write
around	covers	four	kinds	now	sing	two	years
away	do	friend	know	of	small	under	yellow
baby	does	full	laugh	off	soil	until	you
be	done	funny	learning	old	some	use	young
bear	don't	give	light	one	sometimes	very	your
because	door	go	like	open	soon	walk	
been	down	goes	little	or	starts	want	
before	draw	good	live	our	story	warms	
began	earth	great	long	out	sure	was	
begins	eat	green	look	over	take	wash	
bird	eight	ground	loudly	own	talk	watch	
blue	every	grow	make	paper	the	water	
both	eyes	have	many	pictures	their	we	
boy	fall	he	maybe	play	there	were	

Decoding skills taught to date: consonants *m*, *s*, *c*, *t*; short *a*; consonant *n*; consonant *d*; consonant *p*; consonant *f*; short *i*; consonant *r*; consonant *h*; /z/ spelled *s*; consonant *b*; consonant *g* (hard); short *o*; consonant *l*; consonant *x*; inflection -*s*; short *e*; consonant *y*; consonant *w*; consonant *k*; consonant *v*; consonant *j*; short *u*; /kw/ spelled *qu*; consonant *z*; final consonants *ll*; final consonants *ss*; consonants -*ck*; final consonants *ff*; final consonants *zz*; blends with *r*; blends with *l*; blends with *s*; final blend *mp*; final blend *nt*; final blend *nd*; final blend *st*; digraph *th*; ending -*s*; ending -*es*; ending -*ed* /ed/; ending -*ed* /d/; ending -*ed* /t/; ending -*ing*; digraphs *ch*, *tch*; possessives with '*s*; digraph *sh*; digraph *wh*; digraph *ph*; contractions '*s*, *n't*; long *a* (CVC*e*); soft *c* /s/; /j/ spelled *g*, *dge*; long *i* (CVC*e*); digraphs *kn*, *gn*; digraph *wr*; digraph *mb*; long *o* (CV, CVC*e*); long *u* (CVC*e*); long *e* (*e*, *ee*); long *e* (CVC*e*, *ea*); final consonants *ng*; final consonants *nk*; long *a* (*ai*, *ay*); contractions '*ll*, '*d*; long *o* (*ow*, *oa*); contractions '*ve*, '*re*; compound words; short *e* (*ea*); *r*-controlled *ar*; *r*-controlled *or*, *ore*; *r*-controlled *er*, *ir*; *r*-controlled *ur*; /o͞o/ spelled *oo*; closed syllables (CVC); /o͞o/ spelled *ou*, *ew*; /o͞o/ spelled *oo*

Joon Hee sets the blooms in the sun at noon. He gives them food, too. They bloom, bloom, bloom!

4

Joon's Big Blooms

Joon Hee grows lots of big blooms in his room.

1

Joon Hee puts the roots in the pot. Then he gets his tools. He drops a scoop of dirt in the pot.

The blooms are drooping! Joon Hee must fix the blooms. They need sun and food.

Glue Clues

DECODABLE WORDS

Target Skill: /o͞o/ spelled *u*, *ue*

clue	glue	Stu's	true
clues	Stu	Sue	truth

Previously Taught Skills

are	have	make	rug	took
be	in	making	see	use
close	is	me	so	went
find	it	much	soon	will
for	know	need	spots	yelled
gift	lead	nice	thank	you
go	like	now	that	
good	line	on	they	
has	look	place	this	

SKILLS APPLIED IN WORDS IN STORY: consonants *m, s, t, c*; short *a*; consonant *n*; consonant *d*; consonant *p*; consonant *f*; short *i*; consonant *r*; consonant *h*; /z/ spelled *s*; consonant *g* (hard); short *o*; consonant *l*; inflection -*s*; short *e*; consonant *y*; consonant *w*; consonant *k*; consonant *v*; short *u*; final consonants *ll*; blends with *r*; blends with *l*; blends with *s*; digraph *th*; ending -*s*; ending -*ed* /d/; ending -*ing*; digraph *ch*; possessives with '*s*; long *a* (CVCe); soft *c* /s/; long *i* (CVCe); digraph *kn*; long *o* (CV, CVCe); long *u* (CVCe); long *e* (*e, ee*); long *e* (*ea*); final consonants *nk*; long *o* (*ow*); *r*-controlled *ar*; /o͞o/ spelled *oo*; /o͞o/ spelled *oo*; /o͞o/ spelled *u, ue*

HIGH-FREQUENCY WORDS

a	friend	my	said	to
door	I	out	the	where

Houghton Mifflin Harcourt

Glue Clues

High-Frequency Words Taught to Date

Grade 1

a	brown	few	here	never	said	today	would
about	by	find	hold	new	see	together	write
after	call	first	house	night	shall	too	years
again	car	five	how	no	she	try	yellow
all	carry	fly	I	noise	show	two	you
almost	cold	follow	into	nothing	sing	under	young
along	come	food	is	now	small	until	your
and	could	for	kinds	of	soil	use	
animal	country	four	know	off	some	very	
are	covers	friend	laugh	old	sometimes	walk	
around	do	full	learning	one	soon	warms	
away	does	funny	light	open	starts	was	
baby	done	give	like	or	story	wash	
be	don't	go	little	our	sure	watch	
bear	door	goes	live	out	take	water	
because	down	good	long	over	talk	we	
been	draw	great	look	own	the	were	
before	earth	green	loudly	paper	their	what	
began	eat	ground	make	pictures	there	where	
begins	eight	grow	many	play	these	who	
bird	every	have	maybe	pull	they	why	
blue	eyes	he	me	put	think	window	
both	fall	hear	more	read	those	with	
boy	far	help	mother	ready	three	work	
bring	father	her	my	right	to	world	

Decoding skills taught to date: consonants *m, s, c, t;* short *a;* consonant *n;* consonant *d;* consonant *p;* consonant *f;* short *i;* consonant *r;* consonant *h;* /z/ spelled *s;* consonant *b;* consonant *g* (hard); short *o;* consonant *l;* consonant *x;* inflection *-s;* short *e;* consonant *y;* consonant *w;* consonant *k;* consonant *v;* consonant *j;* short *u;* /kw/ spelled *qu;* consonant *z;* final consonants *ll;* final consonants *ss;* consonants *-ck;* final consonants *ff;* final consonants *zz;* blends with *r;* blends with *l;* blends with *s;* final blend *mp;* final blend *nt;* final blend *nd;* final blend *st;* digraph *th;* ending *-s;* ending *-es;* ending *-ed* /ed/; ending *-ed* /d/; ending *-ed* /t/; ending *-ing;* digraphs *ch, tch;* possessives with *'s;* digraph *sh;* digraph *wh;* digraph *ph;* contractions *'s, n't;* long *a* (CVCe); soft *c* /s/; /j/ spelled *g, dge;* long *i* (CVCe); digraphs *kn, gn;* digraph *wr;* digraph *mb;* long *o* (CV, CVCe); long *u* (CVCe); long *e* (*e, ee*); long *e* (CVCe, *ea*); final consonants *ng;* final consonants *nk;* long *a* (*ai, ay*); contractions *'ll, 'd;* long *o* (*ow, oa*); contractions *'ve, 're;* compound words; short *e* (*ea*); *r*-controlled *ar; r*-controlled *or, ore; r*-controlled *er, ir; r*-controlled *ur;* /o͝o/ spelled *oo;* closed syllables (CVC); /o͞o/ spelled *ou, ew;* /o͞o/ spelled *oo;* /o͞o/ spelled *u, ue*

"It is the truth, Sue," said Stu.
"I took that glue to make this
gift for you!"

"Thank you, Stu!" yelled Sue.
"It is such a nice gift. I like it
so much. You are a good, good
friend for making this for me."

4

Glue Clues

"I will need glue soon," said
Sue. "Where is my glue? It has
to be in a place that is close.
I know! Now I will go look for
clues."

1

"Look, clues! I see glue spots on this rug. They are in a line. I will find out where the glue spots lead!"

The glue spots went to Stu's door. "Stu, I have a clue," said Sue. "Is it true that you have my glue? I will need to use it soon."

Your Book Is Due, Ruth

DECODABLE WORDS

Target Skill: /o͞o/ spelled *u*, *ue*

Blue	overdue	Ruth's	truth
due	Ruth	true	

Previously Taught Skills

asked	dad	is	slid	took
be	dime	it	take	will
book	her	Miss	thank	you
books	in	must	that	
box	into	not	this	

SKILLS APPLIED IN WORDS IN STORY: consonants *m, s, t*; short *a*; consonant *d*; short *i*; consonant *r*; consonant *h*; /z/ spelled *s*; consonant *b*; short *o*; consonant *l*; consonant *x*; inflection *-s*; consonant *w*; consonant *k*; short *u*; final consonants *ll*; final consonants *ss*; blends with *r*; blends with *l*; blends with *s*; final blend *st*; ending *-ed* /d/; digraph *th*; ending *-s*; possessives with *'s*; compound words; long *a* (CVCe); long *i* (CVCe); long *e* (e); final consonants *nk*; *r*-controlled *er*; /o͞o/ spelled *oo*; /o͞o/ spelled *ou*; /o͞o/ spelled *oo*; /o͞o/ spelled *u, ue*

HIGH-FREQUENCY WORDS

a	over	the	your
again	put	to	
my	said	today	

Houghton Mifflin Harcourt

Your Book Is Due, Ruth

High-Frequency Words Taught to Date

Grade 1

a	brown	few	here	never	said	today	would
about	by	find	hold	new	see	together	write
after	call	first	house	night	shall	too	years
again	car	five	how	no	she	try	yellow
all	carry	fly	I	noise	show	two	you
almost	cold	follow	into	nothing	sing	under	young
along	come	food	is	now	small	until	your
and	could	for	kinds	of	soil	use	
animal	country	four	know	off	some	very	
are	covers	friend	laugh	old	sometimes	walk	
around	do	full	learning	one	soon	warms	
away	does	funny	light	open	starts	was	
baby	done	give	like	or	story	wash	
be	don't	go	little	our	sure	watch	
bear	door	goes	live	out	take	water	
because	down	good	long	over	talk	we	
been	draw	great	look	own	the	were	
before	earth	green	loudly	paper	their	what	
began	eat	ground	make	pictures	there	where	
begins	eight	grow	many	play	these	who	
bird	every	have	maybe	pull	they	why	
blue	eyes	he	me	put	think	window	
both	fall	hear	more	read	those	with	
boy	far	help	mother	ready	three	work	
bring	father	her	my	right	to	world	

Decoding skills taught to date: consonants *m, s, c, t*; short *a*; consonant *n*; consonant *d*; consonant *p*; consonant *f*; short *i*; consonant *r*; consonant *h*; /z/ spelled *s*; consonant *b*; consonant *g* (hard); short *o*; consonant *l*; consonant *x*; inflection -*s*; short *e*; consonant *y*; consonant *w*; consonant *k*; consonant *v*; consonant *j*; short *u*; /kw/ spelled *qu*; consonant *z*; final consonants *ll*; final consonants *ss*; consonants -*ck*; final consonants *ff*; final consonants *zz*; blends with *r*; blends with *l*; blends with *s*; final blend *mp*; final blend *nt*; final blend *nd*; final blend *st*; digraph *th*; ending -*s*; ending -*es*; ending -*ed* /ed/; ending -*ed* /d/; ending -*ed* /t/; ending -*ing*; digraphs *ch, tch*; possessives with '*s*; digraph *sh*; digraph *wh*; digraph *ph*; contractions '*s, n't*; long *a* (CVC*e*); soft *c* /s/; /j/ spelled *g, dge*; long *i* (CVC*e*); digraphs *kn, gn*; digraph *wr*; digraph *mb*; long *o* (CV, CVC*e*); long *u* (CVC*e*); long *e* (*e, ee*); long *e* (CVC*e, ea*); final consonants *ng*; final consonants *nk*; long *a* (*ai, ay*); contractions '*ll,* '*d*; long *o* (*ow, oa*); contractions '*ve,* '*re*; compound words; short *e* (*ea*); *r*-controlled *ar*; *r*-controlled *or, ore*; *r*-controlled *er, ir*; *r*-controlled *ur*; /o͞o/ spelled *oo*; closed syllables (CVC); /o͞o/ spelled *ou, ew*; /o͝o/ spelled *oo*; /o͞o/ spelled *u, ue*

Ruth slid a dime into the box.
"My books will not be overdue again," said Ruth.

"Thank you!" said Miss Blue.

4

Your Book Is Due, Ruth

"Ruth, your book is due," said Ruth's dad. "Take it over to Miss Blue."

1

Ruth took her book to Miss Blue.

"Miss Blue, is it true that my book is due today?" asked Ruth.

"Ruth, the truth is that your book is overdue," said Miss Blue. "You must put a dime in this box."

It Is June!

DECODABLE WORDS

Target Skill: /o͞o/ spelled *u_e* (CVC*e*)

Bruce	June	Luke's	spruce	tune
Duke	Luke	prune	tube	

Previously Taught Skills

as	help	is	Mom	sing	will
called	helped	it	picked	this	you
game	his	let's	pup	up	

SKILLS APPLIED IN WORDS IN STORY: consonants *m, s, c, t*; short *a*; consonant *n*; consonant *d*; consonant *p*; short *i*; consonant *r*; consonant *h*; /z/ spelled *s*; consonant *b*; consonant *g* (hard); short *o*; consonant *l*; short *e*; consonant *y*; consonant *w*; consonant *k*; consonant *j*; short *u*; final consonants *ll*; consonants *-ck*; blends with *r*; blends with *s*; ending *-ed* /d/; digraph *ch*; contraction *'s*; long *a* (CVC*e*); soft *c* /s/; final consonants *ng*; /o͞o/ spelled *ou*; /o͞o/ spelled *oo*; /o͞o/ spelled *u_e* (CVC*e*)

HIGH-FREQUENCY WORDS

a	house	the
do	I	
every	said	

 Houghton Mifflin Harcourt.

It Is June!

High-Frequency Words Taught to Date

Grade 1

a	bring	fall	he	many	paper	talk	wash
about	brown	far	hear	maybe	pictures	the	watch
after	by	father	help	me	play	their	water
again	call	few	her	more	pull	there	we
all	car	find	here	mother	put	these	were
almost	carry	first	hold	my	read	they	what
along	cold	five	house	never	ready	think	where
and	come	fly	how	new	right	those	who
animal	could	follow	I	night	said	three	why
are	country	food	into	no	see	to	window
around	covers	for	is	noise	shall	today	with
away	do	four	kinds	nothing	she	together	work
baby	does	friend	know	now	show	too	world
be	don't	funny	laugh	of	sing	try	would
because	done	give	learning	off	small	two	write
been	door	go	light	old	soil	under	years
before	down	goes	like	one	some	until	yellow
began	draw	good	little	open	sometimes	use	you
begins	earth	great	live	or	soon	very	young
bird	eat	green	long	our	starts	walk	your
blue	eight	ground	look	out	story	want	
both	every	grow	loudly	over	sure	warms	
boy	eyes	have	make	own	take	was	

Decoding skills taught to date: consonants *m, s, c, t*; short *a*; consonant *n*; consonant *d*; consonant *p*; consonant *f*; short *i*; consonant *r*; consonant *h*; /z/ spelled *s*; consonant *b*; consonant *g*; short *o*; consonant *l*; consonant *x*; inflection *-s*; short *e*; consonant *y*; consonant *w*; consonant *k*; consonant *v*; consonant *j*; short *u*; /kw/ spelled *qu*; consonant *z*; final consonants *ll*; final consonants *ss*; consonants *ck*; final consonants *ff*; final consonants *zz*; blends with *r*; blends with *l*; blends with *s*; final blend *mp*; final blend *nt*; final blend *nd*; final blend *st*; digraph *th*; ending *-s*; ending *-es*; ending *-ed* /ed/; ending *-ed* /d/; ending *-ed* /t/; ending *-ing*; digraphs *ch, tch*; possessives with *'s*; digraph *sh*; digraph *wh*; digraph *ph*; contractions *'s, n't*; long *a* (CVC*e*); soft *c* /s/; /j/ spelled *g, dge*; long *i* (CVC*e*); digraphs *kn, gn*; digraph *wr*; digraph *mb*; long *o* (CV, CVC*e*); long *u* (CVC*e*); long *e* (*e, ee*); long *e* (CVC*e, ea*); final consonants *ng*; final consonants *nk*; long *a* (*ai, ay*); contractions *'ll, 'd*; long *o* (*ow, oa*); contractions *'ve, 're*; compound words; short *e* (*ea*); r-controlled *ar*; r-controlled *or, ore*; r-controlled *er, ir*; r-controlled *ur*; vowel digraph *oo* /ŏŏ/; closed syllables (CVC); /oo/ spelled *oo, ou*; /oo/ spelled *ew*; /oo/ spelled *u, ue*; /oo/ spelled *u_e*

"Let's do this every June!"
said Mom.

4

It Is June!

"Bruce! Luke!" called Mom.
"It is June! Will you help spruce
up the house?"

1

"I will prune this spruce,"
said Bruce. "As I prune, I will
sing a tune!"

Luke picked up his tube game.
Luke's pup, Duke, helped, too!

2

3

Spruce Tune

DECODABLE WORDS

Target Skill: /o͞o/ spelled *u_e* (CVCe)

Bruce	June	lute	tune
flute	Luke	spruce	

Previously Taught Skills

big	hit	likes	names	street
her	is	lives	on	up
his	it	makes	plays	

SKILLS APPLIED IN WORDS IN STORY: consonants *m, s, c, t*; consonant *n*; consonant *p*; consonant *f*; short *i*; consonant *r*; consonant *h*; /z/ spelled *s*; consonant *b*; consonant *g* (hard); short *o*; consonant *l*; inflection *-s*; consonant *y*; consonant *k*; consonant *v*; consonant *j*; short *u*; blends with *r*; blends with *l*; blends with *s*; ending *-s*; long *a* (CVCe); soft *c* /s/; long *i* (CVCe); long *e* (ee); long *a* (ay); r-controlled *er*; /o͞o/ spelled *u_e* (CVCe)

HIGH-FREQUENCY WORDS

a

Houghton Mifflin Harcourt.

/o͞o/ spelled *u_e* (CVCe)

BOOK 156

Spruce Tune

SPRUCE

High-Frequency Words Taught to Date

Grade 1

a	boy	eyes	grow	loudly	over	sure	was
about	bring	fall	have	make	own	take	wash
after	brown	far	he	many	paper	talk	watch
again	by	father	hear	maybe	pictures	the	water
all	call	few	help	me	play	their	we
almost	car	find	her	more	pull	there	were
along	carry	first	here	mother	put	these	what
and	cold	five	hold	my	read	they	where
animal	come	fly	house	never	ready	think	who
are	could	follow	how	new	right	those	why
around	country	food	I.	night	said	three	window
away	covers	for	into	no	see	to	with
baby	do	four	is	noise	shall	today	work
be	does	friend	kinds	nothing	she	together	world
bear	done	full	know	now	show	too	would
because	don't	funny	laugh	of	sing	try	write
been	door	give	learning	off	small	two	years
before	down	go	light	old	soil	under	yellow
began	draw	goes	like	one	some	until	you
begins	earth	good	little	open	sometimes	use	young
bird	eat	great	live	or	soon	very	your
blue	eight	green	long	our	starts	walk	
both	every	ground	look	out	story	warms	

Decoding skills taught to date: consonants *m, s, c, t;* short *a;* consonant *n;* consonant *d;* consonant *p;* consonant *f;* short *i;* consonant *r;* consonant *h;* /z/ spelled *s;* consonant *b;* consonant *g;* short *o;* consonant *l;* consonant *x;* inflection *-s;* short *e;* consonant *y;* consonant *w;* consonant *k;* consonant *v;* consonant *j;* short *u;* /kw/ spelled *qu;* consonant *z;* final consonants *ll;* final consonants *ss;* consonants *ck;* final consonants *ff;* final consonants *zz;* blends with *r;* blends with *l;* blends with *s;* final blend *mp;* final blend *nt;* final blend *nd;* final blend *st;* digraph *th;* ending *-s;* ending *-es;* ending *-ed* /ed/; ending *-ed* /d/; ending *-ed* /t/; ending *-ing;* digraphs *ch, tch;* possessives with *'s;* digraph *sh;* digraph *wh;* digraph *ph;* contractions *'s, n't;* long *a* (CVC*e*); soft *c* /s/; /j/ spelled *g, dge;* long *i* (CVC*e*); digraphs *kn, gn;* digraph *wr;* digraph *mb;* long *o* (CV, CVC*e*); long *u* (CVC*e*); long *e* (*e, ee*); long *e* (CVC*e, ea*); final consonants *ng;* final consonants *nk;* long *a* (*ai, ay*); contractions *'ll, 'd;* long *o* (*ow, oa*); contractions *'ve, 're;* compound words; short *e* (*ea*); *r*-controlled *ar;* *r*-controlled *or, ore;* *r*-controlled *er, ir;* *r*-controlled *ur;* /o͝o/ spelled *oo;* closed syllables (CVC); /o͞o/ spelled *ou, ew;* /o͞o/ spelled *oo;* /o͞o/ spelled *u, ue;* /o͞o/ spelled *u_e* (CVC*e*)

"Spruce Tune" is a big hit on Spruce Street!

4

Spruce Tune

Luke lives on Spruce Street. Luke makes up a tune. Luke names it "Spruce Tune."

1

Bruce likes "Spruce Tune."
Bruce plays "Spruce Tune" on
his flute.

June likes "Spruce Tune."
June plays "Spruce Tune" on
her lute.

Al and Scout

DECODABLE WORDS

Target Skill: /ou/ spelled *ou, ow*

bounded	ground	out	pout	scowled
couch	house	outside	round	slouched
down	now	pounded	Scout	

Previously Taught Skills

Al	go	kept	rain	wet
and	hat	Mom	sat	you
can	he	on	then	
don't	his	onto	went	

SKILLS APPLIED IN WORDS IN STORY: consonants *m, s, t, c,* short *a;* consonant *n;* consonant *d;* consonant *p;* short *i;* consonant *r;* consonant *h;* /z/ spelled *s;* consonant *b;* consonant *g* (hard); short *o;* consonant *l;* short *e;* consonant *y;* consonant *w;* consonant *k;* blends with *r;* blends with *l;* blends with *s;* final blend *nt;* final blend *nd;* digraph *th;* ending *-ed* /ed/; ending *-ed* /d/; digraph *ch;* contraction *n't;* long *i* (CVCe); long *o* (CV); long *e* (*e*), long *a* (*ai*); compound words; /ou/ spelled *ou, ow*

HIGH-FREQUENCY WORDS

all	of	said
around	put	the

Houghton Mifflin Harcourt

Al and Scout

High-Frequency Words Taught to Date

Grade 1

a	brown	family	hear	more	please	their	what
about	buy	far	help	mother	pull	there	where
after	by	father	her	my	put	these	who
again	call	few	here	myself	read	they	why
all	car	find	hold	never	ready	think	window
almost	carry	first	house	new	right	those	with
along	city	five	how	night	said	three	work
and	cold	fly	I	no	school	to	world
animal	come	follow	into	noise	see	today	would
are	could	food	is	nothing	seven	together	write
around	country	for	kinds	now	shall	too	years
away	covers	four	know	of	she	try	yellow
baby	do	friend	laugh	off	show	two	you
be	does	full	learning	old	sing	under	young
bear	done	funny	light	one	small	until	your
because	don't	give	like	open	soil	use	
been	door	go	little	or	some	very	
before	down	goes	live	our	sometimes	walk	
began	draw	good	long	out	soon	warms	
begins	earth	great	look	over	starts	was	
bird	eat	green	loudly	own	story	wash	
blue	eight	ground	make	paper	sure	watch	
both	every	grow	many	party	take	water	
boy	eyes	have	maybe	pictures	talk	we	
bring	fall	he	me	play	the	were	

Decoding skills taught to date: consonants *m, s, c, t*; short *a*; consonant *n*; consonant *d*; consonant *p*; consonant *f*; short *i*; consonant *r*; consonant *h*; /z/ spelled *s*; consonant *b*; consonant *g* (hard); short *o*; consonant *l*; consonant *x*; inflection *-s*; short *e*; consonant *y*; consonant *w*; consonant *k*; consonant *v*; consonant *j*; short *u*; /kw/ spelled *qu*; consonant *z*; final consonants *ll*; final consonants *ss*; consonants *-ck*; final consonants *ff*; final consonants *zz*; blends with *r*; blends with *l*; blends with *s*; final blend *mp*; final blend *nt*; final blend *nd*; final blend *st*; digraph *th*; ending *-s*; ending *-es*; ending *-ed* /ed/; ending *-ed* /d/; ending *-ed* /t/; ending *-ing*; digraphs *ch, tch*; possessives with *'s*; digraph *sh*; digraph *wh*; digraph *ph*; contractions *'s, n't*; long *a* (CVC*e*); soft *c* /s/; /j/ spelled *g, dge*; long *i* (CVC*e*); digraphs *kn, gn*; digraph *wr*; digraph *mb*; long *o* (CV, CVC*e*); long *u* (CVC*e*); long *e* (*e, ee*); long *e* (CVC*e, ea*); final consonants *ng*; final consonants *nk*; long *a* (*ai, ay*); contractions *'ll, 'd*; long *o* (*ow, oa*); contractions *'ve, 're*; compound words; short *e* (*ea*); r-controlled *ar*; r-controlled *or, ore*; r-controlled *er, ir*; r-controlled *ur*; /o͝o/ spelled *oo*; closed syllables (CVC); /o͞o/ spelled *ou, ew*; /o͞o/ spelled *oo*; /o͞o/ spelled *u, ue*; /ou/ spelled *ou, ow*

Al and Scout

Al and Scout slouched on the couch. Al scowled. Outside, the rain pounded down.

1

Al and Scout bounded out onto the wet ground. And the rain kept falling down all around town!

4

Mom said, "Don't pout, Al.
You and Scout can go out now."

© Houghton Mifflin Harcourt Publishing Company

Al sat down. He put on his
round hat. Then he and Scout
went out of the house.

No Gown Downtown

DECODABLE WORDS

Target Skill: /ou/ spelled *ou, ow*

crown	found	gown	sound
downtown	frowned	proud	

Previously Taught Skills

am	did	no	that	will
and	just	not	then	you
can	make	Rose	this	
can't	Mom	she	wear	

SKILLS APPLIED IN WORDS IN STORY: consonants *m, s, t, c*; short *a*; consonant *n*; consonant *d*; consonant *p*; consonant *f*; short *i*; consonant *r*; consonant *h*; consonant *g* (hard); short *o*; consonant *l*; short *e*; consonant *y*; consonant *w*; consonant *j*; short *u*; final consonants *ll*; blends with *r*; final blend *nd*; digraph *th*; ending -*ed* /d/; digraph *sh*; contraction *n't*; long *a* (CVC*e*); long *o* (CV, CVC*e*); long *e* (*e*); compound words; short *e* (*ea*); /ou/ spelled *ou, ow*

HIGH-FREQUENCY WORDS

a	I	said
again	of	your

Houghton Mifflin Harcourt

/ou/ spelled *ou, ow*

BOOK 158

No Gown Downtown

High-Frequency Words Taught to Date

Grade 1

a	bring	eyes	grow	make	own	starts	warms
about	brown	fall	have	many	paper	story	was
after	buy	family	he	maybe	party	sure	wash
again	by	far	hear	me	pictures	take	watch
all	call	father	help	more	play	talk	water
almost	car	few	her	mother	please	the	we
along	carry	find	here	my	pull	their	were
and	city	first	hold	myself	put	there	what
animal	cold	five	house	never	read	these	where
are	come	fly	how	new	ready	they	who
around	could	follow	I	night	right	think	why
away	country	food	into	no	said	those	window
baby	covers	for	is	noise	school	three	with
be	do	four	kinds	nothing	see	to	work
bear	does	friend	know	now	seven	today	world
because	done	full	laugh	of	shall	together	would
been	don't	funny	learning	off	she	too	write
before	door	give	light	old	show	try	years
began	down	go	like	one	sing	two	yellow
begins	draw	goes	little	open	small	under	you
bird	earth	good	live	or	soil	until	young
blue	eat	great	long	our	some	use	your
both	eight	green	look	out	sometimes	very	
boy	every	ground	loudly	over	soon	walk	

Decoding skills taught to date: consonants *m, s, c, t;* short *a;* consonant *n;* consonant *d;* consonant *p;* consonant *f;* short *i;* consonant *r;* consonant *h;* /z/ spelled *s;* consonant *b;* consonant *g* (hard); short *o;* consonant *l;* consonant *x;* inflection *-s;* short *e;* consonant *y;* consonant *w;* consonant *k;* consonant *v;* consonant *j;* short *u;* /kw/ spelled *qu;* consonant *z;* final consonants *ll;* final consonants *ss;* consonants *-ck;* final consonants *ff;* final consonants *zz;* blends with *r,* blends with *l,* blends with *s;* final blend *mp;* final blend *nt;* final blend *nd;* final blend *st;* digraph *th;* ending *-s;* ending *-es;* ending *-ed* /ed/; ending *-ed* /d/; ending *-ed* /t/; ending *-ing;* digraphs *ch, tch;* possessives with *'s;* digraph *sh;* digraph *wh;* digraph *ph;* contractions *'s, n't;* long *a* (CVC*e*); soft *c* /s/; /j/ spelled *g, dge;* long *i* (CVC*e*); digraphs *kn, gn;* digraph *wr;* digraph *mb;* long *o* (CV, CVC*e*); long *u* (CVC*e*); long *e* (*e, ee*); long *e* (CVC*e, ea*); final consonants *ng;* final consonants *nk;* long *a* (*ai, ay*); contractions *'ll, 'd;* long *o* (*ow, oa*); contractions *'ve, 're;* compound words; short *e* (*ea*); *r*-controlled *ar;* *r*-controlled *or, ore;* *r*-controlled *er, ir;* *r*-controlled *ur;* /o͞o/ spelled *oo;* closed syllables (CVC); /o͞o/ spelled *ou, ew;* /o͞o/ spelled *oo;* /o͞o/ spelled *u, ue;* /o͞o/ spelled *u_e* (CVC*e*); /ou/ spelled *ou, ow*

"I am proud of you, Rose," said Mom. "We will have fun downtown. Then you can wear your crown and gown again!"

4

No Gown Downtown

Rose found a crown and a gown. "I will wear this crown and gown downtown," said Rose.

1

"No, Rose," said Mom. "You can't wear that crown and gown downtown."

Rose did not make a sound. She just frowned.

Ten Coins

DECODABLE WORDS

Target Skill: */oi/ spelled oy, oi*

coins	foil	moist	spoil
Floyd	joy	pointed	toy

Previously Taught Skills

big	got	meal	pulled	will
cake	had	Mom	snack	with
did	he	not	store	you
eat	his	off	ten	
for	in	or	this	
gave	man	placed	went	

SKILLS APPLIED IN WORDS IN STORY: consonants *m, s, t, c*; short *a*; consonant *n*; consonant *d*; consonant *p*; consonant *f*; short *i*; consonant *r*; consonant *h*; /z/ spelled *s*; consonant *b*; consonant *g* (hard); short *o*; consonant *l*; short *e*; consonant *y*; consonant *w*; consonant *v*; consonant *j*; final consonants *ll*; final consonants *ff*; blends with *l*; blends with *s*; final blend *st*; final blend *nt*; digraph *th*; ending *-ed* /ed/; ending *-ed* /d/; long *a* (CVCe); soft *c* /s/; long *e* (e); long *e* (ea); *r*-controlled *or*; /o͞o/ spelled *ou*; /oi/ spelled *oy, oi*

HIGH-FREQUENCY WORDS

a	called	I	said	to
buy	do	maybe	the	your

/oi/ spelled *oy, oi*

BOOK 159

Ten Coins

High-Frequency Words Taught to Date

Grade 1

a	brown	family	hear	more	please	their	what
about	buy	far	help	mother	pull	there	where
after	by	father	her	my	put	these	who
again	call	few	here	myself	read	they	why
all	car	find	hold	never	ready	think	window
almost	carry	first	house	new	right	those	with
along	city	five	how	night	said	three	work
and	cold	fly	I	no	school	to	world
animal	come	follow	into	noise	see	today	would
are	could	food	is	nothing	seven	together	write
around	country	for	kinds	now	shall	too	years
away	covers	four	know	of	she	try	yellow
baby	do	friend	laugh	off	show	two	you
be	does	full	learning	old	sing	under	young
bear	done	funny	light	one	small	until	your
because	don't	give	like	open	soil	use	
been	door	go	little	or	some	very	
before	down	goes	live	our	sometimes	walk	
began	draw	good	long	out	soon	warms	
begins	earth	great	look	over	starts	was	
bird	eat	green	loudly	own	story	wash	
blue	eight	ground	make	paper	sure	watch	
both	every	grow	many	party	take	water	
boy	eyes	have	maybe	pictures	talk	we	
bring	fall	he	me	play	the	were	

Decoding skills taught to date: consonants *m, s, c, t*; short *a*; consonant *n*; consonant *d*; consonant *p*; consonant *f*; short *i*; consonant *r*; consonant *h*; /z/ spelled *s*; consonant *b*; consonant *g* (hard); short *o*; consonant *l*; consonant *x*; inflection *-s*; short *e*; consonant *y*; consonant *w*; consonant *k*; consonant *v*; consonant *j*; short *u*; /kw/ spelled *qu*; consonant *z*; final consonants *ll*; final consonants *ss*; consonants *-ck*; final consonants *ff*; final consonants *zz*; blends with *r*; blends with *l*; blends with *s*; final blend *mp*; final blend *nt*; final blend *nd*; final blend *st*; digraph *th*; ending *-s*; ending *-es*; ending *-ed* /ed/; ending *-ed* /d/; ending *-ed* /t/; ending *-ing*; digraphs *ch, tch*; possessives with '*s*; digraph *sh*; digraph *wh*; digraph *ph*; contractions '*s*, *n't*; long *a* (CVC*e*); soft *c* /s/; /j/ spelled *g, dge*; long *i* (CVC*e*); digraphs *kn, gn*; digraph *wr*; digraph *mb*; long *o* (CV, CVC*e*); long *u* (CVC*e*); long *e* (*e, ee*); long *e* (CVC*e, ea*); final consonants *ng*; final consonants *nk*; long *a* (*ai, ay*); contractions '*ll*, '*d*; long *o* (*ow, oa*); contractions '*ve*, '*re*; compound words; short *e* (*ea*); *r*-controlled *ar*; *r*-controlled *or, ore*; *r*-controlled *er, ir*; *r*-controlled *ur*; /o͞o/ spelled *oo*; closed syllables (CVC); /o͞o/ spelled *ou, ew*; /o͞o/ spelled *oo*; /o͞o/ spelled *u, ue*; /o͞o/ spelled *u_e* (CVC*e*); /ou/ spelled *ou, ow*; /oi/ spelled *oy, oi*

Floyd pulled the foil off the cake. "For you, Mom!" he said with joy. "I got you this moist cake!"

4

Ten Coins

Floyd had ten coins. "Maybe I will buy a toy," he said.

1

Floyd went to the store.
"Do not eat a snack or you will
spoil your meal," called Mom.

Floyd did not buy a toy. He
pointed to a big, moist cake in
the bakery. Floyd gave the man
his ten coins. The man placed
the cake in foil.

The New Boy

DECODABLE WORDS

Target Skill: /oi/ spelled *oy, oi*

boy	joined	pointed	Troy
join	Joy	Roy	voice

Previously Taught Skills

am	don't	in	new	soft
at	feel	is	next	this
be	first	it	not	want
can	glad	like	now	was
class	he	low	sad	you
desk	her	Miss	she	
did	his	Mom	sit	

SKILLS APPLIED IN WORDS IN STORY: consonants *m, s, t, c*; short *a*; consonant *n*; consonant *d*; consonant *p*; short *i*; consonant *r*; consonant *h*; /z/ spelled *s*; consonant *b*; consonant *g* (hard); short *o*; consonant *l*; consonant *x*; short *e*; consonant *y*; consonant *w*; consonant *k*; consonant *v*; consonant *j*; final consonants *ss*; blends with *r*; blends with *l*; final blend *nt*; final blend *st*; digraph *th*; ending *-ed* /d/; ending *-ed* /ed/; digraph *sh*; contraction *n't*; soft *c* /s/; long *i* (CVCe); long *e* (*e, ee*); long *o* (*ow*); *r*-controlled *er*; /ou/ spelled *ow*; /oi/ spelled *oy, oi*

HIGH-FREQUENCY WORDS

a	here	said	the
day	I	school	to
happy	our	teacher	

© Houghton Mifflin Harcourt Publishing Company

/oi/ spelled *oy, oi*

BOOK 160

The New Boy

High-Frequency Words Taught to Date

Grade 1

a	brown	family	hear	more	please	their	what
about	buy	far	help	mother	pull	there	where
after	by	father	her	my	put	these	who
again	call	few	here	myself	read	they	why
all	car	find	hold	never	ready	think	window
almost	carry	first	house	new	right	those	with
along	city	five	how	night	said	three	work
and	cold	fly	I	no	school	to	world
animal	come	follow	into	noise	see	today	would
are	could	food	is	nothing	seven	together	write
around	country	for	kinds	now	shall	too	years
away	covers	four	know	of	she	try	yellow
baby	do	friend	laugh	off	show	two	you
be	does	full	learning	old	sing	under	young
bear	done	funny	light	one	small	until	your
because	don't	give	like	open	soil	use	
been	door	go	little	or	some	very	
before	down	goes	live	our	sometimes	walk	
began	draw	good	long	out	soon	warms	
begins	earth	great	look	over	starts	was	
bird	eat	green	loudly	own	story	wash	
blue	eight	ground	make	paper	sure	watch	
both	every	grow	many	party	take	water	
boy	eyes	have	maybe	pictures	talk	we	
bring	fall	he	me	play	the	were	

Decoding skills taught to date: consonants *m, s, c, t;* short *a;* consonant *n;* consonant *d;* consonant *p;* consonant *f;* short *i;* consonant *r;* consonant *h;* /z/ spelled *s;* consonant *b;* consonant *g* (hard); short *o;* consonant *l;* consonant *x;* inflection -*s;* short *e;* consonant *y;* consonant *w;* consonant *k;* consonant *v;* consonant *j;* short *u;* /kw/ spelled *qu;* consonant *z;* final consonants *ll;* final consonants *ss;* consonants -*ck;* final consonants *ff;* final consonants *zz;* blends with *r,* blends with *l;* blends with *s;* final blend *mp;* final blend *nt;* final blend *nd;* final blend *st;* digraph *th;* ending -*s;* ending -*es;* ending -*ed* /ed/; ending -*ed* /d/; ending -*ed* /t/; ending -*ing;* digraphs *ch, tch;* possessives with '*s;* digraph *sh;* digraph *wh;* digraph *ph;* contractions '*s, n't;* long *a* (CVC*e*); soft *c* /s/; /j/ spelled *g, dge;* long *i* (CVC*e*); digraphs *kn, gn;* digraph *wr;* digraph *mb;* long *o* (CV, CVC*e*); long *u* (CVC*e*); long *e* (*e, ee*); long *e* (CVC*e, ea*); final consonants *ng;* final consonants *nk;* long *a* (*ai, ay*); contractions '*ll, 'd;* long *o* (*ow, oa*); contractions '*ve, 're;* compound words; short *e* (*ea*); *r*-controlled *ar;* *r*-controlled *or, ore;* *r*-controlled *er, ir;* *r*-controlled *ur;* /o͞o/ spelled *oo;* closed syllables (CVC); /o͞o/ spelled *ou, ew;* /o͞o/ spelled *oo;* /o͞o/ spelled *u, ue;* /o͞o/ spelled *u_e* (CVC*e*); /ou/ spelled *ou, ow;* /oi/ spelled *oy, oi*

The New Boy

Roy was sad. It was his first day at a new school. "Mom, I don't want to be the new boy," said Roy.

Roy joined Joy at her desk. Now he was happy. He did not feel like the new boy!

4

1

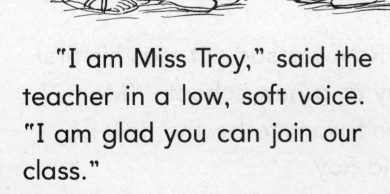

"I am Miss Troy," said the
teacher in a low, soft voice.
"I am glad you can join our
class."

Miss Troy said, "Class, this is
Roy. He is new here."

"Sit here, Roy," said Joy. She
pointed next to her.

2

3

Draw, Draw, Draw

DECODABLE WORDS

Target Skill: /aw/ spelled *aw, au*

Aubree	draws	lawn
draw	fawn	Paul
drawn	hawk	pauses

Previously Taught Skills

and	big	has	then
at	can	he	
Ben	class	on	

SKILLS APPLIED IN WORDS IN STORY: consonant *t, c*; short *a*; consonant *n*; consonant *d*; consonant *p*; consonant *f*; short *i*; consonant *r*; consonant *h*; /z/ spelled *s*; consonant *b*; consonant *g* (hard); short *o*; consonant *l*; inflection *-s*; short *e*; consonant *k*; final consonants *ss*; blends with *r*; blends with *l*; final blend *nd*; digraph *th*; long *e* (*e, ee*); /aw/ spelled *aw, au*

HIGH-FREQUENCY WORDS

a	school	the

Houghton Mifflin Harcourt

Draw, Draw, Draw

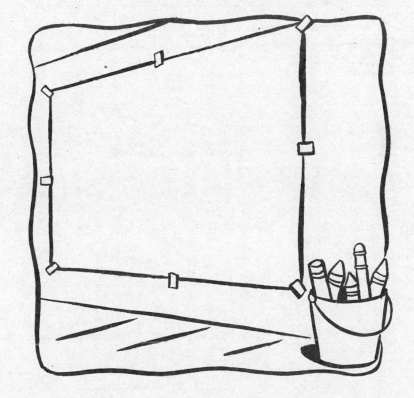

High-Frequency Words Taught to Date

Grade 1

a	brown	fall	have	many	paper	story	warms
about	buy	family	he	maybe	party	sure	was
after	by	far	hear	me	pictures	take	wash
again	call	father	help	more	play	talk	watch
all	car	few	her	mother	please	the	water
almost	carry	find	here	my	pull	their	we
along	city	first	hold	myself	put	there	were
and	cold	five	house	never	read	these	what
animal	come	fly	how	new	ready	they	where
are	could	follow	I	night	right	think	who
around	country	food	into	no	said	those	why
away	covers	for	is	noise	school	three	window
baby	do	four	kinds	nothing	see	to	with
be	does	friend	know	now	seven	today	work
because	done	full	laugh	of	shall	together	world
been	don't	funny	learning	off	she	too	would
before	door	give	light	old	show	try	write
began	down	go	like	one	sing	two	years
begins	draw	goes	little	open	small	under	yellow
bird	earth	good	live	or	soil	until	you
blue	eat	great	long	our	some	use	young
both	eight	green	look	out	sometimes	very	your
boy	every	ground	loudly	over	soon	walk	
bring	eyes	grow	make	own	starts	want	

Decoding skills taught to date: consonant *m, s, t, c*; short *a*; consonant *n*; consonant *d*; consonant *p*; consonant *f*; short *i*; consonant *r*; consonant *h*; /z/ spelled *s*; consonant *b*; consonant *g* (hard); short *o*; consonant *l*; consonant *x*; inflection *–s*; short *e*; consonant *y*; consonant *w*; consonant *k*; consonant *v*; consonant *j*; short *u*; /kw/ spelled *qu*; consonant *z*; final consonants *ll*; final consonants *ss*; consonants *ck*; final consonants *ff*; final consonants *zz*; blends with *r*; blends with *l*; blends with *s*; final blend *mp*; final blend *nt*; final blend *nd*; final blend *st*; digraph *th*; ending *–s*; ending *–es*; ending *–ed* /ed/; ending *–ed* /d/; ending *–ed* /t/; ending *–ing*; digraphs *ch, tch*; possessives with *'s*; digraph *sh*; digraph *wh*; digraph *ph*; contractions *'s, n't*; long *a* (CVC*e*); soft *c* /s/; /j/ spelled *g, dge*; long *i* (CVC*e*); digraphs *kn, gn*; digraph *wr*; digraph *mb*; long *o* (CV, CVC*e*); long *u* (CVC*e*); long *e* (*e, ee*); long *e* (CVC*e, ea*); final consonants *ng*; final consonants *nk*; long *e* (*ea, e_e*); long *a* (*ai, ay*); contractions *'ll, 'd*; long *o* (*ow, oa*); contractions *'ve, 're*; compound words; short *e* (*ea*); *r*-controlled *ar*; *r*-controlled *or, ore*; *r*-controlled *er, ir, ur*; /o͞o/ spelled *oo*; closed syllables (CVC); /o͞o/ spelled *ou, ew*; /o͞o/ spelled *oo*; /o͞o/ spelled *u, ue*; /o͞o/ spelled *u_e* (CVC*e*); /ou/ spelled *ou, ow*; /oi/ spelled *oy, oi*; /aw/ spelled *aw, au*

The class has drawn a hawk and a fawn on a big lawn!

Draw, Draw, Draw

First, Paul draws a big lawn.

Ben pauses. Then he draws
a hawk on the big lawn.

Last, Aubree draws a fawn
on the big lawn.

© Houghton Mifflin Harcourt Publishing Company

Paul

DECODABLE WORDS

Target Skill: /aw/ spelled *aw, au*

cause	jaunt	Paul	prawns
dawn	launch	pause	yawns

Previously Taught Skills

at	from	it's	still
boat	go	looks	time
can't	he	not	will
dock	his	off	
fish	is	on	
for	it	rope	

SKILLS APPLIED IN WORDS IN STORY: consonant *m, s, t, c*; short *a*; consonant *n*; consonant *d*; consonant *p*; consonant *f*; short *i*; consonant *r*; consonant *h*; /z/ spelled *s*; consonant *b*; consonant *g* (hard); short *o*; consonant *l*; inflection –*s*; consonant *y*; consonant *w*; consonant *k*; consonant *j*; final consonants *ll*; consonants *ck*; final consonants *ff*; blends with *r*; blends with *s*; final blend *nt*; ending –*s*; digraph *ch*; digraph *sh*; contractions '*s, n't*; long *i* (CVCe); long *o* (CV, CVCe); long *e (e)*; long *o* (*oa*); *r*-controlled *or*; /o͞o/ spelled *oo*; /aw/ spelled *aw, au*

HIGH-FREQUENCY WORDS

a	the	there	to	wants

Houghton Mifflin Harcourt.

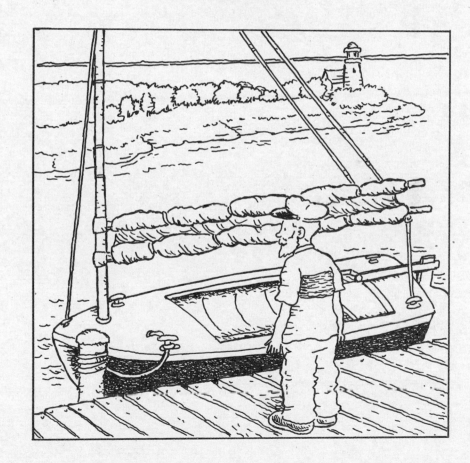

Paul

High-Frequency Words Taught to Date

Grade 1

a	buy	far	help	mother	pull	there	what
about	by	father	her	my	put	these	where
after	call	few	here	myself	read	they	who
again	car	find	hold	never	ready	think	why
all	carry	first	house	new	right	those	window
almost	city	five	how	night	said	three	with
along	cold	fly	I	no	school	to	work
and	come	follow	into	noise	see	today	world
animal	could	food	is	nothing	seven	together	would
are	country	for	kinds	now	shall	too	write
around	covers	four	know	of	she	try	years
away	do	friend	laugh	off	show	two	yellow
baby	does	full	learning	old	sing	under	you
be	done	funny	light	one	small	until	young
because	don't	give	like	open	soil	use	your
been	door	go	little	or	some	very	
before	down	goes	live	our	sometimes	walk	
began	draw	good	long	out	soon	want	
begins	earth	great	look	over	starts	warms	
bird	eat	green	loudly	own	story	was	
blue	eight	ground	make	paper	sure	wash	
both	every	grow	many	party	take	watch	
boy	eyes	have	maybe	pictures	talk	water	
bring	fall	he	me	play	the	we	
brown	family	hear	more	please	their	were	

Decoding skills taught to date: consonant *m, s, t, c*; short *a*; consonant *n*; consonant *d*; consonant *p*; consonant *f*; short *i*; consonant *r*; consonant *h*; /z/ spelled *s*; consonant *b*; consonant *g* (hard); short *o*; consonant *l*; consonant *x*; inflection *–s*; short *e*; consonant *y*; consonant *w*; consonant *k*; consonant *v*; consonant *j*; short *u*; /kw/ spelled *qu*; consonant *z*; final consonants *ll*; final consonants *ss*; consonants *ck*; final consonants *ff*; final consonants *zz*; blends with *r*; blends with *l*; blends with *s*; final blend *mp*; final blend *nt*; final blend *nd*; final blend *st*; digraph *th*; ending *–s*; ending *–es*; ending *–ed* /ed/; ending *–ed* /d/; ending *–ed* /t/; ending *–ing*; digraphs *ch, tch*; possessives with *'s*; digraph *sh*; digraph *wh*; digraph *ph*; contractions *'s, n't*; long *a* (CVC*e*); soft *c* /s/; /j/ spelled *g, dge*; long *i* (CVC*e*); digraphs *kn, gn*; digraph *wr*; digraph *mb*; long *o* (CV, CVC*e*); long *u* (CVC*e*); long *e* (*e, ee*); long *e* (CVC*e, ea*); final consonants *ng*; final consonants *nk*; long *e* (*ea, e_e*); long *a* (*ai, ay*); contractions *'ll, 'd*; long *o* (*ow, oa*); contractions *'ve, 're*; compound words; short *e* (*ea*); r-controlled *ar*; r-controlled *or, ore*; r-controlled *er, ir, ur*; /o͞o/ spelled *oo*; closed syllables (CVC); /o͞o/ spelled *ou, ew*; /o͞o/ spelled *oo*; /o͞o/ spelled *u, ue*; /o͞o/ spelled *u_e* (CVC*e*); /ou/ spelled *ou, ow*; /oi/ spelled *oy, oi*; /aw/ spelled *aw, au*

Paul is off on his jaunt! It's time to fish for prawns at dawn.

Paul

It is dawn. Paul yawns. He wants to fish for prawns.

Paul can't launch his boat
from the dock!
 There is a pause. The boat
will not go.

The boat still will not go.
Paul looks for the cause. It is
the rope!

Clapping and Tapping

DECODABLE WORDS

Target Skill: **ending *-ing*: drop *e*; double consonant**

chatting	dining	sipping	spinning
clapping	hopping	skipping	tapping
dancing	joking	smiling	

Previously Taught Skills

and	has	is	Nate	stoop
bedroom	he	jumping	on	Tess
crunching	her	Kim	playing	
glass	his	look	she	
hands	in	munching	springing	

SKILLS APPLIED IN WORDS IN STORY: consonants *m, s, t, c*; short *a*; consonant *n*; consonant *d*; consonant *p*; short *i*; consonant *r*; consonant *h*; /z/ spelled *s*; consonant *b*; consonant *g* (hard); short *o*; consonant *l*; short *e*; consonant *k*; consonant *j*; short *u*; final consonants *ss*; blends with *r*; blends with *l*; blends with *s*; final blend *mp*; final blend *nd*; ending *-s*; ending *-ing*; digraph *ch*; digraph *sh*; long *a* (CVCe); soft *c* /s/; long *i* (CVCe); long o (CVCe); long e (e); final consonants *ng*; long *a* (ay); compound words; *r*-controlled *er*; closed syllables (CVC); /o͞o/ spelled *oo*; ending *-ing*: drop *e*, double consonant

HIGH-FREQUENCY WORDS

a	do(ing)	the	what
are	learning	they	window

Houghton Mifflin Harcourt

Clapping and Tapping

High-Frequency Words Taught to Date

Grade 1

a	bring	eyes	have	maybe	pictures	sure	want
about	brown	fall	he	me	play	surprised	warms
above	buy	family	hear	more	please	take	was
after	by	far	help	mother	pull	talk	wash
again	call	father	her	my	pushed	teacher	watch
all	car	few	here	myself	put	the	water
almost	carry	find	hold	never	read	their	we
along	city	first	house	new	ready	there	were
and	cold	five	how	night	right	these	what
animal	come	fly	I	no	said	they	where
are	could	follow	into	noise	school	think	who
around	country	food	is	nothing	see	those	why
away	covers	for	kinds	now	seven	three	window
baby	do	four	know	of	shall	to	with
be	does	friend	laugh	off	she	today	work
bear	done	full	learning	old	show	together	world
because	don't	funny	light	one	sing	too	would
been	door	give	like	open	small	toward	write
before	down	go	little	or	soil	try	years
began	draw	goes	live	our	some	two	yellow
begins	earth	good	long	out	sometimes	under	you
bird	eat	great	look	over	soon	until	young
blue	eight	green	loudly	own	starts	use	your
both	even	ground	make	paper	story	very	
boy	every	grow	many	party	studied	walk	

Decoding skills taught to date: consonants *m, s, t, c*; short *a*; consonant *n*; consonant *d*; consonant *p*; consonant *f*; short *i*; consonant *r*; consonant *h*; /z/ spelled *s*; consonant *b*; consonant *g* (hard); short *o*; consonant *l*; consonant *x*; inflection *s*; short *e*; consonant *y*; consonant *w*; consonant *k*; consonant *v*; consonant *j*; short *u*; /kw/ spelled *qu*; consonant *z*; final consonants *ll*; final consonants *ss*; consonants *ck*; final consonants *ff*; final consonants *zz*; blends with *r*; blends with *l*; blends with *s*; final blends *mp*; final blend *nt*; final blend *nd*; final blend *st*; digraph *th*; ending -*s*; ending -*es*; ending -*ed* /ed/; ending -*ed* /d/; ending -*ed* /t/; ending -*ing*; digraphs *ch, tch*; possessives with *'s*; digraph *sh*; digraph *wh*; digraph *ph*; contractions with *'s* and *n't*; long *a* (CVC*e*); soft *c* /s/; /j/ spelled *g* and *dge*; long *i* (CVC*e*); digraphs *kn, gn*; digraph *wr*; digraph *mb*; long *o* (CV, CVC*e*); long *u* (CVC*e*); long *e* (*e, ee*); long *e* (CVC*e, ea*); final consonants *ng*; final consonants *nk*; long *e* (*ea, e_e*); long *a* (*ai, ay*); contractions *'ll* and *'d*; long *o* (*ow, oa*); contractions *'ve* and *'re*; compound words; short *e* (*ea*); r-controlled *ar*; r-controlled *or* and *ore*; r-controlled *er, ir*; r-controlled *ur*; /o͝o/ spelled *oo*; closed syllables (CVC); /o͞o/ spelled *ou, ew*; /o͞o/ spelled *oo*, /o͞o/ spelled *u, ue*; /o͞o/ spelled *u_e* (CVC*e*); /ou/ spelled *ou, ow*; /oi/ spelled *oy, oi*; /aw/ spelled *aw, au*; ending -*ing*: drop *e*, double consonant

What are Tess, Nate, and Kim doing on the stoop? They are smiling, chatting, joking, playing, and learning.

Clapping and Tapping

Look in the window. Tess is clapping, tapping, dancing, and spinning.

Nate has a glass in his hands. He is dining, munching, crunching, and sipping.

Kim is in her bedroom. She is skipping, hopping, jumping, and springing.

Rising, Shining, Setting

DECODABLE WORDS

Target Skill: **ending *-ing*: drop *e*; double consonant**

chasing	gliding	humming	shining
dozing	hiding	rising	tapping
flipping	hopping	setting	waking

Previously Taught Skills

and	food	is	now
bees	hare	its	owl
birds	her	just	sun
bugs	hole	lots	toads
cub	home	mom	
for	in	moon	

SKILLS APPLIED IN WORDS IN STORY: consonants *m, s, t, c*; short *a*; consonant *n*; consonant *d*; consonant *p*; consonant *f*; short *i*; consonant *r*; consonant *h*; /z/ spelled *s*; consonant *b*; consonant *g* (hard); short *o*; consonant *l*; inflection *-s*; short *e*; consonant *w*; consonant *k*; consonant *j*; short *u*; consonant *z*; blends with *l*; final blend *nd*; final blend *st*; digraph *th*; ending *-s*; digraph *ch*; digraph *sh*; long *a* (CVCe); long *i* (CVCe); long *o* (CVCe); long *e* (ee); final consonants *ng*; long *o* (oa); *r*-controlled *or*; *r*-controlled *er*; *r*-controlled *ir*; /o͞o/ spelled *oo*; /ou/ spelled *ow*; ending *-ing*: drop *e*, double consonant

HIGH-FREQUENCY WORDS

a	are	of
animal(s)	other	the

Houghton Mifflin Harcourt.

© Houghton Mifflin Harcourt Publishing Company

Rising, Shining, Setting

High-Frequency Words Taught to Date

Grade 1

a	bring	eyes	have	maybe	pictures	sure	want
about	brown	fall	he	me	play	surprised	warms
above	buy	family	hear	more	please	take	was
after	by	far	help	mother	pull	talk	wash
again	call	father	her	my	pushed	teacher	watch
all	car	few	here	myself	put	the	water
almost	carry	find	hold	never	read	their	we
along	city	first	house	new	ready	there	were
and	cold	five	how	night	right	these	what
animal	come	fly	I	no	said	they	where
are	could	follow	into	noise	school	think	who
around	country	food	is	nothing	see	those	why
away	covers	for	kinds	now	seven	three	window
baby	do	four	know	of	shall	to	with
be	does	friend	laugh	off	she	today	work
bear	done	full	learning	old	show	together	world
because	don't	funny	light	one	sing	too	would
been	door	give	like	open	small	toward	write
before	down	go	little	or	soil	try	years
began	draw	goes	live	our	some	two	yellow
begins	earth	good	long	out	sometimes	under	you
bird	eat	great	look	over	soon	until	young
blue	eight	green	loudly	own	starts	use	your
both	even	ground	make	paper	story	very	
boy	every	grow	many	party	studied	walk	

Decoding skills taught to date: consonants *m, s, t, c*; short *a*; consonant *n*; consonant *d*; consonant *p*; consonant *f*; short *i*; consonant *r*; consonant *h*; /z/ spelled *s*; consonant *g* (hard); consonant *b*; short *o*; consonant *l*; consonant *x*; inflection *s*; short *e*; consonant *y*; consonant *w*; consonant *k*; consonant *v*; consonant *j*; short *u*; /kw/ spelled *qu*; consonant *z*; final consonants *ll*; final consonants *ss*; consonants *ck*, final consonants *ff*; final consonants *zz*; blends with *r*; blends with *l*; blends with *s*; final blend *mp*; final blend *nt*; final blend *nd*; final blend *st*; digraph *th*; ending *-s*; ending *-es*; ending *-ed* /ed/; ending *-ed* /d/; ending *-ed* /t/; ending *-ing*; possessives with *'s*; digraph *sh*; digraph *wh*; digraph *ph*; contractions with *'s* and *n't*; long *a* (CVC*e*); soft *c* /s/; /j/ spelled *g, dge*; long *i* (CVC*e*); digraphs *kn, gn*; digraph *wr*; digraph *mb*; long *o* (CV, CVCe); long *u* (CVC*e*); long *e* (*e, ee*); long *e* (CVC*e, ea*); final consonants *ng*; final consonants *nk*; long *e* (*ea, e_e*); long *a* (*ai, ay*); contractions *'ll* and *'d*; long *o* (*ow, oa*); contractions *'ve* and *'re*; compound words; short *e* (*ea*); r-controlled *ar*; r-controlled *or* and *ore*; r-controlled *er, ir*; r-controlled *ur*; /o͝o/ spelled *oo*; closed syllables (CVC); /o͞o/ spelled *ou, ew*; /o͞o/ spelled *oo*; /o͞o/ spelled *u, ue*; /o͞o/ spelled *u_e* (CVC*e*); /ou/ spelled *ou, ow*; /oi/ spelled *oy, oi*; /aw/ spelled *aw, au*; ending *-ing*: drop *e*, double consonant

The moon is rising. Lots of animals are dozing. Owl is just now waking.

4

BOOK 164

Rising, Shining, Setting

The sun is rising. Bees are humming. Birds are tapping for food.

1

The sun is shining. Bugs are flipping and gliding. A mom is chasing her cub.

© Houghton Mifflin Harcourt Publishing Company

The sun is setting. Toads are hopping home. A hare is hiding in its hole.

Nate Dotted and Dabbed

DECODABLE WORDS

Target Skill: **ending -ed: drop e; double consonant**

dabbed	liked	stopped
dotted	mopped	traced
dropped	pasted	used
hugged	smiled	

Previously Taught Skills

and	his	onto	then
beads	it	paint	up
gave	lot	spilled	with
Gran	Nate	string	

SKILLS APPLIED IN WORDS IN STORY: consonant *m, s, t*; short *a*; consonant *n*; consonant *d*; consonant *p*; short *i*; consonant *r*; consonant *h*; /z/ spelled *s*; consonant *b*; consonant *g* (hard); short *o*; consonant *l*; short *e*; consonant *w*; consonant *k*; consonant *v*; short *u*; final consonants *ll*; blends with *r*; blends with *s*; final blend *nt*; final blend *nd*; final blend *st*; digraph *th*; ending *-ed /ed/*; ending *-ed /t/*; ending *-ed /d/*; long *a* (CVCe); soft *c /s/*; long *i* (CVCe); long *u* (CVCe); final consonants *ng*; long *e* (ea); long *a* (ai); compound words; ending *-ed*: drop *e*, double consonant

HIGH-FREQUENCY WORDS

a	again	eight	picture	the

© Houghton Mifflin Harcourt Publishing Company

Houghton Mifflin Harcourt.

Nate Dotted and Dabbed

High-Frequency Words Taught to Date

Grade 1

a	bring	eyes	have	maybe	pictures	sure	want
about	brown	fall	he	me	play	surprised	warms
above	buy	family	hear	more	please	take	was
after	by	far	help	mother	pull	talk	wash
again	call	father	her	my	pushed	teacher	watch
all	car	few	here	myself	put	the	water
almost	carry	find	hold	never	read	their	we
along	city	first	house	new	ready	there	were
and	cold	five	how	night	right	these	what
animal	come	fly	I	no	said	they	where
are	could	follow	into	noise	school	think	who
around	country	food	is	nothing	see	those	why
away	covers	for	kinds	now	seven	three	window
baby	do	four	know	of	shall	to	with
be	does	friend	laugh	off	she	today	work
bear	done	full	learning	old	show	together	world
because	don't	funny	light	one	sing	too	would
been	door	give	like	open	small	toward	write
before	down	go	little	or	soil	try	years
began	draw	goes	live	our	some	two	yellow
begins	earth	good	long	out	sometimes	under	you
bird	eat	great	look	over	soon	until	young
blue	eight	green	loudly	own	starts	use	your
both	even	ground	make	paper	story	very	
boy	every	grow	many	party	studied	walk	

Decoding skills taught to date: consonant *m, s, t, c*; short a; consonant *n*; consonant *d*; consonant *p*; consonant *f*; short i; consonant *r*; consonant *h*; /z/ spelled *s*; consonant *b*; consonant *g* (hard); short o; consonant *l*; consonant *x*; inflection *s*; short *e*; consonant *y*; consonant *w*; consonant *k*; consonant *v*; consonant *j*; short *u*; /kw/ spelled *qu*; consonant *z*; final consonants *ll*; final consonants *ss*; consonants *ck*; final consonants *ff*; final consonants *zz*; blends with *r*; blends with *l*; blends with *s*; final blend *mp*; final blend *nt*; final blend *nd*; final blend *st*; digraph *th*; ending -*s*; ending -*es*; ending -*ed* /ed/; ending -*ed* /d/; ending -*ed* /t/; ending -*ing*; possessives with '*s*; digraph *sh*; digraph *wh*; digraph *ph*; contractions with '*s* and *n't*; long *a* (CVC*e*); soft *c* /s/; /j/ spelled *g, dge*; long *i* (CVC*e*); digraphs *kn, gn*; digraph *wr*; digraph *mb*; long *o* (CV, CVC*e*); long *u* (CVC*e*); long *e* (*e, ee*); long *e* (CVC*e, ea*); final consonants *ng*; final consonants *nk*; long *e* (*ea, e_e*); long a (*ai, ay*); contractions with '*ll* and '*d*; long *o* (*ow, oa*); contractions with '*ve* and '*re*; compound words; short *e* (*ea*); r-controlled *ar*; r-controlled *or* and *ore*; r-controlled *er ir*; r-controlled *ur*; /o͞o/ spelled *oo*; closed syllables (CVC); /o͞o/ spelled *ou, ew*; /o͞o/ spelled *oo*; /o͞o/ spelled *u, ue*; /o͞o/ spelled *u_e* (CVCe); /ou/ spelled *ou, ow*; /oi/ spelled *oy, oi*; /aw/ spelled *aw, au*; ending –*ing*: drop *e*, double consonant; ending -*ed*: drop *e*, double consonant

Nate Dotted and Dabbed

Nate traced a picture. Nate dropped the picture. Nate traced it again.

Nate gave Gran his picture. Gran liked it. Gran smiled and hugged Nate.

4

1

Nate dotted and dabbed his picture with paint. Nate used a lot. Nate spilled it. Nate mopped it up.

Nate pasted eight beads and string onto his picture. Then, Nate stopped.

We Baked

BOOK 166

DECODABLE WORDS

Target Skill: **ending *-ed*: drop *e*; double consonant**

baked	iced	shopped	tasted
begged	rubbed	sliced	whipped

Previously Taught Skills

and	can't	lot	our	we
big	eat	more	pan	with
cake	eggs	nice	things	
can	for	oil	wait	

SKILLS APPLIED IN WORDS IN STORY: consonants *m, s, t, c*; short *a*; consonant *n*; consonant *d*; consonant *p*; consonant *f*; short *i*; consonant *r*; /z/ spelled *s*; consonant *b*; consonant *g* (hard); short *o*; consonant *l*; short *e*; consonant *w*; consonant *k*; short *u*; blends with *l*; blends with *s*; final blend *st*; final blend *nd*; digraph *th*; ending *-s*; ending *-ed* /ed/; ending *-ed* /t/; ending *-ed* /d/; digraph *sh*; contractions with *n't*; digraph *wh*; long *a* (CVCe); soft *c* /s/; long *i* (CVCe); long *e* (e); long *e* (ea); long *a* (ai); final consonants *ng*; *r*-controlled *or* and *ore*; /ou/ spelled *ou*; /oi/ spelled *oi*; ending *-ed*: drop *e*, double consonant

HIGH-FREQUENCY WORDS

a	of	to
have	some	until

We Baked

High-Frequency Words Taught to Date

Grade 1

a	bring	eyes	have	maybe	pictures	sure	want
about	brown	fall	he	me	play	surprised	warms
above	buy	family	hear	more	please	take	was
after	by	far	help	mother	pull	talk	wash
again	call	father	her	my	pushed	teacher	watch
all	car	few	here	myself	put	the	water
almost	carry	find	hold	never	read	their	we
along	city	first	house	new	ready	there	were
and	cold	five	how	night	right	these	what
animal	come	fly	I	no	said	they	where
are	could	follow	into	noise	school	think	who
around	country	food	is	nothing	see	those	why
away	covers	for	kinds	now	seven	three	window
baby	do	four	know	of	shall	to	with
be	does	friend	laugh	off	she	today	work
bear	done	full	learning	old	show	together	world
because	don't	funny	light	one	sing	too	would
been	door	give	like	open	small	toward	write
before	down	go	little	or	soil	try	years
began	draw	goes	live	our	some	two	yellow
begins	earth	good	long	out	sometimes	under	you
bird	eat	great	look	over	soon	until	young
blue	eight	green	loudly	own	starts	use	your
both	even	ground	make	paper	story	very	
boy	every	grow	many	party	studied	walk	

Decoding skills taught to date: consonant *m, s, t, c*; short a; consonant *n*; consonant *d*; consonant *p*; consonant *f*; short *i*; consonant *r*; consonant *h*; /z/ spelled *s*; consonant *b*; consonant *g* (hard); short *o*; consonant *l*; consonant *x*; inflection *s*; short *e*; consonant *y*; consonant *w*; consonant *k*; consonant *v*; consonant *j*; short *u*; /kw/ spelled *qu*; consonant *z*; final consonants *ll*; final consonants *ss*; consonants *ck*; final consonants *ff*; final consonants *zz*; blends with *r*; blends with *l*; blends with *s*; final blend *mp*; final blend *nt*; final blend *nd*; final blend *st*; digraph *th*; ending *-s*; ending *-es*; ending *-ed* /ed/; ending *-ed* /d/; ending *-ed* /t/; ending *-ing*; possessives with *'s*; digraph *sh*; digraph *wh*; digraph *ph*; contractions with *'s* and *n't*; long *a* (CVC*e*); soft *c* /s/; /j/ spelled *g, dge*; long *i* (CVC*e*); digraphs *kn, gn*; digraph *wr*; digraph *mb*; long *o* (CV, CVC*e*); long *u* (CVC*e*); long *e* (*e, ee*); long *e* (CVC*e, ea*); final consonants *ng*; final consonants *nk*; long *e* (*ea, e_e*); long *a* (*ai, ay*); contractions with *'ll* and *'d*; long *o* (*ow, oa*); contractions with *'ve* and *'re*; compound words; short *e* (*ea*); r-controlled *ar*; r-controlled *or* and *ore*; r-controlled *er ir*; r-controlled *ur*; /o͞o/ spelled *oo*, closed syllables (CVC); /o͞o/ spelled *ou, ew*; /o͞o/ spelled *oo*; /o͞o/ spelled *u, ue*; /o͞o/ spelled *u_e* (CVC*e*); /ou/ spelled *ou, ow*; /oi/ spelled *oy, oi*; /aw/ spelled *aw, au*; ending *-ing*: drop *e*, double consonant; ending *-ed*: drop *e*, double consonant

We tasted and tasted. We tasted our baked, iced cake. We begged and begged. We begged for more iced cake.

We Baked

We shopped and shopped. We shopped for things to eat. We whipped and whipped. We whipped a lot of eggs.

We rubbed and rubbed a pan with oil. We baked and baked a nice, big cake. We can't wait until we can have some cake.

We iced and iced. We iced our nice, baked cake. We sliced and sliced. We sliced our nice, baked cake.

Billy in the City

DECODABLE WORDS

Target Skill: long *e* spelled *y, ie*

Billy	city	hilly	yield
brief	fields	sleepy	

Previously Taught Skills

and	Dad	in	ride	time
at	first	last	see	towns
be	go	let	stay	went
big	got	long	stop	will
bus	Gran	not	streets	you
can	had	on	that	
cars	hope	pleased	this	

SKILLS APPLIED IN WORDS IN STORY: consonants *m, s, t, c*; short *a*; consonant *n*; consonant *d*; consonant *p*; consonant *f*; short *i*; consonant *r*; consonant *h*; /z/ spelled *s*; consonant *b*; *consonant g* (hard); short *o*; consonant *l*; short *e*; consonant *y*; consonant *w*; short *u*; final consonants *ll*; blends with *r*; blends with *l*; blends with *s*; final blend *nt*; final blend *nd*; final blend *st*; digraph *th*; ending -*s*; ending -*ed* /*d*/; soft *c* /s/; long *i* (CVCe); long *o* (CV, CVCe); long *e* (*ea*); final consonants *ng*; long *e* (*e, ee*); long *a* (*ay*); *r*-controlled *ir*; *r*-controlled *ar*; /o͞o/ spelled *ou*; /ou/ spelled *ow*; long *e* spelled *y* and *ie*

HIGH-FREQUENCY WORDS

a	I	the	to	were
by	said	they	was	

Houghton Mifflin Harcourt.

Billy in the City

High-Frequency Words Taught to Date

Grade 1

a	brown	family	help	my	put	their	were
about	buy	far	her	myself	read	there	what
above	by	father	here	never	ready	these	where
after	call	few	hold	new	right	they	who
again	car	find	house	night	said	think	why
all	carry	first	how	no	school	those	window
almost	city	five	I	noise	see	three	with
along	cold	fly	into	nothing	seven	to	work
and	come	follow	is	now	shall	today	world
animal	could	food	kinds	of	she	together	would
are	country	for	know	off	show	too	write
around	covers	four	laugh	old	sing	toward	years
away	do	friend	learning	one	small	try	yellow
baby	does	full	light	open	soil	two	you
be	done	funny	like	or	some	under	young
bear	don't	give	little	our	sometimes	until	your
because	door	go	live	out	soon	use	
been	down	goes	long	over	starts	very	
before	draw	good	look	own	story	walk	
began	earth	great	loudly	paper	studied	want	
begins	eat	green	make	party	sure	warms	
bird	eight	ground	many	pictures	surprised	was	
blue	even	grow	maybe	play	take	wash	
both	every	have	me	please	talk	watch	
boy	eyes	he	more	pull	teacher	water	
bring	fall	hear	mother	pushed	the	we	

Decoding skills taught to date: consonants *m, s, t, c*; short *a*; consonant *n*; consonant *d*; consonant *p*; consonant *f*; short *i*; consonant *r*; consonant *h*; /z/ spelled *s*; consonant *b*; consonant *g* (hard); short *o*; consonant *l*; consonant *x*; inflection *-s*; short *e*; consonant *y*; consonant *w*; consonant *k*; consonant *v*; consonant *j*; short *u*; /kw/ spelled *qu*; consonant *z*; final consonants *ll*; final consonants *ss*; consonants *ck*; final consonants *ff*; final consonants *zz*; blends with *r*, blends with *l*, blends with *s*; final blend *mp*; final blend *nt*; final blend *nd*; final blend *st*; digraph *th*; ending *-s*; ending *-es*; ending *-ed* /d/; ending *-ed* /ed/; ending *-ed* /t/; ending *-ing*; digraphs *ch, tch*; possessives with *'s*; digraph *sh*; digraph *wh*; digraph *ph*; contractions with *'s* and *n't*; long *a* (CVCe); soft *c* /s/; /j/ spelled *g, dge*; long *i* (CVCe); digraphs *kn, gn*; digraph *wr*; digraph *mb*; long *o* (CV, CVCe); long *u* (CVCe); long *e* (*e, ee*); long *e* (CVCe, *ea*); final consonants *ng*; final consonants *nk*; long *e* (*ea, e_e*); long *a* (*ai, ay*); contractions *'ll* and *'d*; long *o* (*ow, oa*); contractions *'ve* and *'re*; compound words; short *e* spelled *ea*; r-controlled *ar*; r-controlled *or* and *ore*; r-controlled *er, ir, ur*; /o͞o/ spelled *oo*; closed syllables (CVC); /o͞o/ spelled *ou, ew*; /o͞o/ spelled *oo*; /o͞o/ spelled *u, ue*; /o͞o/ spelled *u_e* (CVCe); /ou/ spelled *ou, ow*; /oi/ spelled *oy, oi*; /aw/ spelled *aw, au*; ending *-ing*: drop *e*, double consonant; ending *-ed*: drop *e*, double consonant; long *e* spelled *y, ie*

Billy and Dad went to see
Gran. Gran was happy.

"I hope you can stay, and
that this time will not be brief,"
said Gran.

4

Billy in the City

Billy and Dad went to see the
city. They got on a big bus.

1

The ride was long. They went by fields and towns. Billy got sleepy.

At last, Billy and Dad got to the city. The city streets were hilly. The bus had to stop and yield to let cars go first.

Messy Willy

DECODABLE WORDS

Target Skill: **long e spelled y, ie**

brief	fluffy	sticky	Willy's
candy	messy	sudsy	
chief	shriek	Willy	

Previously Taught Skills

am	did	had	now	very
and	fix	is	she	we
ate	fur	mess	so	will
bath	gave	Mom	this	you
candy	got	not	too	

SKILLS APPLIED IN WORDS IN STORY: consonants *m, s, t, c*; short *a*; consonant *n*; consonant *d*; consonant *f*; short *i*; consonant *r*; consonant *h*; /z/ spelled *s*; consonant *b*; consonant *g* (hard); short *o*; consonant *l*; consonant *x*; short *e*; consonant *y*; consonant *w*; consonant *k*; consonant *v*; short *u*; final consonants *ll*; final consonants *ss*; consonants *ck*; final consonants *ff*; blends with *r*; blends with *l*; blends with *s*; final blend *nd*; digraph *th*; digraph *ch*; possessives with '*s*; digraph *sh*; long *a* (CVCe); long *o* (CV); long *e* (e); *r*-controlled *ur*; /o͞o/ spelled *ou*; /o͞o/ spelled *oo*; /ou/ spelled *ow*; long *e* spelled *y, ie*

HIGH-FREQUENCY WORDS

a	are	my	some
again	I	said	today

Houghton Mifflin Harcourt.

Messy Willy

High-Frequency Words Taught to Date

Grade 1

a	brown	family	help	my	put	their	were
about	buy	far	her	myself	read	there	what
above	by	father	here	never	ready	these	where
after	call	few	hold	new	right	they	who
again	car	find	house	night	said	think	why
all	carry	first	how	no	school	those	window
almost	city	five	I	noise	see	three	with
along	cold	fly	into	nothing	seven	to	work
and	come	follow	is	now	shall	today	world
animal	could	food	kinds	of	she	together	would
are	country	for	know	off	show	too	write
around	covers	four	laugh	old	sing	toward	years
away	do	friend	learning	one	small	try	yellow
baby	does	full	light	open	soil	two	you
be	done	funny	like	or	some	under	young
bear	don't	give	little	our	sometimes	until	your
because	door	go	live	out	soon	use	
been	down	goes	long	over	starts	very	
before	draw	good	look	own	story	walk	
began	earth	great	loudly	paper	studied	want	
begins	eat	green	make	party	sure	warms	
bird	eight	ground	many	pictures	surprised	was	
blue	even	grow	maybe	play	take	wash	
both	every	have	me	please	talk	watch	
boy	eyes	he	more	pull	teacher	water	
bring	fall	hear	mother	pushed	the	we	

Decoding skills taught to date: consonants *m, s, t, c*; short *a*; consonant *n*; consonant *d*; consonant *p*; consonant *f*; short *i*; consonant *r*; consonant *h*; /z/ spelled *s*; consonant *b*; consonant *g* (hard); short *o*; consonant *l*; consonant *x*; inflection *-s*; short *e*; consonant *y*; consonant *w*; consonant *k*; consonant *v*; consonant *j*; short *u*; /kw/ spelled *qu*; consonant *z*; final consonants *ll*; final consonants *ss*; consonants *ck*; final consonants *ff*; final consonants *zz*; blends with *r*; blend with *l*; blends with *s*; final blend *mp*; final blend *nt*; final blend *nd*; final blend *st*; digraph *th*; ending *-s*; ending *-es*; ending *-ed* /d/; ending *-ed* /ed/; ending *-ed* /t/; ending *-ing*; digraphs *ch, tch*; possessives with *'s*; digraph *sh*; digraph *wh*; digraph *ph*; contractions *'s* and *n't*; long *a* (CVC*e*); soft *c* /s/; /j/ spelled *g, dge*; long *i* (CVC*e*); digraphs *kn, gn*; digraph *wr*; digraph *mb*; long *o* (CV, CVC*e*); long *u* (CVC*e*); long *e* (*e, ee*); long *e* (CVC*e, ea*); final consonants *ng*; final consonants *nk*; long *a* (*ai, ay*); long *e* (*ea, e_e*); contractions *'ll* and *'d*; long *o* (*ow, oa*); contractions *'ve* and *'re*; compound words; short *e* (*ea*); r-controlled *ar*; r-controlled *or* and *ore*; r-controlled *er, ir, ur*; /o͞o/ spelled *oo*; closed syllables (CVC); /o͞o/ spelled *ou, ew*; /o͞o/ spelled *oo*; /o͞o/ spelled *u, ue*; /o͞o/ spelled *u_e* (CVC*e*); /ou/ spelled *ou, ow*; /oi/ spelled *oy, oi*; /aw/ spelled *aw, au*; ending *–ing*: drop *e*, double consonant; ending *-ed*: drop *e*, double consonant; long *e* spelled *y, ie*

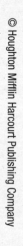

Messy Willy

Willy had very fluffy fur.

Mom gave Willy a brief sudsy bath. Now Willy is fluffy again.

4

1

Willy ate some sticky candy.
Willy's fur got so sticky and
messy.

"Mom! I am too sticky," said
Willy.

Mom did not shriek. She said,
"You are my chief mess today.
We will fix this."

Cindy Studies

DECODABLE WORDS

Target Skill: endings *-es*, *-ed*: change *y* to *i*

copied	hurried	studies

Previously Taught Skills

an	got	it	she	with
as	her	job	show	you
big	for	knew	spelling	
Cindy	good	list	test	
copy	home	Mom	took	

SKILLS APPLIED IN WORDS IN STORY: consonants *m, s, t, c*, short *a*; consonant *n*; consonant *d*; consonant *p*; consonant *f*; short *i*; consonant *h*; /z/ spelled *s*; consonant *b*; consonant *g* (hard); short *o*; consonant *l*; consonant *w*; short *e*; consonant *y*; consonant *k*; consonant *j*; short *u*; final consonants *ll*; blends with *s*; final blend *st*; digraph *th*; ending *-ing*; digraph *sh*; soft *c* /s/; digraph *kn;* long o (CVCe); long e (e); final consonants *ng*; long o (ow); *r*-controlled *or*; *r*-controlled *er*; *r*-controlled *ur*; /o͝o/ spelled *oo*; /o͞o/ spelled *ou*; long e spelled *y*; endings *-es, ed*: change *y* to *i*

HIGH-FREQUENCY WORDS

a	I	school	walk(s)
could	of	the	
do	said	to	

Houghton Mifflin Harcourt.

Cindy Studies

High-Frequency Words Taught to Date

Grade 1

a	bring	eyes	have	maybe	pictures	sure	want
about	brown	fall	he	me	play	surprised	warms
above	buy	family	hear	more	please	take	was
after	by	far	help	mother	pull	talk	wash
again	call	father	her	my	pushed	teacher	watch
all	car	few	here	myself	put	the	water
almost	carry	find	hold	never	read	their	we
along	city	first	house	new	ready	there	were
and	cold	five	how	night	right	these	what
animal	come	fly	I	no	said	they	where
are	could	follow	into	noise	school	think	who
around	country	food	is	nothing	see	those	why
away	covers	for	kinds	now	seven	three	window
baby	do	four	know	of	shall	to	with
be	does	friend	laugh	off	she	today	work
bear	done	full	learning	old	show	together	world
because	don't	funny	light	one	sing	too	would
been	door	give	like	open	small	toward	write
before	down	go	little	or	soil	try	years
began	draw	goes	live	our	some	two	yellow
begins	earth	good	long	out	sometimes	under	you
bird	eat	great	look	over	soon	until	young
blue	eight	green	loudly	own	starts	use	your
both	even	ground	make	paper	story	very	
boy	every	grow	many	party	studied	walk	

Decoding skills taught to date: consonant *m, s, t, c;* short *a;* consonant *n;* consonant *d;* consonant *p;* consonant *f;* short *i;* consonant *r;* consonant *h;* /z/ spelled *s;* consonant *b;* consonant *g* (hard); short *o;* consonant *l;* consonant *x;* inflection *-s;* short *e;* consonant *y;* consonant *w;* consonant *k;* consonant *v;* consonant *j;* short *u;* /kw/ spelled *qu;* consonant *z;* final consonants: *ll;* final consonants: *ss;* consonants *ck;* final consonants: *ff;* final consonants: *zz;* blends with *r;* blends with *l;* blends with *s;* final blend: *mp;* final blend: *nt;* final blend: *nd;* final blend: *st;* digraph *th;* ending *-s;* ending *-es;* ending *-ed* /ed/; ending *-ed* /d/; ending *-ed* /t/; ending *-ing;* digraphs *ch, tch;* digraph *sh;* digraph *wh;* digraph *ph;* possessives with *'s;* contractions *'s* and *n't;* long *a* (CVC*e*); soft *c* /s/; /j/ spelled *g* and *dge;* long *i* (CVC*e*); digraphs *kn, gn;* digraph *wr;* digraph *mb;* long *o* (CV/CVC*e*); long *u* (CVC*e*); long *e* (*e, ee*); long *e* (CVC*e, ea*); final consonants *ng;* final consonants *nk;* long *e* (*ea, e_e*); long *a* (*ai, ay*); contractions *'ll* and *'d;* long *o* (*ow, oa*); contractions *'ve* and *'re;* compound words; short *e* spelled *ea;* r-controlled *ar;* r-controlled *or, ore;* r-controlled *er, ir, ur;* /o͞o/ spelled *oo;* closed syllables (CVC); /o͞o/ spelled *ou, ew;* /o͞o/ spelled *oo;* /o͞o/ spelled *u, ue;* /o͞o/ spelled *u_e* (CVC*e*); /ou/ spelled *ou, ow;* /oi/ spelled *oy, oi;* /aw/ spelled *aw, au;* ending *-ing:* drop *e,* double consonant; ending *-ed:* drop *e,* double consonant; long *e* spelled *y, ie;* endings *-es, -ed,* change *y* to *i*

Cindy Studies

Cindy studies for a big spelling test. She studies, studies, studies.

Cindy hurried home with the copy of her test. Mom said, "Good job! I knew you could do it!"

4

1

Cindy studies her spelling list as she walks to school. She studies, studies, studies.

Cindy took the test. She got an A! She copied the test to show her mom.

Milly Carries the Berries

DECODABLE WORDS

Target Skill: endings -*es*, -*ed*: change *y* to *i*

berries

Previously Taught Skills

and	good	like	picked	tasted
but	grabbed	looked	pie	too
Dad	has	Milly	reached	
day	her	no	she	
did	home	now	so	
for	into	pail	started	

SKILLS APPLIED IN WORDS IN STORY: consonants *m, s, t, c*; short *a*; consonant *n*; consonant *d*; consonant *p*; short *i*; consonant *r*; consonant *h*; /z/ spelled *s*; consonant *b*; consonant *g* (hard); consonant *l*; short *e*; consonant *k*; short *u*; final consonants *ll*; consonants -*ck*; blends with *r*; blends with *s*; digraph *th*; ending -*s*; ending -*ed* /ed/; ending -*ed* /t/; ending -*ed* /d/; final blend -*nd*; final blend -*st*; digraph *ch*; digraph *sh*; long *a* (CVCe); long *i* (CVCe); long *o* (CV/CVCe); long *e* (e); long *e* (ea); long *a* (*ai, ay*); compound words; *r*-controlled *ar*; *r*-controlled *er*; /o͞o/ spelled *oo*; closed syllables (CVC); /o͞o/ spelled *oo*; /ou/ spelled *ow*; ending -*ed*: double consonant; long *e* spelled *y*; endings -*es*, -*ed*: change *y* to *i*

HIGH-FREQUENCY WORDS

a	full	one	they
carry (**carried**)	(in)to	some	
carry (**carries**)	of	the	

© Houghton Mifflin Harcourt Publishing Company

Milly Carries the Berries

High-Frequency Words Taught to Date

Grade 1

a	bring	eyes	have	maybe	pictures	sure	want
about	brown	fall	he	me	play	surprised	warms
above	buy	family	hear	more	please	take	was
after	by	far	help	mother	pull	talk	wash
again	call	father	her	my	pushed	teacher	watch
all	car	few	here	myself	put	the	water
almost	carry	find	hold	never	read	their	we
along	city	first	house	new	ready	there	were
and	cold	five	how	night	right	these	what
animal	come	fly	I	no	said	they	where
are	could	follow	into	noise	school	think	who
around	country	food	is	nothing	see	those	why
away	covers	for	kinds	now	seven	three	window
baby	do	four	know	of	shall	to	with
be	does	friend	laugh	off	she	today	work
bear	done	full	learning	old	show	together	world
because	don't	funny	light	one	sing	too	would
been	door	give	like	open	small	toward	write
before	down	go	little	or	soil	try	years
began	draw	goes	live	our	some	two	yellow
begins	earth	good	long	out	sometimes	under	you
bird	eat	great	look	over	soon	until	young
blue	eight	green	loudly	own	starts	use	your
both	even	ground	make	paper	story	very	
boy	every	grow	many	party	studied	walk	

Decoding skills taught to date: consonant *m, s, t, c*; short *a*; consonant *n*; consonant *d*; consonant *p*; consonant *f*; short *i*; consonant *r*; consonant *h*; /z/ spelled *s*; consonant *b*; consonant *g* (hard); short *o*; consonant *l*; consonant *x*; inflection -*s*; short *e*; consonant *y*; consonant *w*; consonant *k*; consonant *v*; consonant *j*; short *u*; /kw/ spelled *qu*; consonant *z*; final consonants: *ll*; final consonants: *ss*; consonants *ck*; final consonants: *ff*; final consonants: *zz*; blends with *r*; blends with *l*; blends with *s*; final blend: *mp*; final blend: *nt*; final blend: *nd*; final blend: *st*; digraph *th*; ending -*s*; ending -*es*; ending -*ed* /ed/; ending -*ed* /d/; ending -*ed* /t/; ending -*ing*; digraphs *ch, tch*; digraph *sh*; digraph *wh*; digraph *ph*; possessives with *'s*; contractions *'s* and *n't*; long *a* (CVC*e*); soft *c* /s/; /j/ spelled *g* and *dge*; long *i* (CVC*e*); digraphs *kn, gn*; digraph *wr*; digraph *mb*; long *o* (CV/CVC*e*); long *u* (CVC*e*); long *e* (*e, ee*); long *e* (CVC*e*, *ea*); final consonants *ng*; final consonants *nk*; long *e* (*ea, e_e*); long *a* (*ai, ay*); contractions with *'ll* and *'d*; long *o* (*ow, oa*); contractions *'ve* and *'re*; compound words; short *e* spelled *ea*; r-controlled *ar*; r-controlled *or, ore*; r-controlled *er, ir, ur*; /o͞o/ spelled *oo*; closed syllables (CVC); /o͞o/ spelled *ou, ew*; /o͞o/ spelled *oo*; /o͞o/ spelled *u, ue*; /o͞o/ spelled *u_e* (CVC*e*); /ou/ spelled *ou, ow*; /oi/ spelled *oy, oi*; /aw/ spelled *aw, au*; ending –*ing*: drop *e*, double consonant; ending -*ed*: drop *e*, double consonant; long *e* spelled *y, ie*; endings -*es*, -*ed*, change *y* to *i*

Now Dad has a full pail of berries, but Milly has no berries!

4

Milly Carries the Berries

Milly and Dad like treats. So one day they picked berries.

1

Dad and Milly started home.
Dad carried a full pail of berries.
Milly did too.

The berries looked so good.
Milly reached into her pail. She
grabbed some berries. They
tasted good, too!

The Bike Ride

DECODABLE WORDS

Target Skill: **ending -er**

faster	louder	shorter	steeper
harder	quicker	smarter	

Previously Taught Skills

and	dived	let's	ride	tree
ate	down	miles	rode	up
be	for	Mule	see	we
bees	getting	next	Sheep	went
bike	got	on	take	will
big	had	our	tea	
but	hills	peaches	that	
buzz	hive	ran	then	
buzzed	jumped	rest	time	

SKILLS APPLIED IN WORDS IN STORY: consonants *m, s, t*; short *a*; consonant *n*; consonant *d*; consonant *p*; consonant *f*; short *i*; consonant *r*; consonant *h*; /z/ spelled *s*; consonant *b*; consonant *g* (hard); short *o*; consonant *l*; consonant *x*; inflection *–s*; short *e*; consonant *w*; consonant *k*; consonant *v*; consonant *j*; short *u*; /kw/ spelled *qu*; consonant *z*; final consonants *ll*; consonants *ck*; final consonants *zz*; blends with *r*; blends with *s*; final blend *mp*; final blend *nt*; final blend *nd*; final blend *st*; digraph *th*; ending *–s*; ending *–es*; ending *–ed* /d/; ending *–ed* /t/; ending *–ing*; digraph *ch*; digraph *sh*; digraph *wh*; contractions with *'s*; long *a* (CVCe); long *i* (CVCe); long *o* (CVCe); long *u* (CVCe); long *e* (*e, ee*); long *e* (*ea*); *r*-controlled *ar*; *r*-controlled *or*; /ou/ spelled *ou, ow*; ending *-ing*: double consonant; ending *-er*

HIGH-FREQUENCY WORDS

a	I	the	to	what
do	said	they	was	

High-Frequency Words Taught to Date

Grade 1

a	brown	fall	hear	mother	pull	teacher	we
about	buy	family	help	my	pushed	the	were
above	by	far	her	myself	put	their	what
after	call	father	here	near	read	there	where
again	car	few	high	never	ready	these	who
all	carry	find	hold	new	right	they	why
almost	city	first	house	night	said	think	window
along	cold	five	how	no	school	those	with
always	come	fly	I	noise	see	three	work
and	could	follow	into	nothing	seven	to	world
animal	country	food	is	now	shall	today	would
are	covers	for	kinds	of	she	together	write
around	different	four	know	off	show	too	years
away	do	friend	laugh	old	sing	toward	yellow
baby	does	full	learning	once	small	try	you
be	done	funny	light	one	soil	two	young
bear	don't	give	like	open	some	under	your
because	door	go	little	or	sometimes	until	
been	down	goes	live	our	soon	use	
before	draw	good	long	out	starts	very	
began	earth	great	look	over	stories	walk	
begins	eat	green	loudly	own	story	want	
bird	eight	ground	make	paper	studied	warms	
blue	enough	grow	many	party	sure	was	
both	even	happy	maybe	pictures	surprised	wash	
boy	every	have	me	play	take	watch	
bring	eyes	he	more	please	talk	water	

Decoding skills taught to date: consonants *m, s, t, c*; short *a*; consonant *n*; consonant *d*; consonant *p*; consonant *f*; short *i*; consonant *r*; consonant *h*; /z/ spelled *s*; consonant *b*; consonant *g* (hard); short *o*; consonant *l*; consonant *x*; inflection *-s*; short *e*; consonant *y*; consonant *w*; consonant *k*; consonant *v*; consonant *j*; short *u*; /kw/ spelled *qu*; consonant *z*; final consonants *ll*; final consonants *ss*; consonants *-ck*; final consonants *ff*; final consonants *zz*; blends with *r*; blends with *l*; blends with *s*; final blend *mp*; final blend *nt*; final blend *nd*; final blend *st*; digraph *th*; ending *-s*; ending *-es*; ending *-ed* /ed/; ending *-ed* /d/; ending *-ed* /t/; ending *-ing*; digraphs *ch, tch*; possessives with *'s*; digraph *sh*; digraph *wh*; digraph *ph*; contractions *'s, n't*; long *a* (CVC*e*); soft *c* /s/; /j/ spelled *g, dge*; long *i* (CVC*e*); digraphs *kn, gn*; digraph *wr*; digraph *mb*; long *o* (CV, CVC*e*); long *u* (CVC*e*); long *e* (*e, ee*); long *e* (CVC*e, ea*); final consonants *ng*; final consonants *nk*; long *e* (*ea, e_e*); long *a* (*ai, ay*); contractions *'ll* and *'d*; long *o* (*ow, oa*); contractions *'ve* and *'re*; compound words; short *e* (*ea*); r-controlled *ar*; r-controlled *or* and *ore*; r-controlled *er, ir, ur*; /o͞o/ spelled *oo*; closed syllables (CVC); /o͞o/ spelled *ou, ew*; /o͞o/ spelled *oo*; /o͞o/ spelled *u, ue*; /o͞o/ spelled *u_e* (CVC*e*); /ou/ spelled *ou, ow*; /oi/ spelled *oy, oi*; /aw/ spelled *aw, au*; ending *–ing*: drop *e*, double consonant; ending *-ed*: drop *e*, double consonant; long *e* spelled *y, ie*; ending *-er*

The bees dived down. They went faster and faster. But Mule and Sheep ran quicker.

"We will be smarter next time," said Sheep. "We will take a shorter bike ride."

4

The Bike Ride

Sheep and Mule went on a bike ride. They rode for miles. The hills got steeper. The ride was getting harder. "Let's rest next to that tree," said Sheep.

1

Mule and Sheep ate peaches.
They had tea.

Then Mule jumped up. "I see
a big hive," said Mule.

"Buzz, buzz. What do we see
next to our tree?" said the bees.
The bees buzzed louder.

2

3

The Bear

DECODABLE WORDS

Target Skill: ending *-er*

cooler	deeper	faster	shorter	thicker

Previously Taught Skills

and	den	grows	on	stores
as	eats	her	out	takes
at	fat	in	piles	them
bear	feeds	is	play	then
bear's	first	its	she	up
born	food	keeps	sleeps	warm
brown	for	land	slow	way
cubs	fur	last	smells	wind
crawls	goes	looks	snow	winter
days	grow	lot	spring	

SKILLS APPLIED IN WORDS IN STORY: consonants *m*, *s*, *t*, *c*; short *a*; consonant *n*; consonant *d*; consonant *p*; consonant *f*; short *i*; consonant *r*; consonant *h*; /z/ spelled *s*; consonant *b*; consonant *g* (hard); short *o*; consonant *l*; inflection *-s*; short *e*; consonant *w*; consonant *k*; short *u*; final consonants *ll*; consonants *ck*; blends with *r*; blends with *l*; blends with *s*; final blend *nd*; final blend *st*; digraph *th*; ending *-s*; ending *-es*; possessives with *'s*; digraph *sh*; long *a* (CVCe); long *i* (CVCe); long *o* (CV); long *e* (*e*, *ee*); long *e* (*ea*); final consonants *ng*; long *a* (*ay*); long *o* (*ow*); short *e* (*ea*); *r*-controlled *ar*; *r*-controlled (*or*, *ore*); *r*-controlled *er*; *r*-controlled *ir*; *r*-controlled *ur*; /o͞o/ spelled *oo*; closed syllables (CVC); /o͝o/ spelled *oo*; /ou/ spelled *ou*; /aw/ spelled *aw*; ending *-er*

HIGH-FREQUENCY WORDS

a	of	the
are	mother	

Houghton Mifflin Harcourt.

The Bear

High-Frequency Words Taught to Date

Grade 1

a	bring	every	happy	many	paper	story	walk
about	brown	eyes	have	maybe	party	studied	want
above	buy	fall	he	me	pictures	sure	warms
after	by	family	hear	more	play	surprised	was
again	call	far	help	mother	please	take	wash
all	car	father	her	my	pull	talk	watch
almost	carry	few	here	myself	pushed	teacher	water
along	city	find	high	near	put	the	we
always	cold	first	hold	never	read	their	were
and	come	five	house	new	ready	there	what
animal	could	fly	how	night	right	these	where
are	country	follow	I	no	said	they	who
around	covers	food	into	noise	school	think	why
away	different	for	is	nothing	see	those	window
baby	do	four	kinds	now	seven	three	with
be	does	friend	know	of	shall	to	work
bear	done	full	laugh	off	she	today	world
because	don't	funny	learning	old	show	together	would
been	door	give	light	once	sing	too	write
before	down	go	like	one	small	toward	years
began	draw	goes	little	open	soil	try	yellow
begins	earth	good	live	or	some	two	you
bird	eat	great	long	our	sometimes	under	young
blue	eight	green	look	out	soon	until	your
both	enough	ground	loudly	over	starts	use	
boy	even	grow	make	own	stories	very	

Decoding skills taught to date: consonants *m, s, t, c*; short *a*; consonant *n*; consonant *d*; consonant *p*; consonant *f*; short *i*; consonant *r*; consonant *h*; /z/ spelled *s*; consonant *b*; consonant *g* (hard); short *o*; consonant *l*; consonant *x*; inflection *-s*; short *e*; consonant *y*; consonant *w*; consonant *k*; consonant *v*; consonant *j*; short *u*; /kw/ spelled *qu*; final consonants *ll*; final consonants *ss*; consonants *-ck*; final consonants *ff*; final consonants *zz*; blends with *r*; blends with *l*; blends with *s*; final blend *mp*; final blend *nt*; final blend *nd*; final blend *st*; digraph *th*; ending *-s*; ending *-es*; ending *-ed* /ed/; ending *-ed* /d/; ending *-ed* /t/; ending *-ing*; digraphs *ch, tch*; possessives with *'s*; digraph *sh*; digraph *wh*; digraph *ph*; contractions *'s, n't*; long *a* (CVC*e*); soft *c* /s/; /j/ spelled *g, dge*; long *i* (CVC*e*); digraphs *kn, gn*; digraph *wr*; digraph *mb*; long *o* (CV, CVC*e*); long *u* (CVC*e*); long *e* (*e, ee*); long *e* (CVC*e, ea*); final consonants *ng*; final consonants *nk*; long *e* (*ea, e_e*); long *a* (*ai, ay*); contractions *'ll* and *'d*; long *o* (*ow, oa*); contractions *'ve* and *'re*; compound words; short *e* (*ea*); *r*-controlled *ar*; *r*-controlled *or* and *ore*; *r*-controlled *er*; *r*-controlled *ir*; *r*-controlled *ur*; /o͞o/ spelled *oo*; closed syllables (CVC); /o͞o/ spelled *ou, ew*; /o͞o/ spelled *oo*; /o͞o/ spelled *u, ue*; /o͞o/ spelled *u_e* (CVC*e*); /ou/ spelled *ou, ow*; /oi/ spelled *oy, oi*; /aw/ spelled *aw, au*; ending *-ing*: drop *e*, double consonant; ending *-ed*: drop *e*, double consonant; long *e* spelled *y, ie*; ending *-er*

At last it is spring. The bear
takes her cubs out of the den.
She is slow at first. Then she
goes faster. She looks for food
as the cubs play.

The Bear

The brown bear smells the
wind. Winter is on its way. The
bear eats a lot. She stores fat.
Her fur grows thicker.

© Houghton Mifflin Harcourt Publishing Company

Days grow shorter. The land is cooler. The bear crawls in her den and sleeps. Snow piles up deeper and deeper.

The bear's cubs are born in the winter. The mother feeds them. She keeps them warm.

Clean Kittens

DECODABLE WORDS

Target Skill: ending -*est*

cleanest	fastest	neatest	shortest

Previously Taught Skills

am	get	kittens	neat	three
and	gets	know	noise	time
bed	hats	made	panted	treat
clean	in	marched	pick	too
cleans	is	masks	played	up
did	Kat	mess	ready	we
don't	Ken	Mom	room	which
for	Kip	much	that	will
games	kitten	must	this	you

SKILLS APPLIED IN WORDS IN STORY: consonants *m, t, s, c*; short *a*; consonant *n*; consonant *d*; consonant *p*; consonant *f*; short *i*; consonant *r*; consonant *h*; /z/ spelled *s*; consonant *g* (hard); short *o*; consonant *l*; inflection -*s*; short *e*; consonant *y*; consonant *w*; consonant *k*; short *u*; final consonants *ll*; final consonants *ss*; consonants -*ck*; blends with *r*; blends with *l*; blends with *s*; final blend *nd*; final blend *st*; digraph *th*; ending -*s*; ending -*ed* /ed/; ending -*ed* /d/; ending -*ed* /t/; digraph *ch*; digraph *sh*; digraph *wh*; long *a* (CVCe); long *i* (CVCe); digraph *kn*; long *e* (*e, ee*); long *e* (*ea*); long *a* (*ay*); long *o* (*ow*); short *e* (*ea*); *r*-controlled *ar*; *r*-controlled *or*; contractions with *n't*; /o͞o/ spelled *ou*; closed syllables (CVC); /o͞o/ spelled *oo*; /oi/ spelled *oi*; long *e* spelled *y*; ending -*est*

HIGH-FREQUENCY WORDS

a	I	the
are	said	they

Houghton Mifflin Harcourt

Clean Kittens

High-Frequency Words Taught to Date

Grade 1

a	bring	every	happy	many	paper	story	walk
about	brown	eyes	have	maybe	party	studied	want
above	buy	fall	he	me	pictures	sure	warms
after	by	family	hear	more	play	surprised	was
again	call	far	help	mother	please	take	wash
all	car	father	her	my	pull	talk	watch
almost	carry	few	here	myself	pushed	teacher	water
along	city	find	high	near	put	the	we
always	cold	first	hold	never	read	their	were
and	come	five	house	new	ready	there	what
animal	could	fly	how	night	right	these	where
are	country	follow	I	no	said	they	who
around	covers	food	into	noise	school	think	why
away	different	for	is	nothing	see	those	window
baby	do	four	kinds	now	seven	three	with
be	does	friend	know	of	shall	to	work
bear	done	full	laugh	off	she	today	world
because	don't	funny	learning	old	show	together	would
been	door	give	light	once	sing	too	write
before	down	go	like	one	small	toward	years
began	draw	goes	little	open	soil	try	yellow
begins	earth	good	live	or	some	two	you
bird	eat	great	long	our	sometimes	under	young
blue	eight	green	look	out	soon	until	your
both	enough	ground	loudly	over	starts	use	
boy	even	grow	make	own	stories	very	

Decoding skills taught to date: consonants *m, s, t,* c; short *a;* consonant *n;* consonant *d;* consonant *p;* consonant *f;* short *i;* consonant *r;* consonant *h;* /z/ spelled *s;* consonant *b;* consonant *g* (hard); short *o;* consonant *l;* consonant *x;* inflection *-s;* short *e;* consonant *y;* consonant *w;* consonant *k;* consonant *v;* consonant *j;* short *u;* /kw/ spelled *qu;* consonant *z;* final consonants *ll;* final consonants *ss;* consonants *-ck;* final consonants *ff;* final consonants *zz;* blends with *r,* blends with *l,* blends with *s;* final blend *mp;* final blend *nt;* final blend *nd;* final blend *st;* digraph *th;* ending *-s;* ending *-es;* ending *-ed* /ed/; ending *-ed* /d/; ending *-ed* /t/; ending *-ing;* digraphs *ch, tch;* possessives with *'s;* digraph *sh;* digraph *wh;* digraph *ph;* contractions with *'s* and *n't;* long *a* (CVC*e*); soft *c* /s/; /j/ spelled *g, dge;* long *i* (CVC*e*), digraphs *kn, gn;* digraph *wr;* digraph *mb;* long *o* (CV, CVC*e*); long *u* (CVC*e*); long *e* (*e, ee*); long *e* (CVC*e, ea*); final consonants *ng;* final consonants *nk;* long *e* (*ea, e_e*); long *a* (*ai, ay*); contractions *'ll* and *'d;* long *o* (*ow, oa*); contractions *'ve* and *'re;* compound words; short *e* (*ea*); *r*-controlled *ar, r*-controlled *or* and *ore; r*-controlled *er, r*-controlled *ir, r*-controlled *ur;* /o͞o/ spelled *oo;* closed syllables (CVC); /o͞o/ spelled *ou, ew,* /o͞o/ spelled *oo;* /o͞o/ spelled *u, ue;* /o͞o/ spelled *u_e* (CVC*e*); /ou/ spelled *ou, ow;* /oi/ spelled *oy, oi;* /aw/ spelled *aw, au;* ending *–ing:* drop *e,* double consonant; ending *-ed:* drop *e,* double consonant; long *e* spelled *y, ie;* ending *-er,* ending *-est*

Clean Kittens

"This room is neat!" said Mom.
"Which kitten gets a treat?"
"We don't know," panted Kip,
Kat, and Ken. "We did too much.
We are ready for bed."

The three kittens played
games. They marched and made
noise. They made hats and
masks. They made a mess.

4

1

"You must pick up this mess,"
Mom said. "The kitten that
cleans in the shortest time will
get a treat."

"I am the cleanest kitten,"
said Kip.

"I am the neatest kitten,"
said Kat.

"I am the fastest kitten,"
said Ken.

The Band

DECODABLE WORDS

Target Skill: ending -est

deepest	loudest	softest	sweetest

Previously Taught Skills

and	ding	hit	Pat	sweet
band	drum	horn	play	time
bell	flute	it	played	Tom
blew	for	Jack	she	toot
boom	had	let's	shook	tweet
can	he	loud	soft	we
class	her	Meg	songs	
deep	his	now	sound	

SKILLS APPLIED IN WORDS IN STORY: consonants *m, s, t, c*; short *a*; consonant *n*; consonant *d*; consonant *p*; consonant *f*; short *i*; consonant *r*; consonant *h*; /z/ spelled *s*; consonant *b*; consonant *g* (hard); short *o*; consonant *l*; short *e*; consonant *w*; consonant *k*; consonant *j*; short *u*; final consonants *ll*; final consonants *ss*; consonants *-ck*; blends with *r*; blends with *l*; blends with *s*; final blend *nd*; ending *-s*; ending *-ed* /d/; digraph *sh*; contractions with *'s*; long *i* (CVCe); long *e* (*e, ee*); final consonants *ng*; long *a* spelled *ay*; *r*-controlled *or*; *r*-controlled *er*; /o͞o/ spelled *oo*; /o͞o/ spelled *ou, ew*; /o͞o/ spelled *oo*; /o͞o/ spelled *u_e* (CVCe); /ou/ spelled *ou, ow*; ending *-est*

HIGH-FREQUENCY WORDS

a	I	the	together
are	said	they	was

Houghton Mifflin Harcourt.

The Band

High-Frequency Words Taught to Date

Grade 1

a	bring	every	happy	many	paper	story	walk
about	brown	eyes	have	maybe	party	studied	want
above	buy	fall	he	me	pictures	sure	warms
after	by	family	hear	more	play	surprised	was
again	call	far	help	mother	please	take	wash
all	car	father	her	my	pull	talk	watch
almost	carry	few	here	myself	pushed	teacher	water
along	city	find	high	near	put	the	we
always	cold	first	hold	never	read	their	were
and	come	five	house	new	ready	there	what
animal	could	fly	how	night	right	these	where
are	country	follow	I	no	said	they	who
around	covers	food	into	noise	school	think	why
away	different	for	is	nothing	see	those	window
baby	do	four	kinds	now	seven	three	with
be	does	friend	know	of	shall	to	work
bear	done	full	laugh	off	she	today	world
because	don't	funny	learning	old	show	together	would
been	door	give	light	once	sing	too	write
before	down	go	like	one	small	toward	years
began	draw	goes	little	open	soil	try	yellow
begins	earth	good	live	or	some	two	you
bird	eat	great	long	our	sometimes	under	young
blue	eight	green	look	out	soon	until	your
both	enough	ground	loudly	over	starts	use	
boy	even	grow	make	own	stories	very	

Decoding skills taught to date: consonants *m, s, t,* c; short *a*; consonant *n*; consonant *d*; consonant *p*; consonant *f*; short *i*; consonant *r*; consonant *h*; /z/ spelled *s*; consonant *b*; consonant *g* (hard); short *o*; consonant *l*; consonant *x*; inflection -*s*; short *e*; consonant *y*; consonant *w*; consonant *k*; consonant *v*; consonant *j*; short *u*; /kw/ spelled *qu*; consonant *z*; final consonants *ll*; final consonants *ss*; consonants -*ck*; final consonants *ff*; final consonants *zz*; blends with *r*; blends with *l*; blends with *s*; final blend *mp*; final blend *nt*; final blend *nd*; final blend *st*; digraph *th*; ending -*s*; ending -*es*; ending -*ed* /ed/; ending -*ed* /t/; ending -*ed* /d/; ending -*ing*; digraphs *ch, tch*; possessives with *'s*; digraph *sh*; digraph *wh*; digraph *ph*; contractions with *'s* and *n't*; long *a* (CVC*e*); soft *c* /s/; /j/ spelled *g, dge*; long *i* (CVC*e*), digraphs *kn, gn*; digraph *wr*; digraph *mb*; long *o* (CV, CVC*e*); long *u* (CVC*e*); long *e* (*e, ee*); long *e* (CVC*e, ea*); final consonants *ng*; final consonants *nk*; long *e* (*ea, e_e*); long *a* (*ai, ay*); contractions with *'ll* and *'d*; long *o* (*ow, oa*); contractions *'ve* and *'re*; compound words; short *e* spelled *ea*; *r*-controlled *ar*; *r*-controlled *or* and *ore*; *r*-controlled *er, ir*; *r*-controlled *ur*; /o͞o/ spelled *oo*; closed syllables (CVC); /o͞o/ spelled *ou, ew*; /o͞o/ spelled *oo*; /o͞o/ spelled *u, ue*; /o͞o/ spelled *u_e* (CVC*e*); /ou/ spelled *ou, ow*; /oi/ spelled *oy, oi*; /aw/ spelled *aw, au*; ending −*ing*: drop *e*, double consonant; ending -*ed*: drop *e*, double consonant; long *e* spelled *y, ie*; ending -*er*; ending -*est*

"Let's play songs together,"
said Tom. They played loud,
sweet, deep, and soft.

   "Now we are a band,"
said Meg.

The Band

It was time for band class.
Tom had a drum. Meg had a
horn. Jack had a flute. Pat had
a bell.

   "Let's play," they said.

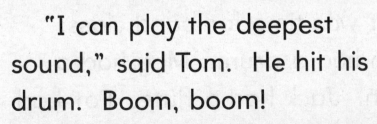

"I can play the deepest
sound," said Tom. He hit his
drum. Boom, boom!

"I can play the softest sound,"
said Pat. She shook her bell.
Ding, ding!

"I can play the sweetest
sound," said Jack. He played his
flute. Tweet, tweet!

"I can play the loudest
sound," said Meg. She blew her
horn. Toot, toot!

Baker Joy

DECODABLE WORDS

Target Skill: ending *-er*: drop *e*, double consonant

baker	later	winner

Previously Taught Skills

added	eggs	Joy	out	this
and	good	meal	pan	time
bake	got	milk	she	up
be	grows	mix	shelf	went
bowl	he	mixed	stuff	when
bread	her	mixer	taste	with
can	how	mixing	tastes	yes
corn	in	needed	teach	
dad	is	off	then	
dry	it	our	things	

SKILLS APPLIED IN WORDS IN STORY: consonants *m, s, t, c,* short *a*; consonant *n*; consonant *d*; consonant *p*; consonant *f*; short *i*; consonant *r*; consonant *h*; /z/ spelled *s*; consonant *b*; consonant *g* (hard); short *o*; consonant *l*; consonant *x*, inflection *s*; short *e*; consonant *y*; consonant *w*; consonant *k*; consonant *j*; short *u*; final consonants *ff*; blends wlth *r*; blend with *l*; final blend *nd*; final blend *st*; digraph *th*; ending *-s*; ending *-ed /ed/*; ending *-ed /t/*; ending *-ing*; digraph *ch*; digraph *sh*; digraph *wh*; long *a* (CVC*e*); long *i* (CVC*e*); long *e (e, ee)*; long *e (ea)*; final consonants *ng*; long *o (ow)*; short *e* spelled *ea*; *r*-controlled *or*; *r*-controlled *er*; /o͞o/ spelled *oo*; /ou/ spelled *ou, ow*; /oi/ spelled *oy*; ending *-ed*; long *e* spelled *y*; ending *-er*; ending *-er*: drop *e*: double consonant

HIGH-FREQUENCY WORDS

a	happy	said	to
done	learning	the	was
great	put	they	

© Houghton Mifflin Harcourt Publishing Company

Baker Joy

CORN MEAL

High-Frequency Words Taught to Date

Grade 1

a	brown	fall	hear	mother	pull	teacher	we
about	buy	family	help	my	pushed	the	were
above	by	far	her	myself	put	their	what
after	call	father	here	near	read	there	where
again	car	few	high	never	ready	these	who
all	carry	find	hold	new	right	they	why
almost	city	first	house	night	said	think	window
along	cold	five	how	no	school	those	with
always	come	fly	I	noise	see	three	work
and	could	follow	into	nothing	seven	to	world
animal	country	food	is	now	shall	today	would
are	covers	for	kinds	of	she	together	write
around	different	four	know	off	show	too	years
away	do	friend	laugh	old	sing	toward	yellow
baby	does	full	learning	once	small	try	you
be	done	funny	light	one	soil	two	young
bear	don't	give	like	open	some	under	your
because	door	go	little	or	sometimes	until	
been	down	goes	live	our	soon	use	
before	draw	good	long	out	starts	very	
began	earth	great	look	over	stories	walk	
begins	eat	green	loudly	own	story	want	
bird	eight	ground	make	paper	studied	warms	
blue	enough	grow	many	party	sure	was	
both	even	happy	maybe	pictures	surprised	wash	
boy	every	have	me	play	take	watch	
bring	eyes	he	more	please	talk	water	

Decoding skills taught to date: consonants *m, s, t, c*, short *a*; consonant *n*; consonant *d*; consonant *p*; consonant *f*; short *i*; consonant *r*; consonant *h*; /z/ spelled *s*; consonant *b*; consonant *g* (hard); short *o*; consonant *l*; consonant *x*; inflection *s*; short *e*; consonant *y*; consonant *w*; consonant *k*; consonant *v*; consonant *j*; short *u*; /kw/ spelled *qu*; consonant *z*; final consonants *ll*; final consonants *ss*; consonants *ck*; final consonants *ff*; final consonants *zz*; blends with *r*; blends with *l*; blends with *s*; final blend *mp*; final blend *nt*; final blend *nd*; final blend *st*; digraph *th*; ending *-s*; ending *-es*; ending *-ed* /ed/; ending *-ed* /t/; ending *-ed* /d/; ending *-ing*; possessives with *'s*; digraph *sh*; digraph *wh*; digraph *ph*; contractions with *'s* and *n't*; long *a* (CVCe); soft *c* /s/; /j/ spelled *g, dge*; long *i* (CVCe); digraphs *kn, gn*; digraph *wr*; digraph *mb*; long *o* (CV, CVCe); long *u* (CVCe); long *e* (*e, ee*); long *e* (CVCe, *ea*); final consonants *ng*; final consonants *nk*; long *e* (*ea, e_e*); long *a* (*ai, ay*); contractions *'ll, 'd*; long *o* (*ow, oa*); contractions *'ve* and *'re*; compound words; short *e* (*ea*); r-controlled *ar*; r-controlled *or, ore*; r-controlled *er, ir*; r-controlled *ur*; /o͞o/ spelled *oo*; closed syllables (CVC); /o͞o/ spelled *ou, ew*; /o͝o/ spelled *oo*; /o͞o/ spelled *u, ue*; /o͞o/ spelled *u_e* (CVCe); /ou/ spelled *ou, ow*; /oi/ spelled *oy, oi*; /aw/ spelled *aw, au*; ending *-ing*: drop *e*, double consonant; ending *-ed*: drop *e*, double consonant; long *e* spelled *y, ie*; ending *-er*; ending *-est*; ending *-er*: drop *e*, double consonant

Later, Dad said, "It is time to taste our corn bread."

"This tastes good," said Joy.

"Yes," said Dad. "Our bread is a winner!"

4

Baker Joy

Joy can be a baker when she grows up. She is learning how to bake with her dad. She is happy he can teach her. He is a great baker.

1

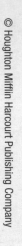

Dad got things he needed off the shelf. He needed milk, corn meal mix, eggs, a bowl, and a mixer. Dad and Joy put the dry stuff in the bowl. They added eggs and mixed in milk.

When the mixing was done, Dad and Joy got out a pan. They put the mix in the pan. Then they put it in to bake.

Mark Runs

DECODABLE WORDS

Target Skill: ending *-er*: drop *e*, double consonant

bigger	runner	runners	upper	winner

Previously Taught Skills

and	faster	in	much	think
at	finish	is	off	time
be	first	jumped	race	training
best	get	kids	ready	up
bigger	going	line	run	warming
cheered	grade	looked	runs	went
county	he	looks	sorts	when
dad	helping	Mark	sound	yay
drills	him	Mark's	starter	
ended	his	meet	than	

SKILLS APPLIED IN WORDS IN STORY: consonants *m, s, t, c,* short *a;* consonant *n;* consonant *d;* consonant *p;* consonant *f;* short *i;* consonant *r;* consonant *h; /z/* spelled *s;* consonant *b;* consonant *g* (hard); short *o;* consonant *l;* inflection *s;* short *e;* consonant *y;* consonant *w;* consonant *k;* consonant *j;* short *u;* final consonants *ll;* final consonants *ff;* blends with *l;* blends with *s;* final blend *-nt;* final blend *-nd;* final blend *-st;* blends with *r;* digraph *th;* ending *-s;* ending *-ed /ed/;* ending *-ed /t/;* ending *-ed /d/;* ending *-ing;* digraph *ch;* possessives with *'s;* digraph *sh;* digraph *wh;* contractions *n't;* long *a* (CVCe); soft *c /s/;* long *i* (CVCe); long *o* (CV); long *e* (*e, ee*); final consonants *nk;* long *a* (*ai, ay*); short *e* spelled *ea; r*-controlled *ar; r*-controlled *or; r*-controlled *ir; /o͞o/* spelled *oo;* closed syllables (CVC); */ou/* spelled *ou;* long *e* spelled *y;* ending *-er;* ending *-er:* drop *e*, double consonant

HIGH-FREQUENCY WORDS

all	father	the	was(n't)
began	of	to	
family	some	was	

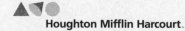
Houghton Mifflin Harcourt.

Mark Runs

High-Frequency Words Taught to Date

Grade 1

a	brown	fall	hear	mother	pull	teacher	we
about	buy	family	help	my	pushed	the	were
above	by	far	her	myself	put	their	what
after	call	father	here	near	read	there	where
again	car	few	high	never	ready	these	who
all	carry	find	hold	new	right	they	why
almost	city	first	house	night	said	think	window
along	cold	five	how	no	school	those	with
always	come	fly	I	noise	see	three	work
and	could	follow	into	nothing	seven	to	world
animal	country	food	is	now	shall	today	would
are	covers	for	kinds	of	she	together	write
around	different	four	know	off	show	too	years
away	do	friend	laugh	old	sing	toward	yellow
baby	does	full	learning	once	small	try	you
be	done	funny	light	one	soil	two	young
bear	don't	give	like	open	some	under	your
because	door	go	little	or	sometimes	until	
been	down	goes	live	our	soon	use	
before	draw	good	long	out	starts	very	
began	earth	great	look	over	stories	walk	
begins	eat	green	loudly	own	story	want	
bird	eight	ground	make	paper	studied	warms	
blue	enough	grow	many	party	sure	was	
both	even	happy	maybe	pictures	surprised	wash	
boy	every	have	me	play	take	watch	
bring	eyes	he	more	please	talk	water	

Decoding skills taught to date: consonants *m, s, t, c,* short *a;* consonant *n;* consonant *d;* consonant *p;* consonant *f;* short *i;* consonant *r;* consonant *h;* /z/ spelled *s;* consonant *b;* consonant *g* (hard); short *o;* consonant *l;* consonant *x;* inflection *s;* short *e;* consonant *y;* consonant *w;* consonant *k;* consonant *v;* consonant *j;* short *u;* /kw/ spelled *qu;* consonant *z;* final consonants *ll;* final consonants *ss;* consonants *ck,* final consonants *ff;* final consonants *zz;* blends with *r;* blends with *l;* blends with *s;* final blend *mp;* final blend *nt;* final blend *nd;* final blend *st;* ending *-s;* ending *-es;* ending *-ed* /ed/; ending *-ed* /t/; ending *-ed* /d/; ending *-ing;* possessives with *'s;* digraph *sh;* digraph *wh;* digraph *ph;* contractions with *'s* and *n't;* long *a* (CVC*e*); soft *c* /s/; /j/ spelled *g, dge;* long *i* (CVC*e*); digraphs *kn, gn;* digraph *wr;* digraph *mb;* long *o* (CV, CVC*e*); long *u* (CVC*e*); long *e* (*e, ee*); long *e* (CVC*e, ea*); final consonants *ng;* final consonants *nk;* long *e* (*ea, e_e*); long *a* (*ai, ay*); contractions with *'ll, 'd;* long *o* (*ow, oa*); contractions *'ve, 're;* compound words; short *e* (*ea*); r-controlled *ar;* r-controlled *or, ore;* r-controlled *er, ir;* r-controlled *ur;* /o͞o/ spelled *oo;* closed syllables (CVC); /o͞o/ spelled *ou, ew;* /o͝o/ spelled *oo;* /o͞o/ spelled *u, ue;* /o͞o/ spelled *u_e* (CVC*e*); /ou/ spelled *ou, ow,* /oi/ spelled *oy, oi;* /aw/ spelled *aw, au;* ending *–ing:* drop *e,* double consonant; ending *-ed:* drop *e,* double consonant; long *e* spelled *y, ie;* ending *-er;* ending *-est;* ending *-er:* drop *e,* double consonant

Mark Runs

Time to line up. The starter sound went off. Mark ran and ran. He looked at the finish.

When the race ended, Mark was the winner. His family jumped and cheered! "Yay!"

Mark is the best runner in first grade. He is faster than some of the upper grade kids. Mark is training to run in the county meet.

Mark's father is helping him.
Mark and his dad run all sorts
of drills. Mark is going to
be ready.

Mark and his family get to the
county meet. Mark is warming
up. He looks at all the first
grade runners. Some were much
bigger than Mark. Mark began
to think he wasn't the best.

The Nicest Lunch

DECODABLE WORDS

Target Skill: **ending -est: drop e; double consonant**

biggest	finest	reddest
closest	nicest	

Previously Taught Skills

and	food	jar	milk	went
Bob	good	likes	nice	will
bread	got	lunch	pal	with
Brown	he	made	peanut	you
butter	his	make	Rose	
eat	it's	me	then	
ever	jam	met	too	

SKILLS APPLIED IN WORDS IN STORY: consonants *m, s, c, t*; short *a*; consonant *n*; consonant *d*; consonant *p*; consonant *f*; short *i*; consonant *r*; consonant *h*; /z/ spelled *s*; consonant *b*; consonant *g* (hard); short *o*; consonant *l*; inflection -*s*; short *e*; consonant *y*; consonant *w*; consonant *k*; consonant *v*; consonant *j*; short *u*; final consonants *ll*; blends with *r*; blends with *l*; final blend *nt*; final blend *nd*; final blend *st*; digraph *th*; ending -*s*; digraph *ch*; contraction '*s*; long *a* (CVCe); soft *c* /s/; long *i* (CVCe); long *o* (CVCe); long *e* (e); long *e* (ea); compound words; short *e* (ea); r-controlled *ar*; r-controlled *er*; /o͞o/ spelled *oo*; /o͞o/ spelled *ou*; /o͞o/ spelled *oo*; ending -*est*: drop e, double consonant; /ou/ spelled *ow*

HIGH-FREQUENCY WORDS

a	find	of	to
buy	friend	said	was
could	have	the	

Houghton Mifflin Harcourt.

The Nicest Lunch

High-Frequency Words Taught to Date

Grade 1

a	bring	every	happy	many	paper	story	walk
about	brown	eyes	have	maybe	party	studied	want
above	buy	fall	he	me	pictures	sure	warms
after	by	family	hear	more	play	surprised	was
again	call	far	help	mother	please	take	wash
all	car	father	her	my	pull	talk	watch
almost	carry	few	here	myself	pushed	teacher	water
along	city	find	high	near	put	the	we
always	cold	first	hold	never	read	their	were
and	come	five	house	new	ready	there	what
animal	could	fly	how	night	right	these	where
are	country	follow	I	no	said	they	who
around	covers	food	into	noise	school	think	why
away	different	for	is	nothing	see	those	window
baby	do	four	kinds	now	seven	three	with
be	does	friend	know	of	shall	to	work
bear	done	full	laugh	off	she	today	world
because	don't	funny	learning	old	show	together	would
been	door	give	light	once	sing	too	write
before	down	go	like	one	small	toward	years
began	draw	goes	little	open	soil	try	yellow
begins	earth	good	live	or	some	two	you
bird	eat	great	long	our	sometimes	under	young
blue	eight	green	look	out	soon	until	your
both	enough	ground	loudly	over	starts	use	
boy	even	grow	make	own	stories	very	

Decoding skills taught to date: consonants *m, s, c, t*; short *a*; consonant *n*; consonant *d*; consonant *p*; consonant *f*; short *i*; consonant *r*; consonant *h*; /z/ spelled *s*; consonant *b*; consonant *g* (hard); short *o*; consonant *l*; consonant *x*; inflection *-s*; short *e*; consonant *y*; consonant *w*; consonant *k*; consonant *v*; consonant *j*; short *u*; /kw/ spelled *qu*; consonant *z*; final consonants *ll*; final consonants *ss*; consonants *ck*; final consonants *ff*; final consonants *zz*; blends with *r*; blends with *l*; blends with *s*; final blend *mp*; final blend *nt*; final blend *nd*; final blend *st*; digraph *th*; ending *-s*; ending *-es*; ending *-ed* /ed/; ending *-ed* /d/; ending *-ed* /t/; ending *-ing*; digraphs *ch, tch*; possessives with *'s*; digraph *sh*; digraph *wh*; digraph *ph*; contractions *'s, n't*; long *a* (CVC*e*); soft *c* /s/; /j/ spelled *g, dge*; long *i* (CVC*e*); digraphs *kn, gn*; digraph *wr*; digraph *mb*; long *o* (CV, CVC*e*); long *u* (CVC*e*); long *e* (*e, ee*); long *e* (CVC*e, ea*); final consonants *ng*; final consonants *nk*; long *e* (*ea, e_e*); long *a* (*ai, ay*); contractions *'ll, 'd*; long *o* (*ow, oa*); contractions *'ve, 're*; compound words; short *e* (*ea*); r-controlled *ar*; r-controlled *or, ore*; r-controlled *er, ir*; r-controlled *ur*; /o͞o/ spelled *oo*; closed syllables (CVC); /o͞o/ spelled *ou, ew*; /o͞o/ spelled *oo*; /o͞o/ spelled *u, ue*; /o͞o/ spelled *u_e* (CVC*e*); /ou/ spelled *ou, ow*; /oi/ spelled *oy, oi*; /aw/ spelled *aw, au*; ending *-ing*: drop *e*, double consonant; ending *-ed*: drop *e*, double consonant; long *e* spelled *y, ie*; endings *-es, -ed*: change *y* to *i*; ending *-er*; ending *-est* ending *-er*: drop *e*, double consonant; ending *-est*: drop *e*, double consonant

Bob and Rose made lunch.
It was the finest lunch ever.
"It's nice to have lunch with a
good friend," said Rose.

BOOK 177

The Nicest Lunch

Bob Brown likes to eat peanut
butter. He likes milk, too.
Bob went to buy food to make
the nicest lunch.

© Houghton Mifflin Harcourt Publishing Company

Bob got bread and milk. He got the biggest jar of peanut butter and the reddest jam he could find.

Then Bob met his closest pal, Rose. He said, "Will you have lunch with me?"

The Nicest Day

DECODABLE WORDS

Target Skill: ending *-est*: drop *e*, double consonant

cutest	nicest	widest

Previously Taught Skills

and	flash	jiffy	room	top
Annie	for	know	see	up
asked	get	later	she	wait
at	go	looked	shorts	week
be	going	mom	smile	what
bus	good	my	smiled	woke
came	got	nice	stepped	you
clothes	her	on	such	
day	in	out	summer	
do	is	outfit	swimming	
dress	it	outside	that	
dressed	it's	picked	things	
enjoy	jean	red	this	

SKILLS APPLIED IN WORDS IN STORY: consonant *n*; consonant *d*; consonant *p*; consonant *f*; short *i*; consonant *r*; consonant *h*; /z/ spelled *s*; consonant *b*; consonant *g* (hard); short *o*; consonant *l*; short *e*; consonant *y*; consonant *w*; consonant *k*; consonant *j*; short *u*; /kw/ spelled *qu*; final consonants *ss*; consonants *ck*, blends with *r*; blends with *l*; blends with *s*; final blend *nd*; final blend *st*; digraph *th*; ending *-s*; ending *-ed* /d/; ending *-ed* /t/; ending *-ing*; digraph *ch*; digraph *sh*; long *a* (CVC*e*); soft *c* /s/; long *i* (CVC*e*); digraph *kn*; long *o* (CV, CVC*e*); long *e* (*e*); long *e* (*ea*); final consonants *ng*; long *e* (*ea*); long *a* (*ay*); long *o* (*ow*); compound words; *r*-controlled (*or*); *r*-controlled *er*; /ōō/ spelled *oo*; closed syllables (CVC); /ōō/ spelled *ou*; /ōō/ spelled *oo*; /ou/ spelled *ou*; /oi/ spelled *oy*; ending *–ing*: double consonant; ending *-ed*: drop *e*, double consonant; ending *-est*; ending *–est*: drop *e*

HIGH-FREQUENCY WORDS

a	do	of	school	to	what
are	I	said	the	to(day)	

The Nicest Day

High-Frequency Words Taught to Date

Grade 1

a	brown	fall	hear	mother	pull	teacher	we
about	buy	family	help	my	pushed	the	were
above	by	far	her	myself	put	their	what
after	call	father	here	near	read	there	where
again	car	few	high	never	ready	these	who
all	carry	find	hold	new	right	they	why
almost	city	first	house	night	said	think	window
along	cold	five	how	no	school	those	with
always	come	fly	I	noise	see	three	work
and	could	follow	into	nothing	seven	to	world
animal	country	food	is	now	shall	today	would
are	covers	for	kinds	of	she	together	write
around	different	four	know	off	show	too	years
away	do	friend	laugh	old	sing	toward	yellow
baby	does	full	learning	once	small	try	you
be	done	funny	light	one	soil	two	young
bear	don't	give	like	open	some	under	your
because	door	go	little	or	sometimes	until	
been	down	goes	live	our	soon	use	
before	draw	good	long	out	starts	very	
began	earth	great	look	over	stories	walk	
begins	eat	green	loudly	own	story	want	
bird	eight	ground	make	paper	studied	warms	
blue	enough	grow	many	party	sure	was	
both	even	happy	maybe	pictures	surprised	wash	
boy	every	have	me	play	take	watch	
bring	eyes	he	more	please	talk	water	

Decoding skills taught to date: consonants *m, s, t, c*; short *a*; consonant *n*; consonant *d*; consonant *p*; consonant *f*; short *i*; consonant *r*; consonant *h*; /z/ spelled *s*; consonant *b*; consonant *g* (hard); short *o*; consonant *l*; consonant *x*; inflection *s*; short *e*; consonant *y*; consonant *w*; consonant *k*; consonant *v*; consonant *j*; short *u*; /kw/ spelled *qu*; consonant *z*; final consonants *ll*; final consonants *ss*; consonants *ck*; final consonants *ff*; final consonants *zz*; blends with *r*; blends with *l*; blends with *s*; final blend *mp*; final blend *nt*; final blend *nd*; final blend *st*; ending *-s*; ending *-es*; ending *-ed* /ed/; ending *-ed* /t/; ending *-ed* /d/; ending *-ing*; digraphs *ch, tch*; possessives with *'s*; digraph *sh*; digraph *wh*; digraph *ph*; contractions with *'s* and *n't*; long a (CVCe); soft *c* /s/; /j/ spelled *g* and *dge*; long i (CVCe); digraphs *kn, gn*; digraph *wr*; digraph *mb*; long o (CV, CVCe); long u (CVCe); long e (e, ee); long e (CVCe, ea); final consonants *ng*; final consonants *nk*; long e (ea, e_e); long a (ai, ay); contractions with *'ll* and *'d*; long o (ow, oa); contractions with *'ve* and *'re*; compound words; short e spelled *ea*; r-controlled *ar*; r-controlled *or* and *ore*; r-controlled *er, ir*; r-controlled *ur*; /o͞o/ spelled *oo*; closed syllables (CVC); /o͞o/ spelled *ou, ew*; /o͞o/ spelled *oo*; /o͞o/ spelled *u, ue*; /o͞o/ spelled *u_e* (CVCe); /ou/ spelled *ou, ow*; /oi/ spelled *oy, oi*; /aw/ spelled *aw, au*; ending *-ing*: drop e, double consonant; ending *-ed*: drop e, double consonant; long e spelled *y, ie*; ending *-es, -ed*, change y to *i*; ending *-er*; ending *-est*; ending *-er*: drop e, double consonant; ending *-est*: drop e, double consonant

The Nicest Day

Annie stepped outside to wait for the bus. "Do you know what day it is?" Annie asked. "It's the nicest day of the week. I get to go swimming later!"

Annie woke up for school. Her mom came to her room, and she said to dress in summer clothes. "It is going to be the nicest day of the week."

Annie looked at her things.
She picked out her jean shorts
and her red top. "This is good
for such a nice day. It's my
cutest outfit," Annie said.

Annie got dressed in a flash.
Her mom looked at her and said,
"I see that you are set to enjoy
the day."
Annie smiled the widest smile.

The Sandiest Places

DECODABLE WORDS

Target Skill: endings -*er*, -*est*: change *y* to *i*

rainier   sunniest   trickiest

sandiest   thorniest

Previously Taught Skills

contain	holes	much	sandy	these	ways
days	in	not	scales	thirsty	which
desert	inside	on	see	thorns	with
deserts	is	places	snakes	thorny	without
for	it	plant	stay	time	you
get	keep	plants	survive	toads	
help	long	rain	than	until	
here	many	rains	them	way	

SKILLS APPLIED IN WORDS IN STORY: consonants *m, s, c, t*; short *a*; consonant *n*; consonant *d*; consonant *p*; consonant *f*; short *i*; consonant *r*; consonant *h*; /z/ spelled *s*; consonant *g* (hard); short *o*; consonant *l*; inflection -*s;* short *e*; consonant *y*; consonant *w*; consonant *k*; consonant *v*; short *u*; blends with *l*; blends with *s*; final blend *nt*; final blend *nd;* final blend *st*; digraph *th*; ending *s*; ending -*es*; ending -*s*; digraph *ch*; possessives with *'s*; digraph *wh*; long *a* (CVCe); soft *c* /s/; long *i* (CVCe); long *o* (CVCe); long *e* (ee); long *e* (CVCe); final consonants -*ng*; long *a* (ai, ay); long *o* (oa); compound words; *r*-controlled *or*; *r*-controlled *er, ir*; *r*-controlled *ur*; closed syllables (CVC); long *e* spelled *y*; /o͞o/ spelled *ou*; /ou/ spelled *ou*; -*er*, -*est*: change *y* to *i*

HIGH-FREQUENCY WORDS

a	away	have	water
animal(s)	cover(ed)	the	won't
are	do	to	world('s)

Houghton Mifflin Harcourt.

The Sandiest Places

High-Frequency Words Taught to Date

Grade 1

a	buy	far	here	never	right	think	with
about	by	father	high	new	said	those	work
above	call	few	hold	night	school	three	world
after	car	find	house	no	see	to	would
again	carry	first	how	noise	seven	today	write
all	city	five	I	nothing	shall	together	years
almost	cold	fly	into	now	she	too	yellow
along	come	follow	is	of	show	toward	you
always	could	food	kinds	off	sing	try	young
and	country	for	know	old	small	two	your
animal	covers	four	laugh	once	soil	under	
are	different	friend	learning	one	some	until	
around	do	full	light	open	sometimes	use	
away	does	funny	like	or	soon	very	
baby	done	give	little	our	starts	walk	
be	don't	go	live	out	stories	want	
bear	door	goes	long	over	story	warms	
because	down	good	look	own	studied	was	
been	draw	great	loudly	paper	sure	wash	
before	earth	green	make	party	surprised	watch	
began	eat	ground	many	pictures	take	water	
begins	eight	grow	maybe	play	talk	we	
bird	enough	happy	me	please	teacher	were	
blue	even	have	more	pull	the	what	
both	every	he	mother	pushed	their	where	
boy	eyes	hear	my	put	there	who	
bring	fall	help	myself	read	these	why	
brown	family	her	near	ready	they	window	

Decoding skills taught to date: consonants *m, s, c, t;* short *a;* consonant *n;* consonant *d;* consonant *p;* consonant *f;* short *i;* consonant *r;* consonant *h;* /z/ spelled *s;* consonant *b;* consonant *g* (hard); short *o;* consonant *l;* consonant *x;* inflection *-s;* short *e;* consonant *y;* consonant *w;* consonant *k;* consonant *v;* consonant *j;* short *u;* /kw/ spelled *qu;* consonant *z;* final consonants *ll;* final consonants *ss;* consonants *ck;* final consonants *ff;* final consonants *zz;* blends with *r;* blends with *l;* blends with *s;* final blend *mp;* final blend *nt;* final blend *nd;* final blend *st;* digraph *th;* ending *-s;* ending *-es;* ending *-ed* /ed/; ending *-ed* /d/; ending *-ed* /t/; ending *-ing;* digraphs *ch, tch;* possessives with *'s;* digraph *sh;* digraph *wh;* digraph *ph;* contractions *'s, n't;* long *a* (CVC*e*); soft *c* /s/; /j/ spelled *g, dge;* digraphs *kn, gn;* digraph *wr;* digraph *mb;* long *o* (CV, CVC*e*); long *u* (CVC*e*); long *e* (*e, ee*); long *e* (CVC*e, ea*); final consonants *ng;* final consonants *nk;* long *a* (*ai, ay*); contractions *'ll, 'd;* long *o* (*ow, oa*); contractions *'ve, 're;* compound words; short *e* (*ea*); r-controlled *ar;* r-controlled *or, ore;* r-controlled *er, ir;* r-controlled *ur;* /o͞o/ spelled *oo;* closed syllables; /o͞o/ spelled *ou, ew;* /o͝o/ spelled *oo;* /o͞o/ spelled *u, ue;* /o͞o/ spelled *u_e* (CVC*e*); /ou/ spelled *ou, ow;* /oi/ spelled *oy, oi;* /aw/ spelled *aw, au;* ending *-ing:* drop *e,* double consonant; ending *-ed:* drop *e,* double consonant; long *e* spelled *y, ie;* endings *–es, -ed:* change *y* to *i;* ending *–er;* ending *-est;* ending *–er:* drop *e,* double consonant; ending *–est:* drop *e,* double consonant; endings *-er, -est:* change *y* to *i*

Desert snakes are covered with scales. The scales help snakes keep water inside for a long time.

Desert plants and animals have ways to survive without much water. Which way is the trickiest?

4

The Sandiest Places

Deserts do not get much rain. Many places are rainier than deserts.

Deserts are the world's sandiest places.

1

Here are desert plants. These thorny plants contain rain. Thorns keep thirsty animals away. Which plant is the thorniest?

Desert toads stay in sandy holes until it rains. You won't see them on the sunniest days.

The Silliest Queen

DECODABLE WORDS

Target Skill: **endings *-er*, *-est*: change *y* to *i***

funniest	shinier	sillier
happiest	shiniest	silliest

Previously Taught Skills

and	glass	looking	shook	you
asked	glasses	maid	speak	
best	is	not	than	
can't	Kathleen	queen	thing	
did	Kathleen's	rest	yelled	

SKILLS APPLIED IN WORDS IN STORY: consonants *m, s, c, t*; short *a*; consonant *n*; consonant *d*; consonant *p*; consonant *f*; short *i*; consonant *r*; consonant *h*; /z/ spelled *s*; consonant *b*; consonant *g* (hard); short *o*; consonant *l*; short *e*; consonant *y*; consonant *k*; short *u*; /kw/ spelled *qu*; final consonants *ll*; final consonants *ss*; blends with *l*; blends with *s*; final blend *nd*; final blend *st*; digraph *th*; ending *-es*; ending *-ed* /d/; ending *-ed* /t/; ending *-ing*; possessives with *'s*; digraph *sh*; contraction *n't*; long *i* (CVCe); long *e* (ee); long *e* (ea); final consonants *ng*; long *a* (ai); /o͞o/ spelled *oo*; /o͝o/ spelled *oo*; long *e* spelled *y*; endings *-er*, *-est*: change *y* to *i*

HIGH-FREQUENCY WORDS

are	talk	who
said	the	

Houghton Mifflin Harcourt.

The Silliest Queen

High-Frequency Words Taught to Date

Grade 1

a	brown	fall	hear	mother	pull	teacher	we
about	buy	family	help	my	pushed	the	were
above	by	far	her	myself	put	their	what
after	call	father	here	near	read	there	where
again	car	few	high	never	ready	these	who
all	carry	find	hold	new	right	they	why
almost	city	first	house	night	said	think	window
along	cold	five	how	no	school	those	with
always	come	fly	I	noise	see	three	work
and	could	follow	into	nothing	seven	to	world
animal	country	food	is	now	shall	today	would
are	covers	for	kinds	of	she	together	write
around	different	four	know	off	show	too	years
away	do	friend	laugh	old	sing	toward	yellow
baby	does	full	learning	once	small	try	you
be	done	funny	light	one	soil	two	young
bear	don't	give	like	open	some	under	your
because	door	go	little	or	sometimes	until	
been	down	goes	live	our	soon	use	
before	draw	good	long	out	starts	very	
began	earth	great	look	over	stories	walk	
begins	eat	green	loudly	own	story	want	
bird	eight	ground	make	paper	studied	warms	
blue	enough	grow	many	party	sure	was	
both	even	happy	maybe	pictures	surprised	wash	
boy	every	have	me	play	take	watch	
bring	eyes	he	more	please	talk	water	

Decoding skills taught to date: consonants *m, s, c, t*; short *a*; consonant *n*; consonant *d*; consonant *p*; consonant *f*; short *i*; consonant *r*; consonant *h*; /z/ spelled *s*; consonant *b*; consonant *g* (hard); short *o*; consonant *l*; consonant *x*; inflection -*s*; short *e*; consonant *y*; consonant *w*; consonant *k*; consonant *v*; consonant *j*; short *u*; /kw/ spelled *qu*; consonant *z*; final consonants *ll*; final consonants *ss*; consonants *ck*; final consonants *ff*; final consonants *zz*; blends with *r*; blends with *l*; blends with *s*; final blend *mp*; final blend *nt*; final blend *nd*; final blend *st*; digraph *th*; ending -*s*; ending -*es*; ending *ed* /ed/; ending -*ed* /d/; ending -*ed* /t/; ending -*ing*; digraphs *ch, ch*; possessives with *'s*; digraph *sh*; digraph *wh*; digraph *ph*; contractions *'s, n't*; long *a* (CVC*e*); soft *c* /s/; /j/ spelled *g, dge*; long *i* (CVC*e*); digraphs *kn, gn*; digraph *wr*; digraph *mb*; long *o* (CV, CVC*e*); long *u* (CVC*e*); long *e* (*e, ee*); long *e* (CVC*e, ea*); final consonants *ng*; final consonants *nk*; long *a* (*ai, ay*); contractions *'ll, 'd*; long *o* (*ow, oa*); contractions *'ve, 're*; compound words; short *e* (*ea*); r-controlled *ar*; r-controlled *or, ore*; r-controlled *er, ir*; r-controlled *ur*; /o͞o/ spelled *oo*; closed syllables; /o͞o/ spelled *ou, ew*; /o͞o/ spelled *oo*; /o͞o/ spelled *u, ue*; /o͞o/ spelled *u_e* (CVC*e*); /ou/ spelled *ou, ow*; /oi/ spelled *oy, oi*; /aw/ spelled *aw, au*; ending -*ing*: drop *e*, double consonant; ending -*ed*: drop *e*, double consonant; long *e* spelled *y, ie*; endings -*es*, -*ed*: change *y* to *i*; ending -*er*; ending -*est*; ending -*er*: drop *e*, double consonant; ending -*est*: drop *e*, double consonant; endings -*er*, -*est*: change *y* to *i*

"You are sillier!" said the maid. "Looking glasses can't talk!"

The Silliest Queen

Queen Kathleen's best looking glass is shinier than the rest.

Queen Kathleen asked, "Who is the happiest queen?" The shiniest looking glass did not speak.

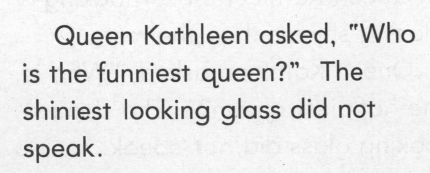

Queen Kathleen asked, "Who is the funniest queen?" The shiniest looking glass did not speak.

Queen Kathleen shook the looking glass and yelled, "You are the silliest thing!"

Rainy Day

DECODABLE WORDS

Target Skill: **syllable** _le_

apple	pickles	twinkle
little	simple	

Previously Taught Skills

and	good	make	rainy	top
asked	hard	meat	set	use
bread	his	Mom	shall	we
can	hmmm	my	side	with
chips	in	need	sister	yes
Dad	is	nice	sounds	
day	it	now	spread	
dishes	let's	okay	such	
for	like	on	tastes	
fun	luckiest	out	that	
get	lunch	raining	them	

SKILLS APPLIED IN WORDS IN STORY: consonants *m, s, t, c*, short *a*; consonant *n*; consonant *d*; consonant *p*; consonant *f*; short *i*; consonant *r*; consonant *h*; /z/ spelled *s*; consonant *b*; consonant *g* (hard); short *o*; consonant *l*; inflection -*s*; short *e*; consonant *y*; consonant *w*; consonant *k*; short *u*; final consonants *ck*, blends with *r*; blends with *s*; final blend *nd*; final blend *st*; digraph *th*; ending -*s*; ending -*es*; ending -*ed* /t/; ending -*ing*; digraph *ch*; digraph *sh*; contraction '*s*; long *a* (CVC*e*); soft *c* /s/; long *i* (CVC*e*); long *o* (CV); long *u* (CVC*e*); long *e* (*e, ee*); long *e* (*ea*); final consonants *ng*; final consonants *nk*; long *a* (*ai, ay*); compound words; short *e* (*ea*); *r*-controlled *ar*; *r*-controlled *or*; *r*-controlled *er*; /o͞o/ spelled *oo*; closed syllable (CVC); /ou/ spelled *ou, ow*; long *e* spelled *y*; ending -*est*: change *y* to *i*; syllable _le_

HIGH-FREQUENCY WORDS

a	eye	said	to
are	I	something	today
do	put	the	what

Houghton Mifflin Harcourt.

Rainy Day

High-Frequency Words Taught to Date

Grade 1

a	brown	fall	hear	mother	pull	teacher	we
about	buy	family	help	my	pushed	the	were
above	by	far	her	myself	put	their	what
after	call	father	here	near	read	there	where
again	car	few	high	never	ready	these	who
all	carry	find	hold	new	right	they	why
almost	city	first	house	night	said	think	window
along	cold	five	how	no	school	those	with
always	come	fly	I	noise	see	three	work
and	could	follow	into	nothing	seven	to	world
animal	country	food	is	now	shall	today	would
are	covers	for	kinds	of	she	together	write
around	different	four	know	off	show	too	years
away	do	friend	laugh	old	sing	toward	yellow
baby	does	full	learning	once	small	try	you
be	done	funny	light	one	soil	two	young
bear	don't	give	like	open	some	under	your
because	door	go	little	or	sometimes	until	
been	down	goes	live	our	soon	use	
before	draw	good	long	out	starts	very	
began	earth	great	look	over	stories	walk	
begins	eat	green	loudly	own	story	want	
bird	eight	ground	make	paper	studied	warms	
blue	enough	grow	many	party	sure	was	
both	even	happy	maybe	pictures	surprised	wash	
boy	every	have	me	play	take	watch	
bring	eyes	he	more	please	talk	water	

Decoding skills taught to date: consonants *m, s, t, c*, short *a*; consonant *n*; consonant *d*; consonant *p*; consonant *f*; short *i*; consonant *r*; consonant *h*; /z/ spelled *s*; consonant *b*; consonant *g* (hard); short *o*; consonant *l*; consonant *x*; inflection *s*; short *e*; consonant *y*; consonant *w*; consonant *k*; consonant *v*; consonant *j*; short *u*; /kw/ spelled *qu*; consonant *z*; final consonants *ll*; final consonants *ss*; consonants *ck*; final consonants *ff*; final consonants *zz*; blends with *r*; blends with *l*; final blend *mp*; final blend *nt*; final blend *nd*; final blend *st*; digraph *th*; ending -*s*; ending -*es*; ending -*ed /ed/*; ending -*ed /t/*; ending -*ed /d/*; ending -*ing*; digraphs *ch, tch*; possessives with *'s*; digraph *sh*; digraph *wh*; digraph *ph*; contractions with *'s* and *n't*; long *a* (CVC*e*); soft *c* /s/; /j/ spelled *g*, *dge*; long *i* (CVC*e*); digraphs *kn, gn*; digraph *wr*; digraph *mb*; long *o* (CV, CVC*e*); long *u* (CVC*e*); long *e* (*e, ee*); long *e* (CVC*e*, *ea*); final consonants *ng*; final consonants *nk*; long *e* (*ea, e_e*); long *a* (*ai ,ay*); contractions *'ll, 'd*; long *o* (*ow, oa*); contractions *'ve, 're*; compound words; short *e* (*ea*); r-controlled *ar*; r-controlled *or, ore*; r-controlled *er, ir*; r-controlled *ur*; /o͞o/ spelled *oo*; closed syllables (CVC); /o͞o/ spelled *ou, ew*; /o͝o/ spelled *oo*; /o͞o/ spelled *u, ue*; /o͞o/ spelled *u_e* (CVC*e*); /ou/ spelled *ou, ow*; /oi/ spelled *oy, oi*; /aw/ spelled *aw, au*; ending -*ing*: drop *e*, double consonant; ending -*ed*: drop *e*, double consonant; long *e* spelled *y, ie*; endings -*ing*, -*ed*: change *y* to *i*; ending -*er*; ending -*est*; ending -*er*: drop *e*, double consonant; ending -*est*: drop *e*, double consonant; endings -*er*, -*est*: change *y* to *i*; syllable _*le*

Now let's get Mom and Dad and set out the dishes. "MOM! DAD!"

"Such a nice lunch! We are the luckiest mom and dad!" Dad said with a twinkle in his eye.

4

Rainy Day

Today, it is raining hard. My little sister and I need to find something to do. I said, "Let's make lunch for Mom and Dad."

"Okay, that sounds like fun."
said my sister.

"Hmmm, what shall we make
for them?" I asked. "Something
that is simple and tastes good."

"We can use bread and meat,"
said my little sister.

"Yes, and let's put a spread
and pickles on top." I said.

"And apple chips on the side,"
my little sister said.

Ben and Frankie

DECODABLE WORDS

Target Skill: syllable _le_

chuckle	freckles	little	tickled
dimples	giggle	rattle	

Previously Taught Skills

and	Frankie	like	play	this
asked	fun	look	rug	those
at	he	looks	sat	went
baby	help	lot	shook	when
Ben	him	me	so	with
Ben's	his	mine	smiled	wow
big	is	Mom	squeak	yes
Dad	it	much	squealed	
feet	just	on	then	

SKILLS APPLIED IN WORDS IN STORY: consonants *m, s, t,* short *a*; consonant *n*; consonant *d*; consonant *p*; consonant *f*; short *i*; consonant *r*; consonant *h*; /z/ spelled *s*; consonant *b*; consonant *g* (hard); short *o*; consonant *l*; inflection *s*; short *e*; consonant *y*; consonant *w*; consonant *k*; consonant *j*; short *u*; /kw/ spelled *qu*; consonants *ck,* blends with *r*; blends with *l*; blends with *s*; final blend *nd*; final blend *st*; digraph *th*; ending *-s*; ending *-ed* /d/; ending *-ed* /t/; digraph *ch*; possessives with '*s*; digraph *sh*; digraph *wh*; long *i* (CVCe); long *o* (CV, CVCe); long *e* (*e, ee*); long *e* (*ea*); final consonants *nk*; long *a* (*ay*); /o͞o/ spelled *oo*; closed syllables (CVC); /o͝o/ spelled *oo*; /ou/ spelled *ow*; long *e* spelled *y, ie*; syllable *_le*

HIGH-FREQUENCY WORDS

a	great	the	you
are	picture	to	yours
does	said	were	

Houghton Mifflin Harcourt.

© Houghton Mifflin Harcourt Publishing Company

syllable _le_

BOOK 182

Ben and Frankie

High-Frequency Words Taught to Date

Grade 1

a	brown	fall	hear	mother	pull	teacher	we
about	buy	family	help	my	pushed	the	were
above	by	far	her	myself	put	their	what
after	call	father	here	near	read	there	where
again	car	few	high	never	ready	these	who
all	carry	find	hold	new	right	they	why
almost	city	first	house	night	said	think	window
along	cold	five	how	no	school	those	with
always	come	fly	I	noise	see	three	work
and	could	follow	into	nothing	seven	to	world
animal	country	food	is	now	shall	today	would
are	covers	for	kinds	of	she	together	write
around	different	four	know	off	show	too	years
away	do	friend	laugh	old	sing	toward	yellow
baby	does	full	learning	once	small	try	you
be	done	funny	light	one	soil	two	young
bear	don't	give	like	open	some	under	your
because	door	go	little	or	sometimes	until	
been	down	goes	live	our	soon	use	
before	draw	good	long	out	starts	very	
began	earth	great	look	over	stories	walk	
begins	eat	green	loudly	own	story	want	
bird	eight	ground	make	paper	studied	warms	
blue	enough	grow	many	party	sure	was	
both	even	happy	maybe	pictures	surprised	wash	
boy	every	have	me	play	take	watch	
bring	eyes	he	more	please	talk	water	

Decoding skills taught to date: consonants *m, s, t, c*; short *a*; consonant *n*; consonant *d*; consonant *p*; consonant *f*; short *i*; consonant *r*; consonant *h*; /z/ spelled *s*; consonant *b*; consonant *g* (hard); short *o*; consonant *l*; consonant *x*; inflection *s*; short *e*; consonant *y*; consonant *w*; consonant *k*; consonant *v*; consonant *j*; short *u*; /kw/ spelled *qu*; consonant *z*; final consonants *ll*; final consonants *ss*; consonants *ck*; final consonants *ff*; final consonants *zz*; blends with *r*; blends with *l*; blends with *s*; final blend *mp*; final blend *nt*; final blend *nd*; final blend *st*; digraph *th*; ending *-s*; ending *-es*; ending *-ed* /ed/; ending *-ed* /t/; ending *-ed* /d/; ending *-ing*; digraphs *ch, tch*; possessives with *'s*; digraph *sh*; digraph *wh*; digraph *ph*; contractions with *'s* and *n't*; long *a* (CVC*e*); soft *c* /s/; /j/ spelled *g, dge*; long *i* (CVC*e*); digraphs *kn, gn*; digraph *wr*; digraph *mb*; long *o* (CV, CVC*e*); long *u* (CVC*e*); long *e* (*e, ee*); long *e* (CVC*e, ea*); final consonants ng; final consonants *nk*; long *e* (*ea, e_e*); long *a* (*ai ,ay*); contractions *'ll, 'd*; long *o* (*ow, oa*); contractions *'ve, 're*; compound words; short *e* (*ea*); r-controlled *ar*; r-controlled (*or, ore*); r-controlled *er, ir*; r-controlled *ur*; /o͞o/ spelled *oo*; closed syllables (CVC); /o͞o/ spelled *ou, ew*; /o͞o/ spelled *oo*; /o͞o/ spelled *u, ue*; /o͞o/ spelled *u_e* (CVC*e*); /ou/ spelled *ou, ow*; /oi/ spelled *oy, oi*; /aw/ spelled *aw, au*; ending –*ing*: drop e, double consonant; ending -*ed*: drop e, double consonant; long *e* spelled *y, ie*; endings –*ing, -ed*: change y to *i*; ending –*er*; ending -*est*; ending –*er*: drop e, double consonant; ending –*est*: drop e, double consonant; endings *-er, -est*: change y to *i*; syllable *_le*

"Like mine?" asked Frankie.

"Yes, Ben looks just like you when you were little. Just look at this picture," said Mom.

"Wow!" said Frankie. "He does look a lot like me!"

4

Ben and Frankie

Baby Ben and Frankie sat on the rug. Frankie tickled Ben's feet.

"Giggle, giggle, giggle, squeak, squeak," squealed Ben.

1

© Houghton Mifflin Harcourt Publishing Company

"Mom, Dad, look at Ben chuckle. It is so much fun to play with him," said Frankie.

"You are a great big help," said Dad.

Ben shook his rattle, and then smiled at Frankie.

"Look at those dimples and freckles," said Frankie.

"His dimples and freckles are just like yours," said Dad.

2

3

White Knight

DECODABLE WORDS

Target Skill: long *i* spelled *-ie*, *-igh*

fight	Knight	pie	sighed	tight
high	might	right	tie	

Previously Taught Skills

am	fell	is	not	toss
and	for	it	on	up
brave	get	just	rope	White
but	hang	like	she	will
came	he	Miss	started	
down	help	Moll	this	

SKILLS APPLIED IN WORDS IN STORY: consonants *m, s, c, t*; short *a*; consonant *n*; consonant *d*; consonant *p*; consonant *f*; short *i*; consonant *r*; consonant *h*; /z/ spelled *s*; consonant *b*; consonant *g* (hard); short *o*; consonant *l*; short *e*; consonant *w*; consonant *k*; consonant *v*; consonant *j*; short *u*; final consonant *ll*; final consonant *ss*; blends with *r*; blends with *s*; final blend *nd*; final blend *st*; digraph *th*; ending *ed* /ĕd/; ending *-ed* /d/; digraph *sh*; digraph *wh*; long *a* (CVCe); long *i* (CVCe); digraph *kn*; long o (CVCe); long e (e); final consonants *ng*; r-controlled *ar*; r-controlled vowel spelled *or*; vowel combination *ow*; long *i* (ie, igh)

HIGH-FREQUENCY WORDS

call(ed)	said	want(ed)
come	some	was
could	to	what
I	the	you

Houghton Mifflin Harcourt.

White Knight

High-Frequency Words Taught to Date

Grade 1

a	bring	eyes	head	me	please	take	water
about	brown	fall	hear	more	pull	talk	we
above	buy	family	heard	mother	pushed	teacher	were
across	by	far	help	my	put	the	what
after	call	father	her	myself	read	their	where
again	car	few	here	near	ready	there	who
all	carry	find	high	never	right	these	why
almost	city	first	hold	new	said	they	window
along	cold	five	house	night	school	think	with
always	come	fly	how	no	second	those	work
and	could	follow	I	noise	see	three	world
animal	country	food	into	nothing	seven	to	would
are	covers	for	is	now	shall	today	write
around	cried	four	kinds	of	she	together	years
away	different	friend	know	off	should	too	yellow
baby	do	full	large	old	show	toward	you
ball	does	funny	laugh	once	sing	try	young
be	done	give	learning	one	small	two	your
bear	don't	go	light	open	soil	under	
because	door	goes	like	or	some	until	
been	down	good	little	our	sometimes	use	
before	draw	great	live	out	soon	very	
began	earth	green	long	over	starts	walk	
begins	eat	ground	look	own	stories	want	
bird	eight	grow	loudly	paper	story	warms	
blue	enough	happy	make	party	studied	was	
both	even	have	many	pictures	sure	wash	
boy	every	he	maybe	play	surprised	watch	

Decoding skills taught to date: consonants *m, s, c, t*; short *a*; consonant *n*; consonant *d*; consonant *p*; consonant *f*; short *i*; consonant *r*; consonant *h*; /z/ spelled *s*; consonant *b*; consonant *g* (hard); short *o*; consonant *l*; consonant *x*; inflection *-s*; short *e*; consonant *y*; consonant *w*; consonant *k*; consonant *v*; consonant *j*; short *u*; /kw/ spelled *qu*; consonant *z*; final consonant *ll*; final consonant *ss*; consonants *-ck*; final consonant *ff*; final consonant *zz*; blends with *r*; blends with *l*; blends with *s*; final blend *-mp*; final blend *-nt*; final blend *-nd*; final blend *st*; digraph *th*; ending *-s*; ending *-es*; ending *-ed* /ed/; ending *-ed* /d/; ending *-ed* /t/; ending *-ing*; digraphs *ch*, *tch*; possessives with *'s*; digraph *sh*; digraph *wh*; digraph *ph*; contractions with *'s* and *n't*; long *a* (CVCe); soft *c* /s/; /j/ spelled *g, dge*; long *i* (CVCe); digraphs *kn, gn*; digraph *wr*; digraph *mb*; long *o* (CV, CVCe); long *u* (CVCe); long *e* (e, ee); long *e* (CVCe, ea); final consonants *ng*; final consonants *nk*; long *e* (ea, e_e); long *a* (ai, ay); contractions *'ll*, *'d*; long *o* (ow, oa); contractions *'ve* and *'re*; compound words; short *e* (ea); r-controlled *ar*; r-controlled (or, ore); r-controlled *er, ir*; r-controlled *ur*; /ōō/ spelled *oo*; closed syllables (CVC); /ōō/ spelled *ou, ew*; /ōō/ spelled *oo*; /ōō/ spelled *u, ue*; /ōō/ spelled *u_e* (CVCe); /ou/ spelled *ou, ow*; /oi/ spelled *oy, oi*; /aw/ spelled *aw, au*; ending *-ing*: drop *e*; double consonant; ending *-ed*: drop *e*; double consonant; long *e* spelled *y, ie*; endings *-ing, -ed*: change *y* to *i*; ending *-er*; ending *-est*; ending *-er*: drop *e*, double consonant; ending *-est*: drop *e*, double consonant; endings *-er, -est*: change *y* to *i*; syllable *_le*; long *i* spelled *ie, igh*

Miss Moll came down the rope. "You might like some pie," she said.

White Knight just sighed.

4

White Knight

White Knight said, "I am brave. I fight for what is right."

1

Miss Moll was up high.
She called, "White Knight!
White Knight!"

White Knight wanted to
help Miss Moll get down. "I will
toss you this rope, Miss Moll.
Tie it tight, and I will come up!"
he said. White Knight started
up, but he could not hang on!
He fell!

High, High Up

DECODABLE WORDS

Target Skill: **long *i* spelled *-ie*, *-igh***

bright	lie	sight
high	night	sunlight

Previously Taught Skills

as	for	look	soon
at	glass	loons	sun
coast	hilltops	see	then
dive	is	shines	this
feed	it	sleeping	up
fish	lake	smooth	wake

SKILLS APPLIED IN WORDS IN STORY: consonants *m, s, c, t*; short *a*; consonant *n*; consonant *d*; consonant *p*; consonant *f*; short *i*; consonant *r*; consonant *h*; /z/ spelled *s*; consonant *g* (hard); short *o*; consonant *l*; inflection *-s*; short *e*; consonant *w*; consonant *k*; consonant *v*; short *u*; final consonant *ll*; final consonant *ss*; blends with *r*; blends with *l*; blends with *s*; final blend *st*; digraph *th*; ending *-s*; ending *-ing*; digraph sh; long *a* (CVCe); long *i* (CVCe); long *e* (ee); long *o* (oa); final consonants *ng*; compound words; *r*-controlled (*or*); /o͞o/ spelled *oo*; /o͝o/ spelled *oo*; long *i* (*ie*, *igh*)

HIGH-FREQUENCY WORDS

a	fly	the	they	under
along	over	their	to	water

Houghton Mifflin Harcourt

High, High Up

High-Frequency Words Taught to Date

Grade 1

a	bring	eyes	head	me	please	take	water
about	brown	fall	hear	more	pull	talk	we
above	buy	family	heard	mother	pushed	teacher	were
across	by	far	help	my	put	the	what
after	call	father	her	myself	read	their	where
again	car	few	here	near	ready	there	who
all	carry	find	high	never	right	these	why
almost	city	first	hold	new	said	they	window
along	cold	five	house	night	school	think	with
always	come	fly	how	no	second	those	work
and	could	follow	I	noise	see	three	world
animal	country	food	into	nothing	seven	to	would
are	covers	for	is	now	shall	today	write
around	cried	four	kinds	of	she	together	years
away	different	friend	know	off	should	too	yellow
baby	do	full	large	old	show	toward	you
ball	does	funny	laugh	once	sing	try	young
be	done	give	learning	one	small	two	your
bear	don't	go	light	open	soil	under	
because	door	goes	like	or	some	until	
been	down	good	little	our	sometimes	use	
before	draw	great	live	out	soon	very	
began	earth	green	long	over	starts	walk	
begins	eat	ground	look	own	stories	want	
bird	eight	grow	loudly	paper	story	warms	
blue	enough	happy	make	party	studied	was	
both	even	have	many	pictures	sure	wash	
boy	every	he	maybe	play	surprised	watch	

Decoding skills taught to date: consonants *m, s, c, t*; short *a*; consonant *n*; consonant *d*; consonant *p*; consonant *f*; short *i*; consonant *r*; consonant *h*; /z/ spelled *s*; consonant *b*; consonant *g* (hard); short *o*; consonant *l*; consonant *x*; inflection -*s*; short *e*; consonant *y*; consonant *w*; consonant *k*; consonant *v*; consonant *j*; short *u*; /kw/ spelled *qu*; consonant *z*; final consonant *ll*; final consonant *ss*; consonants -*ck*; final consonant *ff*; final consonant *zz*; blends with *r*; blends with *l*; blends with *s*; final blend -*mp*; final blend -*nt*; final blend -*nd;* final blend *st*; digraph *th*; ending-*s*; ending-*es*; ending-*ed* /ed/; ending-*ed* /d/; ending-*ed* /t/; ending-*ing*; digraphs *ch, tch*; possessives with *'s*; digraph *sh*; digraph *wh*; digraph *ph*; contractions with *'s* and *n't*; long *a* (CVC*e*); soft *c* /s/; /j/ spelled *g, dge*; long *i* (CVC*e*); digraphs *kn, gn*; digraph *wr*; digraph *mb*; long *o* (CV, CVC*e*); long *u* (CVC*e*); long *e* (*e, ee*); long *e* (CVC*e, ea*); final consonants *ng*; final consonants *nk*; long *e* (*ea, e_e*); long *a* (*ai, ay*); contractions *'ll, 'd*; long *o* (*ow, oa*); contractions *'ve* and *'re*; compound words; short *e* (*ea*); r-controlled *ar*; r-controlled (*or, ore*); r-controlled *er, ir*; r-controlled *ur*; /o͞o/ spelled *oo*; closed syllables (CVC); /o͞o/ spelled *ou, ew*; /o͞o/ spelled *oo*; /o͞o/ spelled *u, ue*; /o͞o/ spelled *u_e* (CVC*e*); /ou/ spelled *ou, ow*; /oi/ spelled *oy, oi*; /aw/ spelled *aw, au*; ending –*ing*: drop *e*, double consonant; ending -*ed*: drop *e*, double consonant; long *e* spelled *y, ie*; endings –*ing, -ed*: change *y* to *i*; ending –*er*; ending -*est*; ending –*er*: drop *e*, double consonant; ending –*est*: drop *e*, double consonant; endings -*er, -est*: change *y* to *i*; syllable _*le*; long *i* spelled *ie, igh*

The bright sun shines on their wings as these loons fly high, high up along the coast. It is a sight to see!

High, High Up

At night this lake is as smooth as glass. Loons lie sleeping.

Soon, bright sunlight shines over the high hilltops. The loons wake up.

Loons stick their heads into the water to look for fish. Then they dive under to feed.

Vy and the Fly

DECODABLE WORDS

Target Skill: long *i* spelled *y*

fly	fry	sky	Vy

Previously Taught Skills

and	dove	in	sat	upset
back	down	is	saw	yelled
bit	fries	it	she	
box	get	no	then	
but	go	on	took	
can	her	sailed	up	

SKILLS APPLIED IN WORDS IN STORY: consonant *c, s, t,* short *a*; consonant *n*; consonant *d*; consonant *p*; consonant *f*; short *i*; consonant *r*; consonant *h*; /z/ spelled *s*; consonant *b*; consonant *g* (hard); short *o*; consonant *l*; consonant *x*; inflection -*s*; short *e*; consonant *y*; consonant *k*; consonant *v*; short *u*; final consonants *ll*; consonants *ck*; blends with *r*; blends with *l*; blends with *s*; final blend *nd*; ending -*s*; ending -*ed* /d/; digraph *sh*; long *o* (CV, CVCe); long *e* (*e*); long *a* spelled *ai*; compound words; *r*-controlled *er*; /o͞o/ spelled *oo*; /ou/ spelled *ow*; /aw/ spelled *aw*; long *i* spelled *ie*; long *i* spelled *y*

HIGH-FREQUENCY WORDS

a	into	the	want(s)
away	of	to	

Houghton Mifflin Harcourt.

Vy and the Fly

High-Frequency Words Taught to Date

Grade 1

a	brown	family	help	myself	ready	these	window
about	buy	far	her	near	right	they	with
above	by	father	here	never	said	think	work
across	call	few	high	new	school	those	world
after	car	find	hold	night	second	three	would
again	carry	first	house	no	see	to	write
all	city	five	how	noise	seven	today	years
almost	cold	fly	I	nothing	shall	together	yellow
along	come	follow	into	now	she	too	you
always	could	food	is	of	should	toward	young
and	country	for	kinds	off	show	try	your
animal	covers	four	know	old	sing	two	
are	cried	friend	large	once	small	under	
around	different	full	laugh	one	soil	until	
away	do	funny	learning	open	some	use	
baby	does	give	light	or	sometimes	very	
ball	done	go	like	our	soon	walk	
be	don't	goes	little	out	starts	want	
bear	door	good	live	over	stories	warms	
because	down	great	long	own	story	was	
been	draw	green	look	paper	studied	wash	
before	earth	ground	loudly	party	sure	watch	
began	eat	grow	make	pictures	surprised	water	
begins	eight	happy	many	play	take	we	
bird	enough	have	maybe	please	talk	were	
blue	even	he	me	pull	teacher	what	
both	every	head	more	pushed	the	where	
boy	eyes	hear	mother	put	their	who	
bring	fall	heard	my	read	there	why	

Decoding skills taught to date: consonants *m, s, t, c,* short *a*; consonant *n*; consonant *d*; consonant *p*; consonant *f*; short *i*; consonant *r*; consonant *h*; /z/ spelled *s*; consonant *b*; consonant *g* (hard); short *o*; consonant *l*; consonant *x*; inflection *s*; short *e*; consonant *y*; consonant *w*; consonant *k*; consonant *v*; consonant *j*; short *u*; /kw/ spelled *qu*; consonant *z*; final consonants *ll*; final consonants *ss*; consonants *ck*; final consonants *ff*; final consonants *zz*; blends with *r*; blends with *l*; blends with *s*; final blend *mp*; final blend *nt*; final blend *nd*; final blend *st*; digraph *th*; ending *-s*; ending *-es*; ending *-ed* /ed/; ending *-ed* /t/; ending *-ed* /d/; ending *-ing*; possessives with *'s*; digraph *sh*; digraph *wh*; digraph *ph*; contractions with *'s* and *n't*; long *a* (CVC*e*); soft *c* /s/; /j/ spelled *g, dge*; long *i* (CVC*e*); digraphs *kn, gn*; digraph *wr*; digraph *mb*; long *o* (CV, CVC*e*); long *u* (CVC*e*); long *e* (*e, ee*); long *e* (CVC*e, ea*); final consonants *ng*; final consonants *nk*; long *e* (*ea, e_e*); long *a* (*ai, ay*); contractions with *'ll* and *'d*; long *o* (*ow, oa*); contractions *'ve* and *'re*; compound words; short *e* (*ea*); r-controlled *ar*; r-controlled (*or, ore*); r-controlled *er, ir*; r-controlled *ur*; /o͝o/ spelled *oo*; closed syllables (CVC); /o͞o/ spelled *ou, ew*; /o͞o/ spelled *oo*; /o͞o/ spelled *u, ue*; /o͞o/ spelled *u_e* (CVC*e*); /ou/ spelled *ou, ow*; /oi/ spelled *oy, oi*; /aw/ spelled *aw, au*; ending *–ing*: drop *e*, double consonant; ending *-ed*: drop *e*, double consonant; long *e* spelled *y, ie*; endings *–ing, -ed*: change *y* to *i*; ending *–er*; ending *-est*; ending *–er*: drop *e*, double consonant; ending *–est*: drop *e*, double consonant; endings *-er, -est*: change *y* to *i*; syllable *_le*; long *i* spelled *ie, igh*; long *i* spelled *y*

Vy and the Fly

Vy saw a fly in the sky. The fly sat on her fry.

Can Vy get her fry? No, the fly is high up in the sky. Vy is a bit upset. She wants her fry back.

4

1

"Go away, fly!" said Vy.
But the fly dove down to her
box of fries.

The fly took a fry. Then it
sailed up into the sky.

2

3

The Spy

DECODABLE WORDS

Target Skill: **long *i* spelled *y***

Cy	dry	spy
Cy's	my	why

Previously Taught Skills

ask	Dad	is	milk	out
asked	did	know	Mom	will
be	drank	knows	must	
cup	his	Lin	not	

SKILLS APPLIED IN WORDS IN STORY: consonants *m, s, t, c,* short *a*; consonant *n*; consonant *d*; consonant *p*; short *i*; consonant *r*; consonant *h*; /z/ spelled *s*; consonant *b*; short *o*; consonant *l*; inflection *s*; consonant *w*; consonant *k*; short *u*; final consonants *ll*; blends with *r*; blends with *s*; final blend *st*; digraph *th*; ending *-ed* /d/; possessives with *'s*; digraph *wh*; soft *c* /s/; digraph *kn*; final consonants *nk*; long *e* (e); long *o* (ow); /ou/ spelled *ou*; long *i* spelled *y*

HIGH-FREQUENCY WORDS

a	find	said	your
family	I	the	

Houghton Mifflin Harcourt.

The Spy

High-Frequency Words Taught to Date

Grade 1

a	bring	eyes	head	me	please	take	water
about	brown	fall	hear	more	pull	talk	we
above	buy	family	heard	mother	pushed	teacher	were
across	by	far	help	my	put	the	what
after	call	father	her	myself	read	their	where
again	car	few	here	near	ready	there	who
all	carry	find	high	never	right'	these	why
almost	city	first	hold	new	said	they	window
along	cold	five	house	night	school	think	with
always	come	fly	how	no	second	those	work
and	could	follow	I	noise	see	three	world
animal	country	food	into	nothing	seven	to	would
are	covers	for	is	now	shall	today	write
around	cried	four	kinds	of	she	together	years
away	different	friend	know	off	should	too	yellow
baby	do	full	large	old	show	toward	you
ball	does	funny	laugh	once	sing	try	young
be	done	give	learning	one	small	two	your
bear	don't	go	light	open	soil	under	
because	door	goes	like	or	some	until	
been	down	good	little	our	sometimes	use	
before	draw	great	live	out	soon	very	
began	earth	green	long	over	starts	walk	
begins	eat	ground	look	own	stories	want	
bird	eight	grow	loudly	paper	story	warms	
blue	enough	happy	make	party	studied	was	
both	even	have	many	pictures	sure	wash	
boy	every	he	maybe	play	surprised	watch	

Decoding skills taught to date: consonants *m, s, t, c,* short a; consonant *n;* consonant *d;* consonant *p;* consonant *f;* short i; consonant *r;* consonant *h;* /z/ spelled *s;* consonant *b;* consonant *g* (hard); short *o;* consonant *l;* consonant *x;* inflection *s;* short *e;* consonant *y;* consonant *w;* consonant *k;* consonant *v;* consonant *j;* short *u;* /kw/ spelled *qu;* consonant *z;* final consonants *ll;* final consonants *ss;* consonants *ck;* final consonants *ff;* final consonants *zz;* blends with *r;* blends with *l;* blends with *s;* final blend *mp;* final blend *nt;* final blend *nd;* final blend *st;* digraph *th;* ending *-s;* ending *-es;* ending /ed/; ending *-ed* /t/; ending *-ed* /d/; ending *-ing;* digraphs *ch, tch;* possessives with *'s;* digraph *sh;* digraph *wh;* digraph *ph;* contractions with *'s* and *n't;* long *a* (CVC*e*); soft *c* /s/; /j/ spelled *g, dge;* long *i* (CVC*e*); digraphs *kn, gn;* digraph *wr;* digraph *mb;* long *o* (CV, CVC*e*); long *u* (CVC*e*); long *e* (*e, ee*); long *e* (CVC*e, ea*); final consonants *ng;* final consonants *nk;* long *e* (*ea, e_e*); long *a* (*ai, ay*); contractions with *'ll* and *'d;* long *o* (*ow, oa*); contractions *'ve* and *'re;* compound words; short *e* (*ea*); r-controlled *ar;* r-controlled (*or, ore*); r-controlled *er, ir,* r-controlled *ur;* /o͞o/ spelled *oo;* closed syllables (CVC); /o͞o/ spelled *ou, ew;* /o͞o/ spelled *oo;* /o͞o/ spelled *u, ue;* /o͞o/ spelled *u_e* (CVC*e*); /ou/ spelled *ou, ow;* /oi/ spelled *oy, oi;* /aw/ spelled *aw, au;* ending *–ing:* drop *e,* double consonant; ending *-ed:* drop *e,* double consonant; long *e* spelled *y, ie;* endings *–ing, -ed:* change *y* to *i;* ending *-er;* ending *-est;* ending *–er:* drop *e,* double consonant; ending *–est:* drop *e,* double consonant; endings *-er, -est:* change *y* to *i;* syllable *_le;* long *i* spelled *ie, igh;* long *i* spelled *y*

The Spy

Lin knows why Cy's cup is dry.
"I drank your milk," said Lin.

Cy must find out why his cup is
dry. Cy will be a spy. "I will ask
my family," said Cy.

"Why is my cup dry?" Cy
asked Dad. Dad did not
know why.

"Why is my cup dry?" Cy
asked Mom. Mom did not
know why.

Mike in the Sky

DECODABLE WORDS

Target Skill: **long *i* spelled *y*: change to *i*, add *-es*, *-ed***

cried	flies	spies
cries	skies	tried

Previously Taught Skills

and	fly	it	streams	wish
be	go	Mike	that	with
blue	got	off	then	writes
down	had	plane	this	zoomed
dream	he	runway	took	
dreamed	his	sky	trees	
far	in	so	up	
fields	is	start	vroom	

SKILLS APPLIED IN WORDS IN STORY: consonants *m, s, t,* c; short *a;* consonant *n;* consonant *d;* consonant *p;* consonant *f;* short *i;* consonant *r;* consonant *h;* /z/ spelled *s;* consonant *b;* consonant *g* (hard); short *o;* consonant *l;* inflection *-s;* short *e;* consonant *w;* consonant *k;* consonant *v;* final consonants *ff;* short *u;* consonant *z;* blends with *r;* blends with *l;* blends with *s;* final blend *nd;* digraph *th;* ending *-s;* ending *-es;* ending *-ed* /d/; digraph *sh;* long *a* (CVCe); long *i* (CVCe); digraph *wr;* long *o* (CV); long *e* (*e, ee, ea*); long *a* (*ay*); compound words; *r*-controlled *ar;* /o͞o/ spelled *oo;* closed syllables (CVC); /o͞o/ spelled *oo;* /o͞o/ spelled *u, ue;* /ou/ spelled *ow;* long *e* (*ie*); long *i* spelled *y;* long *i* spelled *y*: change to *i*, add *-es, -ed*

HIGH-FREQUENCY WORDS

a	I	love	the	want
great	into	over	to	would

Houghton Mifflin Harcourt.

Mike in the Sky

High-Frequency Words Taught to Date

Grade 1

a	boy	even	happy	loudly	own	starts	very
about	bring	every	have	make	paper	stories	walk
above	brown	eyes	he	many	party	story	want
across	buy	fall	head	maybe	pictures	studied	warms
after	by	family	hear	me	play	sure	was
again	call	far	heard	more	please	surprised	wash
all	car	father	help	mother	pull	take	watch
almost	carry	few	her	my	pushed	talk	water
along	city	find	here	myself	put	teacher	we
always	cold	first	high	near	read	the	were
and	come	five	hold	never	ready	their	what
animal	could	fly	house	new	right	there	where
are	country	follow	how	night	said	these	who
around	covers	food	I	no	school	they	why
away	cried	for	into	noise	second	think	window
baby	different	four	is	nothing	see	those	with
ball	do	friend	kinds	now	seven	three	work
be	does	full	know	of	shall	to	world
bear	done	funny	large	off	she	today	would
because	don't	give	laugh	old	should	together	write
been	door	go	learning	once	show	too	years
before	down	goes	light	one	sing	toward	yellow
began	draw	good	like	open	small	try	you
begins	earth	great	little	or	soil	two	young
bird	eat	green	live	our	some	under	your
blue	eight	ground	long	out	sometimes	until	
both	enough	grow	look	over	soon	use	

Decoding skills taught to date: consonants *m, s, t,* c; short *a*; consonant *n*; consonant *d*; consonant *p*; consonant *f*; short *i*; consonant *r*; consonant *h*; /z/ spelled *s*; consonant *b*; consonant *g* (hard); short *o*; consonant *l*; consonant *x*; inflection *-s*; short *e*; consonant *y*; consonant *w*; consonant *k*; consonant *v*; consonant *j*; short *u*; /kw/ spelled *qu*; consonant *z*; final consonants *ll*; final consonants *ss*; consonants *ck*; final consonants *ff*; final consonants *zz*; blends with *r*; blends with *l*; blends with *s*; final blend *mp*; final blend *nt*; final blend *nd*; final blend *st*; digraph *th*; ending *-s*; ending *-es*; ending *-ed* /ed/; ending *-ed* /d/; ending *-ed* /t/; ending *-ing*; digraphs *ch, tch*; possessives with *'s*; digraph *sh*; digraph *wh*; digraph *ph*; contractions *'s, n't*; long *a* (CVC*e*); soft *c* /s/; /j/ spelled *g, dge*; long *i* (CVC*e*); digraphs *kn, gn*; digraph *wr*; digraph *mb*; long *o* (CV, CVC*e*); long *u* (CVC*e*); long *e* (*e, ee*); long *e* (CVC*e, ea*); final consonants *ng*; final consonants *nk*; long e (*ea, e_e*); long *a* (*ai, ay*); contractions *'ll, 'd*; long *o* (*ow, oa*); contractions *'ve, 're*; compound words; short *e* (*ea*); r-controlled *ar*; r-controlled *or, ore*; r-controlled *er, ir, ur*; /o͞o/ spelled *oo*; closed syllables (CVC); /o͞o/ spelled *ou, ew*; /o͞o/ spelled *oo*; /o͞o/ spelled *u, ue*; /o͞o/ spelled *u_e* (CVC*e*); /ou/ spelled *ou, ow*; /oi/ spelled *oy, oi*; /aw/ spelled *aw, au*; ending *–ing*: drop *e*, double consonant; ending *-ed*: drop *e*, double consonant; long *e* spelled *y, ie*; endings *–ing, -ed*: change *y* to *i*; ending *–er*; ending *-est*; ending *–er*: drop *e*, double consonant; ending *–est*: drop *e*, double consonant; endings *-er, -est*: change *y* to *i*; syllable *_le*; long *i* spelled *ie, igh*; long *i* spelled *y*; long *i* spelled *y*: change to *i*, add *–es, -ed*

Mike in the Sky

Mike had a dream.

"I want to go up in the blue skies in a plane. That would be so great!" he cried.

1

Mike flies far in the blue skies. Then he writes with his plane, "I love to fly!"

4

Mike dreamed that he got his wish. He got into a plane and tried to start it. Vroom!!

Mike zoomed down the runway and took off!

"This is great!" Mike cries. He spies trees and streams. He flies over fields.

Fuzz Flies

DECODABLE WORDS

Target Skill: **long *i* spelled *y*; change to *i*, add *-es*, *-ed***

cried	dried	flies	tried	tries

Previously Taught Skills

am	far	ground	nest	try
and	fell	he	off	up
at	Fizz	how	pond	wet
bird	flap	in	so	when
brave	fly	is	saw	wings
but	flying	last	see	
down	Fuzz	Mom	still	

SKILLS APPLIED IN WORDS IN STORY: consonants *m, s, t, c*; short *a*; consonant *n*; consonant *d*; consonant *p*; consonant *f*; short *i*; consonant *r*; consonant *h*; /z/ spelled *s*; consonant *b*; consonant *g* (hard); short *o*; consonant *l*; inflection *-s*; short *e*; consonant *w*; short *u*; final consonants *ll*; final consonants *ff*; final consonants *zz*; blends with *r*; blends with *l*; blends with *s*; final blend *nd*; final blend *st*; ending *-s*; ending *-ed* /d/; ending *-ing*; digraph *wh*; long *a* (CVCe); long *o* (CV); long *e* (*e, ee*); words ending with *ng*; r-controlled *ar*; r-controlled *ir*; /ou/ spelled *ou, ow*; /au/ spelled *aw*; long *i* spelled *y*; long *i* spelled *y*: change to *i*, add *-es, -ed*

HIGH-FREQUENCY WORDS

a	baby	ready	the	was
again	I	said	to	your

Fuzz Flies

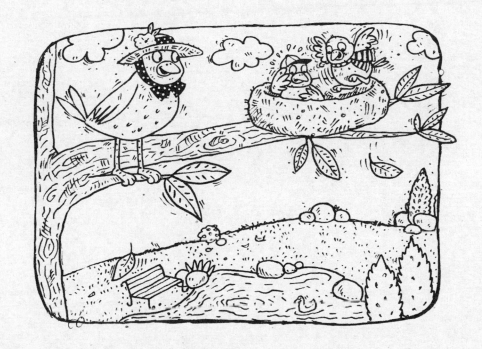

High-Frequency Words Taught to Date

Grade 1

a	boy	even	happy	loudly	own	starts	very
about	bring	every	have	make	paper	stories	walk
above	brown	eyes	he	many	party	story	want
across	buy	fall	head	maybe	pictures	studied	warms
after	by	family	hear	me	play	sure	was
again	call	far	heard	more	please	surprised	wash
all	car	father	help	mother	pull	take	watch
almost	carry	few	her	my	pushed	talk	water
along	city	find	here	myself	put	teacher	we
always	cold	first	high	near	read	the	were
and	come	five	hold	never	ready	their	what
animal	could	fly	house	new	right	there	where
are	country	follow	how	night	said	these	who
around	covers	food	I	no	school	they	why
away	cried	for	into	noise	second	think	window
baby	different	four	is	nothing	see	those	with
ball	do	friend	kinds	now	seven	three	work
be	does	full	know	of	shall	to	world
bear	done	funny	large	off	she	today	would
because	don't	give	laugh	old	should	together	write
been	door	go	learning	once	show	too	years
before	down	goes	light	one	sing	toward	yellow
began	draw	good	like	open	small	try	you
begins	earth	great	little	or	soil	two	young
bird	eat	green	live	our	some	under	your
blue	eight	ground	long	out	sometimes	until	
both	enough	grow	look	over	soon	use	

Decoding skills taught to date: consonants *m, s, t,* c; short *a*; consonant *n*; consonant *d*; consonant *p*; consonant *f*; short *i*; consonant *r*; consonant *h*; /z/ spelled *s*; consonant *b*; consonant *g* (hard); short *o*; consonant *l*; consonant *x*; inflection *-s*; short *e*; consonant *y*; consonant *w*; consonant *k*; consonant *v*; consonant *j*; short *u*; /kw/ spelled *qu*; consonant *z*; final consonants *ll*; final consonants *ss*; consonants *ck*; final consonants *ff*; final consonants *zz*; blends with *r*; blends with *l*; blends with *s*; final blend *mp*; final blend *nt*; final blend *nd*; final blend *st*; digraph *th*; ending *-s*; ending *-es*; ending *-ed* /ed/; ending *-ed* /d/; ending *-ed* /t/; ending *-ing*; digraphs *ch, tch*; possessives with *'s*; digraph *sh*; digraph *wh*; digraph *ph*; contractions *'s* and *n't*; long *a* (CVC*e*); soft *c* /s/; /j/ spelled *g, dge*; long *i* (CVC*e*); digraphs *kn, gn*; digraph *wr*; digraph *mb*; long *o* (CV, CVC*e*); long *u* (CVC*e*); long *e* (*e, ee*); long *e* (CVC*e, ea*); final consonants *ng*; final consonants *nk*; long *e* (*ea, e_e*); long *a* (*ai, ay*); contractions *'ll* and *'d*; long *o* (*ow, oa*); contractions *'ve* and *'re*; compound words; short *e* spelled *ea*; r-controlled *ar*; r-controlled *or, ore*; r-controlled *er, ir, ur*; /o͝o/ spelled *oo*; closed syllables (CVC); /o͞o/ spelled *ou, ew*; /o͞o/ spelled *oo*; /o͞o/ spelled *u, ue*; /o͞o/ spelled *u_e* (CVC*e*); /ou/ spelled *ou, ow*; /oi/ spelled *oy, oi*; /aw/ spelled *aw, au*; ending *–ing*: drop *e*, double consonant; ending *-ed*: drop *e*, double consonant; long *e* spelled *y, ie*; endings *–ing, -ed*: change *y* to *i*; ending *–er*; ending *-est*; ending *–er*: drop *e*, double consonant; ending *–est*: drop *e*, double consonant; endings *-er, -est*: change *y* to *i*; syllable *_le*; long *i* spelled *ie, igh*; long *i* spelled *y*; long *i* spelled *y*: change to *i*, add *–es, -ed*

When Fuzz dried off, he tried again. At last, he was up, up, up! "I am flying!" he cried.

4

Fuzz Flies

Fuzz is ready to fly. But Fuzz is still in the nest.
"The ground is far down," said Fuzz.

1

"Try to flap your wings," said Mom. "See how Fizz flies."

Fuzz saw Fizz fly. Flap, flap, flap! Fuzz was still in the nest.

"A brave baby bird tries and tries," said Mom.

So Fuzz tried and tried. But he fell in the pond. Fuzz was wet!

Goat and Toad's Lunch

DECODABLE WORDS

Target Skill: suffix *-ful*

basketful	handful	painful	restful	thankful

Previously Taught Skills

and	Goat	lift	on	three
ate	go	lighter	our	Toad
basket	hard	loaded	packed	Toad's
cried	hill	lunch	picnic	up
croaked	in	me	rested	with
eat	is	met	spot	
food	it	moaned	things	
for	let's	nice	this	

SKILLS APPLIED IN WORDS IN STORY: consonants *m, s, t, c*; short *a*; consonant *n*; consonant *d*; consonant *p*; consonant *f*; short *i*; consonant *r*; consonant *h*; /z/ spelled *s*; consonant *b*; consonant *g* (hard); short *o*; consonant *l*; short *e*; consonant *w*; consonant *k*; short *u*; double consonants *ll*; consonants *ck*; blends with *r*; blends with *s*; final blend *nd*; final blend *st*; digraph *th*; ending *-s*; ending *-ed* /ed/; ending *-ed* /d/; ending *-ed* /t/; possessives with *'s*; digraph *ch*; contractions *'s*; long *a* (CVC*e*); soft *c* /s/; long *i* (CVC*e*); long *o* (CV); long *e* (ee); final consonants *nk*; long *e* (ea); long *a* (ai); long *o* (oa); contractions *'ve*; closed syllables (CVC); *r*-controlled *ar*; *r*-controlled *or*; *r*-controlled *er*; /o͞o/ spelled *oo*; /ou/ spelled *ou*; ending *-er*; long *i* spelled *igh*; long *e* spelled *y*; ending *-ed*: change *y* to *i*; suffix *-ful*

HIGH-FREQUENCY WORDS

a	I	said	was
carry	I've	the	what
come	of	to	

© Houghton Mifflin Harcourt Publishing Company

suffix *-ful*

BOOK 189

Goat and Toad's Lunch

High-Frequency Words Taught to Date

Grade 1

a	brown	family	heard	more	put	there	why
about	buy	far	help	mother	read	these	window
above	by	father	her	my	ready	they	with
across	call	few	here	myself	right	think	work
after	car	find	high	near	said	those	world
again	carry	first	hold	never	school	thought	would
all	caught	five	house	new	second	three	write
almost	city	fly	how	night	see	to	years
along	cold	follow	I	no	seven	today	yellow
always	come	food	idea	noise	shall	together	you
and	could	for	into	nothing	she	too	young
animal	country	four	is	now	should	took	your
are	covers	friend	kinds	of	show	toward	
around	cried	friendship	know	off	sing	try	
away	different	full	large	old	small	two	
baby	do	funny	laugh	once	soil	under	
ball	does	give	learning	one	some	until	
be	done	go	light	open	sometimes	use	
bear	don't	goes	like	or	soon	very	
beautiful	door	good	listen	our	starts	walk	
because	down	great	little	out	stories	warms	
been	draw	green	live	over	story	was	
before	earth	ground	long	own	studied	wash	
began	eat	grow	look	paper	sure	watch	
begins	eight	happy	loudly	party	surprised	water	
bird	enough	have	make	pictures	take	we	
blue	even	have	many	play	talk	were	
both	every	he	maybe	please	teacher	what	
boy	eyes	head	me	pull	the	where	
bring	fall	hear	minute	pushed	their	who	

Decoding skills taught to date: consonants *m, s, t,* c; short *a*; consonant *n*; consonant *d*; consonant *p*; consonant *f*; short *i*; consonant *r*; consonant *h*; /z/ spelled *s*; consonant *b*; consonant *g* (hard); short *o*; consonant *l*; consonant *x*; inflection -*s*; short *e*; consonant *y*; consonant *w*; consonant *k*; consonant *v*; consonant *j*; short *u*; /kw/ spelled *qu*; consonant *z*; final consonants *ll*; final consonants *ss*; consonants *ck*; final consonants *ff*; final consonants *zz*; blends with *r*; blends with *l*; blends with *s*; final blend *mp*; final blend *nt*; final blend *nd*; final blend *st*; digraph *th*; ending -*s*; ending -*es*; ending -*ed* /ed/; ending -*ed* /d/; ending -*ed* /t/; ending -*ing*; digraphs *ch, tch*; possessives with *'s*; digraph *sh*; digraph *wh*; digraph *ph*; contractions *'s* and *n't*; long *a* (CVC*e*); soft *c* /s/; /j/ spelled *g, dge*; long *i* (CVC*e*); digraphs *kn, gn*; digraph *wr*; digraph *mb*; long *o* (CV, CVC*e*); long *u* (CVC*e*); long *e* (*e, ee*); long *e* (CVC*e, ea*); final consonants *ng*; final consonants *nk*; long *e* (*ea, e_e*); long *a* (*ai, ay*); contractions *'ll* and *'d*; long *o* (*ow, oa*); contractions *'ve* and *'re*; compound words; short *e* spelled *ea*; r-controlled *ar*; r-controlled *or, ore*; r-controlled *er, ir, ur*; /o͝o/ spelled *oo*; closed syllables (CVC); /o͞o/ spelled *ou, ew*; /o͞o/ spelled *oo*; /o͞o/ spelled *u, ue*; /o͞o/ spelled *u_e* (CVC*e*); /ou/ spelled *ou, ow*; /oi/ spelled *oy, oi*; /aw/ spelled *aw, au*; ending –*ing*: drop *e*, double consonant; ending -*ed*: drop *e*, double consonant; long *e* spelled *y, ie*; endings –*ing*, -*ed*: change *y* to *i*; ending –*er*; ending –*est*; ending –*er*: drop *e*, double consonant; ending –*est*: drop *e*, double consonant; endings -*er*, -*est*: change *y* to *i*; syllable _*le*; long *i* spelled *ie, igh*; long *i* spelled *y*; long *i* spelled *y*: change to *i*, add –*es*, -*ed*; suffix -*ful*

suffix *-ful*

BOOK 189

"This is a restful spot for our picnic. Let's eat," cried Toad.

Goat and Toad ate and rested. Goat was thankful for the lighter basket!

Goat and Toad's Lunch

Goat met Toad for a picnic. "Let's go!" said Toad. "I've packed a basketful of food for lunch."

"What is in this basket?"
moaned Goat. "It is a handful
for me to carry."
"I loaded it with three nice
things," croaked Toad.

The basket was hard to lift. It
was painful for Goat to carry.
"Come on," said Toad. "Carry
it up the hill."

Rob Sings a Song

DECODABLE WORDS

Target Skill: **suffix** *–ful*

hopeful	hurtful	joyful	thankful

Previously Taught Skills

am	he	Rabbit	song	wished
bad	his	Rob	smiled	with
but	how	Rob's	sound	
came	in	sang	stay	
can	is	see	teach	
clapped	Lark	she	that	
cried	me	sighed	then	
day	mouth	sing	tune	
didn't	not	sings	up	
good	out	singing	went	

SKILLS APPLIED IN WORDS IN STORY: consonants *m, s, t, c*; short *a*; consonant *n*; consonant *d*; consonant *p*; short *i*; consonant *f*; consonant *r*; consonant *h*; /z/ spelled *s*; consonant *b*; consonant *g* (hard); short *o*; consonant *l*; inflection *-s*; short *e*; consonant *w*; consonant *k*; consonant *j*; short *u*; blends with *r*; blends with *l*; blends with *s*; final blend *nt*; final blend *nd*; digraph *th*; ending *-ed* /d/; ending *-ed* /t/; ending *-ing*; digraph *ch*; possessives with *'s*; digraph *sh*; contractions *n't*; long *a* (CVC*e*); long *i* (CVC*e*); long *o* (CVC*e*); long *u* (CVC*e*); long *e* (*e, ee*); final blend *nk*; long *e* (*ea*); final consonants *ng*; long *a* (*ai, ay*); *r*-controlled *ar*; *r*-controlled *ur*; /o͞o/ spelled *oo*; closed syllables (CVC); /ou/ spelled *ou, ow*; /oi/ spelled *oy*; ending *-ed*: double consonant; long *i* spelled *igh*; suffix *-ful*

HIGH-FREQUENCY WORDS

a	could	of	to	you
always	give	one	was	your
beautiful	I	said	work(ed)	

Houghton Mifflin Harcourt

Rob Sings a Song

High-Frequency Words Taught to Date

Grade 1

a	brown	family	heard	more	put	there	why
about	buy	far	help	mother	read	these	window
above	by	father	her	my	ready	they	with
across	call	few	here	myself	right	think	work
after	car	find	high	near	said	those	world
again	carry	first	hold	never	school	thought	would
all	caught	five	house	new	second	three	write
almost	city	fly	how	night	see	to	years
along	cold	follow	I	no	seven	today	yellow
always	come	food	idea	noise	shall	together	you
and	could	for	into	nothing	she	too	young
animal	country	four	is	now	should	took	your
are	covers	friend	kinds	of	show	toward	
around	cried	friendship	know	off	sing	try	
away	different	full	large	old	small	two	
baby	do	funny	laugh	once	soil	under	
ball	does	give	learning	one	some	until	
be	done	go	light	open	sometimes	use	
bear	don't	goes	like	or	soon	very	
beautiful	door	good	listen	our	starts	walk	
because	down	great	little	out	stories	warms	
been	draw	green	live	over	story	was	
before	earth	ground	long	own	studied	wash	
began	eat	grow	look	paper	sure	watch	
begins	eight	happy	loudly	party	surprised	water	
bird	enough	have	make	pictures	take	we	
blue	even	have	many	play	talk	were	
both	every	he	maybe	please	teacher	what	
boy	eyes	head	me	pull	the	where	
bring	fall	hear	minute	pushed	their	who	

Decoding skills taught to date: consonants *m, s, t, c*; short *a*; consonant *n*; consonant *d*; consonant *p*; consonant *f*; short *i*; consonant *r*; consonant *h*; /z/ spelled *s*; consonant *b*; consonant *g* (hard); short *o*; consonant *l*; consonant *x*; inflection *-s*; short *e*; consonant *y*; consonant *w*; consonant *k*; consonant *v*; consonant *j*; short *u*; /kw/ spelled *qu*; consonant *z*; final consonants *ll*; final consonants *ss*; consonants *ck*; final consonants *ff*; final consonants *zz*; blends with *r*; blends with *l*; blends with *s*; final blend *mp*; final blend *nt*; final blend *nd*; final blend *st*; digraph *th*; ending *-s*; ending *-es*; ending *-ed* /ed/; ending *-ed* /d/; ending *-ed* /t/; ending *-ing*; digraphs *ch, tch*; possessives with *'s*; digraph *sh*; digraph *wh*; digraph *ph*; contractions *'s* and *n't*; long *a* (CVC*e*); soft *c*; soft *c* /s/; /j/ spelled *g, dge*; long *i* (CVC*e*); digraphs *kn, gn*; digraph *wr*; digraph *mb*; long *o* (CV, CVC*e*); long *u* (CVC*e*); long *e* (*e, ee*); long *e* (CVC*e, ea*); final consonants *ng*; final consonants *nk*; long *a* (*ai, ay*); contractions *'ll* and *'d*; long *o* (*ow, oa*) contractions *'ve* and *'re*; compound words; short *e* spelled *ea*; r-controlled *ar*; r-controlled (*or, ore*); r-controlled *er, ir, ur*; /o͞o/ spelled *oo*; closed syllables (CVC); /o͞o/ spelled *ou, ew*; /o͞o/ spelled *oo*; /o͞o/ spelled *u, ue*; /o͞o/ spelled *u_e* (CVC*e*); /ou/ spelled *ou, ow*; /oi/ spelled *oy, oi*; /aw/ spelled *aw, au*; ending *–ing*: drop *e*, double consonant; ending *-ed*: drop *e*, double consonant; long *e* spelled *y, ie*; endings *–ing, -ed*: change *y* to *i*; ending *–er*; ending *-est*; ending *–er*: drop *e*, double consonant; ending *–est*: drop *e*, double consonant; endings *-er, -est*: change *y* to *i*; syllable *_le*; long *i* spelled *ie, igh*; long *i* spelled *y*; long *i* spelled *y*: change to *i*, add *–es, -ed*; suffix *-ful*

Then one day, Rob sang.
Lark clapped. "That was
tuneful," she said.
"I am thankful that you didn't
give up," said Rob. He smiled.

© Houghton Mifflin Harcourt Publishing Company

Rob Sings a Song

Rob Rabbit wished he could
sing. But his singing was not
good. He could not stay in tune.

Rob went to see Lark. "Your singing is joyful," sighed Rob. "I am hopeful you can teach me how to sing."

Lark worked with Rob. But a bad sound always came out of Rob's mouth.

"That is hurtful," cried Lark.

The Big Race

DECODABLE WORDS

Target Skill: **suffix –ly**

badly	loudly	quickly	sadly	slowly
gladly	nicely			

Previously Taught Skills

and	flag	Kit	ran	take
at	for	Lee	rest	turns
Ben	Fran	left	Sam	up
big	Fred	line	same	us
crossed	go	lined	say	went
down	had	need	started	will
dust	he	prize	stop	win
end	huffed	puffed	that's	with
fine	in	race	time	yelled

SKILLS APPLIED IN WORDS IN STORY: consonants *m, s, t,* c; short *a*; consonant *n*; consonant *d*; consonant *p*; consonant *f*; short *i*; consonant *r*; consonant *h*; /z/ spelled *s*; consonant *b*; consonant *g* (hard); short *o*; consonant *l*, short *e*; consonant *y*; consonant *w*; consonant *k*; short *u*; /kw/ spelled *qu*; consonant *z*; final consonants *ll*; final consonants *ss*; consonants *ck*; final consonants *ff*; blends with *r*; blends with *l*; blends with *s*; final blend *nt*; final blend *nd*; final blend *st*; digraph *th*; ending *-s*; ending *–ed* /ed/; ending *–ed* /d/; ending *–ed* /t/; digraph *th*; contractions with *'s*; long *a* (CVC*e*); soft *c* /s/; long *i* (CVC*e*), long *o* (CV); long *e* (*e, ee*); long *a* (*ay*); long *o* (*ow*); r-controlled *ar*; r-controlled *or*; r-controlled *ur*; closed syllable (CVC); /ou/ spelled *ou, ow*; suffix *–ly*

HIGH-FREQUENCY WORDS

animal(s)	I	the	to	you
both	said	they	were	

© Houghton Mifflin Harcourt Publishing Company

The Big Race

High-Frequency Words Taught to Date

Grade 1

a	brown	family	help	mother	read	these	window
about	buy	far	her	my	ready	they	with
above	by	father	here	myself	right	think	work
across	call	few	high	near	said	those	world
after	car	find	hold	never	school	thought	would
again	carry	first	house	new	second	three	write
all	caught	five	how	night	see	to	years
almost	city	fly	I	no	seven	today	yellow
along	cold	follow	idea	noise	shall	together	you
always	come	food	into	nothing	she	too	young
and	could	for	is	now	should	took	your
animal	country	four	kinds	of	show	toward	
are	covers	friend	know	off	sing	try	
around	cried	friendship	large	old	small	two	
away	different	full	laugh	once	soil	under	
baby	do	funny	learning	one	some	until	
ball	does	give	light	open	sometimes	use	
be	done	go	like	or	soon	very	
bear	don't	goes	listen	our	starts	walk	
beautiful	door	good	little	out	stories	warms	
because	down	great	live	over	story	was	
been	draw	green	long	own	studied	wash	
before	earth	ground	look	paper	sure	watch	
began	eat	grow	loudly	party	surprised	water	
begins	eight	happy	make	pictures	take	we	
bird	enough	have	many	play	talk	were	
blue	even	he	maybe	please	teacher	what	
both	every	head	me	pull	the	where	
boy	eyes	hear	minute	pushed	their	who	
bring	fall	heard	more	put	there	why	

Decoding skills taught to date: consonants *m, s, t,* c; short *a*; consonant *n*; consonant *d*; consonant *p*; consonant *f*; short *i*; consonant *r*; consonant *h*; /z/ spelled *s*; consonant *b*; consonant *g* (hard); short *o*; consonant *l*; consonant *x*; inflection *-s*; short *e*; consonant *y*; consonant *w*; consonant *k*; consonant *v*; consonant *j*; short *u*; /kw/ spelled *qu*; consonant *z*; final consonants *ll*; final consonants *ss*; consonants *ck*; final consonants *ff*; final consonants *zz*; blends with *r*, blends with *l*, blends with *s*; final blend *mp*; final blend *nt*; final blend *nd*; final blend *st*; digraph *th*; ending *-s*; ending *-es*; ending *-ed* /ed/; ending *-ed* /d/; ending *-ed* /t/; ending *-ing*; digraphs *ch, tch*; possessives with *'s*; digraph *sh*; digraph *wh*; digraph *ph*; contractions with *'s, n't*; long *a* (CVC*e*); soft *c* /s/; /j/ spelled *g, dge*; long *i* (CVC*e*); digraphs *kn, gn*; digraph *wr*; digraph *mb*; long *o* (CV, CVC*e*); long *u* (CVC*e*); long *e* (*e, ee*); long *e* (CVC*e, ea*); final consonants *ng*; final consonants *nk*; long *a* (*ai, ay*); contractions *'ll* and *'d*; long *o* (*ow, oa*); contractions *'ve* and *'re*; compound words; short *e* spelled *ea*; r-controlled *ar*; r-controlled (*or, ore*); r-controlled *er, ir, ur*; /o͞o/ spelled *oo*; closed syllables (CVC); /o͞o/ spelled *ou, ew*; /o͞o/ spelled *oo*; /o͞o/ spelled *u, ue*; /o͞o/ spelled *u_e* (CVC*e*); /ou/ spelled *ou, ow*; /oi/ spelled *oy, oi*; /aw/ spelled *aw, au*; ending *–ing*: drop *e*, double consonant; ending *-ed*: drop *e*, double consonant; long *e* spelled *y, ie*; endings *–ing, -ed*: change *y* to *i*, ending *–er*, ending *-est*; ending *–er*: drop *e*, double consonant; ending *–est*: drop *e*, double consonant; endings *-er, -est*: change *y* to *i*; syllable *_le*; long *i* spelled *ie, igh*; long *i* spelled *y*, long *i* spelled *y*: change to *i*, add *–es, -ed*; suffix *-ful*; suffix *-ly*

"I gladly say you both win,"
said Sam. "You will need to take
turns with the prize."

"That's fine with us," Fran and
Fred said nicely.

4

The Big Race

The animals lined up for the
big race.

"Go!" yelled Sam loudly.

The flag went down. The race
started.

1

Kit ran badly. Lee ran slowly.
They were sadly left in the dust.
Ben huffed and puffed. He
had to stop and rest.

Fran and Fred ran quickly.
They crossed the end line at the
same time.

Little Fish

DECODABLE WORDS

Target Skill: **suffix** *–ly*

deeply	dimly	quickly	sharply	wisely

Previously Taught Skills

and	down	just	see	why
big	fish	let's	show	will
but	go	likes	so	wishes
can	good	little	swim	you
click	in	long	swims	
Dad	is	looms	teeth	
dark	it	not	them	
deep	its	sea	up	

SKILLS APPLIED IN WORDS IN STORY: consonants *m, s, t, c*; short *a*; consonant *n*; consonant *d*; consonant *p*; consonant *f*; short *i*; consonant *r*; consonant *h*; /z/ spelled *s*; consonant *b*; consonant *g* (hard); short *o*; consonant *l*; inflection *–s*; short *e*; consonant *y*; consonant *w*; consonant *k*; consonant *j*; short *u*; /kw/ spelled *qu*; final consonants *ll*; consonants *ck*; blends with *l*; blends with *s*; final blend *nd*; final blend *st*; digraph *th*; ending *–s*; ending *–es*; digraph *sh*; digraph *wh*; contractions with '*s*; long *i* (CVCe); long *o* (CV); long *e* (*e, ee*); final consonants *ng*; long *e* (*ea*); long *o* (*ow*); short *e* spelled *ea*; r-controlled *ar*; /o͞o/ spelled *oo*; closed syllables (CVC); /o͞o/ spelled *oo*; /o͞o/ spelled *ou, ew*; /ou/ spelled *ow*; /ou/ spelled *ow*; long *e* spelled *y*; syllable *_le*; long *i* spelled *y*; suffix *–ly*

HIGH-FREQUENCY WORDS

a	I	the	water
again	idea	they	
before	said	to	

Houghton Mifflin Harcourt

Little Fish

High-Frequency Words Taught to Date

Grade 1

a	brown	family	heard	more	put	there	why
about	buy	far	help	mother	read	these	window
above	by	father	her	my	ready	they	with
across	call	few	here	myself	right	think	work
after	car	find	high	near	said	those	world
again	carry	first	hold	never	school	thought	would
all	caught	five	house	new	second	three	write
almost	city	fly	how	night	see	to	years
along	cold	follow	I	no	seven	today	yellow
always	come	food	idea	noise	shall	together	you
and	could	for	into	nothing	she	too	young
animal	country	four	is	now	should	took	your
are	covers	friend	kinds	of	show	toward	
around	cried	friendship	know	off	sing	try	
away	different	full	large	old	small	two	
baby	do	funny	laugh	once	soil	under	
ball	does	give	learning	one	some	until	
be	done	go	light	open	sometimes	use	
bear	don't	goes	like	or	soon	very	
beautiful	door	good	listen	our	starts	walk	
because	down	great	little	out	stories	warms	
been	draw	green	live	over	story	was	
before	earth	ground	long	own	studied	wash	
began	eat	grow	look	paper	sure	watch	
begins	eight	happy	loudly	party	surprised	water	
bird	enough	have	make	pictures	take	we	
blue	even	have	many	play	talk	were	
both	every	he	maybe	please	teacher	what	
boy	eyes	head	me	pull	the	where	
bring	fall	hear	minute	pushed	their	who	

Decoding skills taught to date: consonants *m, s, t*, c; short *a*; consonant *n*; consonant *d*; consonant *p*; consonant *f*; short *i*; consonant *r*; consonant *h*; /z/ spelled *s*; consonant *b*; consonant *g* (hard); short *o*; consonant *l*; consonant *x*; inflection -*s*; short *e*; consonant *y*; consonant *w*; consonant *k*; consonant *v*; consonant *j*; short *u*; /kw/ spelled *qu*; consonant *z*; final consonants *ll*; final consonants *ss*; consonants *ck*; final consonants *ff*; final consonants *zz*; blends with *r*; blends with *l*; blends with *s*; final blend *mp*; final blend *nt*; final blend *nd*; final blend *st*; digraph *th*; ending -*s*; ending -*es*; ending -*ed* /ed/; ending -*ed* /d/; ending -*ed* /t/; ending -*ing*; digraphs *ch, tch*; possessives with '*s*; digraph *sh*; digraph *wh*; digraph *ph*; contractions '*s, n't*; long *a* (CVC*e*); soft *c* /s/; /j/ spelled *g, dge*; long *i* (CVC*e*); digraphs *kn, gn*; digraph *wr*; digraph *mb*; long *o* (CV, CVC*e*); long *u* (CVC*e*); long *e* (*e, ee*); long *e* (CVC*e, ea*); final consonants *ng*; final consonants *nk*; long *a* (*ai, ay*); contractions '*ll, 'd*; long *o* (*ow, oa*); contractions '*ve, 're*; compound words; short *e* spelled *ea*; r-controlled *ar*; r-controlled *or, ore*; r-controlled *er, ir, ur*; /ŏŏ/ spelled *oo*; closed syllables (CVC); /ōō/ spelled *ou, ew*; /ōō/ spelled *oo*; /ōō/ spelled *u, ue*; /ōō/ spelled *u_e* (CVC*e*); /ou/ spelled *ou, ow*; /oi/ spelled *oy, oi*; /aw/ spelled *aw, au*; ending –*ing*: drop *e*, double consonant; ending –*ed*: drop *e*, double consonant; long *e* spelled *y, ie*; endings –*ing, -ed*: change *y* to *i*; ending –*er*; ending -*est*; ending –*er*: drop *e*, double consonant; ending –*est*: drop *e*, double consonant; endings -*er, -est*: change *y* to *i*; syllable _*le*; long *i* spelled *ie, igh*; long *i* spelled *y*; long *i* spelled *y*: change to *i*, add –*es, -ed*; suffix -*ful*; suffix -*ly*

A big fish looms before them.
Its long teeth click sharply. Little
fish swims quickly up, up, up.
   "You will not go so deep again
will you," said Dad wisely.

© Houghton Mifflin Harcourt Publishing Company

Little Fish

Little fish likes to swim. He
wishes to swim deep down in the
dark sea.

"It is not a good idea to swim deeply. But let's go and I will show you why," said Dad.

Down, down in the sea they swim. The water is dark. Little fish can just see dimly.

On This Day

DECODABLE WORDS

Target Skill: suffix –y

chilly	rainy	snowy	sunny

Previously Taught Skills

and	day	it	she	warm
be	dry	may	so	wear
big	glasses	mittens	stay	will
boots	hat	Nan	sun	
coat	hot	on	then	
could	if	rain	this	
dark	is	raincoat	too	

SKILLS APPLIED IN WORDS IN STORY: consonants *m, s, t, c*; short *a*; consonant *n*; consonant *d*; consonant *p*; consonant *f*; short *i*; consonant *r*; consonant *h*; /z/ spelled *s*; consonant *b*; consonant *g* (hard); short *o*; consonant *l*, short *e*; consonant *w*; consonant *k*; short *u*; final consonants *ll*; final consonants *ss*; blends with *r*; blends with *l*; blends with *s*; ending –*s*; ending –*es*; final blend *nd*; digraph *th*; digraph *ch*; digraph *sh*; long *o* (CV); long *e* (*e*); long *a* (*ai, ay*); long *o* (*ow, oa*); compound words; short *e* (*ea*); *r*-controlled *ar*; closed syllables (CVC); /o͞o/ spelled *oo*; long *i* spelled *y*; long *e* spelled *y*; suffix –*y*

HIGH-FREQUENCY WORDS

a	put	pull	today	what

© Houghton Mifflin Harcourt Publishing Company

–y

On This Day

High-Frequency Words Taught to Date

Grade 1

a	brown	family	help	mother	read	these	why
about	buy	far	her	my	ready	they	window
above	by	father	here	myself	right	think	with
across	call	few	high	near	said	those	work
after	car	find	hold	never	school	thought	world
again	carry	first	house	new	second	three	would
all	caught	five	how	night	see	to	write
almost	city	fly	I	no	seven	today	years
along	cold	follow	idea	noise	shall	together	yellow
always	come	food	into	nothing	she	too	you
and	could	for	is	now	should	took	young
animal	country	four	kinds	of	show	toward	your
are	covers	friend	know	off	sing	try	
around	cried	friendship	large	old	small	two	
away	different	full	laugh	once	soil	under	
baby	do	funny	learning	one	some	until	
ball	does	give	light	open	sometimes	use	
be	done	go	like	or	soon	very	
bear	don't	goes	listen	our	starts	walk	
beautiful	door	good	little	out	stories	want	
because	down	great	live	over	story	warms	
been	draw	green	long	own	studied	was	
before	earth	ground	look	paper	sure	wash	
began	eat	grow	loudly	party	surprised	watch	
begins	eight	happy	make	pictures	take	water	
bird	enough	have	many	play	talk	we	
blue	even	he	maybe	please	teacher	were	
both	every	head	me	pull	the	what	
boy	eyes	hear	minute	pushed	their	where	
bring	fall	heard	more	put	there	who	

Decoding skills taught to date: consonants *m, s, t,* c; short *a*; consonant *n*; consonant *d*; consonant *p*; consonant *f*, short *i*; consonant *r*; consonant *h*; /z/ spelled *s*; consonant *b*; consonant *g* (hard); short *o*; consonant *l*; consonant *x*; inflection *-s*; short *e*; consonant *y*; consonant *w*; consonant *k*; consonant *v*; consonant *j*; short *u*; /kw/ spelled *qu*; consonant *z*; final consonants *ll*; final consonants *ss*; consonants *ck*; final consonants *ff*; final consonants *zz*; blends with *r*; blends with *l*; blends with *s*; final blend *mp*; final blend *nt*; final blend *nd*; final blend *st*; digraph *th*; ending *-s*; ending *-es*; ending *-ed* /ed/; ending *-ed* /d/; ending *-ed* /t/; ending *-ing*; digraphs *ch, tch*; possessives with *'s*; digraph *sh*; digraph *wh*; digraph *ph*; contractions *'s, n't*; long *a* (CVC*e*); soft *c* /s/; /j/ spelled *g, dge*; long *i* (CVC*e*); digraphs *kn, gn*; digraph *wr*; digraph *mb*; long *o* (CV, CVC*e*); long *u* (CVC*e*); long *e* (*e, ee*); long *e* (CVC*e, ea*); final consonants *ng*; final consonants *nk*; long *a* (*ai, ay*); contractions *'ll, 'd*; long *o* (*ow, oa*); contractions *'ve, 're*; compound words; short *e* spelled *ea*; r-controlled *ar*; r-controlled *or, ore*; r-controlled *er, ir, ur*; /o͞o/ spelled *oo*; closed syllables (CVC); /o͞o/ spelled *ou, ew*; /o͞o/ spelled *oo*; /o͞o/ spelled *u, ue*; /o͞o/ spelled *u_e* (CVC*e*); /ou/ spelled *ou, ow*; /oi/ spelled *oy, oi*; /aw/ spelled *aw, au*; ending *–ing*: drop e, double consonant; ending *-ed*: drop e, double consonant; long *e* spelled *y, ie*; endings *–ing, -ed*: change y to i; ending *–er*; ending *–est*; ending *–er*: drop e, double consonant; ending *–est*: drop e, double consonant; endings *–er, –est*: change y to i; syllable *_le*; long *i* spelled *ie, igh*; long *i* spelled *y*; long *i* spelled *y*: change to i, add *–es, –ed*; suffix *–ful*; suffix *–ly*; suffix *–y*

So what will Nan wear today?

On This Day

It may be sunny and hot today. If it is hot, Nan will put on a sun hat. She will put on dark glasses, too.

It could be rainy. Then Nan will wear a rain hat. She will put on a raincoat and rain boots. She will stay dry.

Today may be snowy and chilly. Then Nan will wear a big hat and coat. She will pull on mittens and boots. She will be warm.

Three Messy Sheep

DECODABLE WORDS

Target Skill: **suffix –y**

bushy	fluffy	messy	mushy
cloudy	fuzzy	muddy	

Previously Taught Skills

and	Fin	in	out	then
Ben	for	is	rain	three
day	gate	look	ran	too
did	get	much	see	way
eat	grass	mud	sheep	we
far	he	nice	sky	went
fell	here	not	soft	
Fen	home	on	splashed	

SKILLS APPLIED IN WORDS IN STORY: consonants *m, s, t, c*; short *a*; consonant *n*; consonant *d*; consonant *p*; consonant *f*; short *i*; consonant *r*; consonant *h*; /z/ spelled *s*; consonant *g* (hard); short *o*; consonant *l*; consonant *b*; short *e*; consonant *y*; consonant *w*; consonant *k*; short *u*; final consonants *ll*; final consonants *ss*; final consonants *ff*; final consonants *zz*; blends with *r*; blends with *l*; blends with *s*; final blend *nt*; final blend *nd*; digraph *th*; ending –*ed* /d/; ending –*ed* /t/; digraph *ch*; digraph *sh*; long *a* (CVCe); soft *c* /s/; long *i* (CVCe), long *o* (CVCe); long *e* (*e, ee*); long *e* (CVCe); long *e* (*ea*); long *a* (*ai, ay*); r-controlled *ar*; r-controlled *or*; /o͞o/ spelled *oo*; /o͝o/ spelled *oo*; vowel digraph *oo*; /ou/ spelled *ou*; long *e* spelled *y*; long *i* spelled *y*; suffix –*y*

HIGH-FREQUENCY WORDS

are	I	open(ed)	the	to
friend(s)	one	said	they	want

© Houghton Mifflin Harcourt Publishing Company

Three Messy Sheep

© Houghton Mifflin Harcourt Publishing Company

High-Frequency Words Taught to Date

Grade 1

a	boy	even	happy	look	over	starts	use
about	bring	every	have	loudly	own	stories	very
above	brown	eyes	he	make	paper	story	walk
across	buy	fall	head	many	party	studied	want
after	by	family	hear	maybe	pictures	sure	warms
again	call	far	heard	me	play	surprised	was
all	car	father	help	minute	please	take	wash
almost	carry	few	her	more	pull	talk	watch
along	caught	find	here	mother	pushed	teacher	water
always	city	first	high	my	put	the	we
and	cold	five	hold	myself	read	their	were
animal	come	fly	house	near	ready	there	what
are	could	follow	how	never	right	these	where
around	country	food	I	new	said	they	who
away	covers	for	idea	night	school	think	why
baby	cried	four	into	no	second	those	window
ball	different	friend	is	noise	see	thought	with
be	do	friendship	kinds	nothing	seven	three	work
bear	does	full	know	now	shall	to	world
beautiful	done	funny	large	of	she	today	would
because	don't	give	laugh	off	should	together	write
been	door	go	learning	old	show	too	years
before	down	goes	light	once	sing	took	yellow
began	draw	good	like	one	small	toward	you
begins	earth	great	listen	open	soil	try	young
bird	eat	green	little	or	some	two	your
blue	eight	ground	live	our	sometimes	under	
both	enough	grow	long	out	soon	until	

Decoding skills taught to date: consonants *m, s, t,* c; short *a*; consonant *n*; consonant *d*; consonant *p*; consonant *f*; short *i*; consonant *r*; consonant *h*; /z/ spelled *s*; consonant *b*; consonant *g* (hard); short *o*; consonant *l*; consonant *x*; inflection *-s*; short *e*; consonant *y*; consonant *w*; consonant *k*; consonant *v*; consonant *j*; short *u*; /kw/ spelled *qu*; consonant *z*; final consonants *ll*; final consonants *ss*; consonants *ck*; final consonants *ff*; final consonants *zz*; blends with *r*; blends with *l*; blends with *s*; final blend *mp*; final blend *nt*; final blend *nd*; final blend *st*; digraph *th*; ending *-s*; ending *-es*; ending *-ed* /ed/; ending *-ed* /d/; ending *-ed* /t/; ending *-ing*; digraphs *ch, tch*; possessives with *'s*; digraph *sh*; digraph *wh*; digraph *ph*; contractions *'s, n't*; long *a* (CVC*e*); soft *c* /s/; /j/ spelled *g, dge*; long *i* (CVC*e*); digraphs *kn, gn*; digraph *wr*; digraph *mb*; long *o* (CV, CVC*e*); long *u* (CVC*e*); long *e* (*e, ee*); long *e* (CVC*e, ea*); final consonants *ng*; final consonants *nk*; long *a* (*ai, ay*); contractions *'ll* and *'d*; long *o* (*ow, oa*); contractions *'ve* and *'re*; compound words; short *e* spelled *ea*; r-controlled *ar*; r-controlled *or, ore*; r-controlled *er, ir, ur*; /o͞o/ spelled *oo*; closed syllables (CVC); /o͞o/ spelled *ou, ew*; /o͞o/ spelled *oo*; /o͞o/ spelled *u, ue*; /o͞o/ spelled *u_e* (CVC*e*); /ou/ spelled *ou, ow*; /oi/ spelled *oy, oi*; /aw/ spelled *aw, au*; ending *-ing*: drop *e*, double consonant; ending *-ed*: drop *e*, double consonant; long *e* spelled *y, ie*; endings *-ing, -ed*: change *y* to *i*; ending *-er*; ending *-est*; ending *-er*: drop *e*, double consonant; ending *-est*: drop *e*, double consonant; endings *-er, -est*: change *y* to *i*; syllable *_le*; long *i* spelled *ie, igh*; long *i* spelled *y*; long *i* spelled *y*: change to *i*, add *-es, -ed*

The sheep ran home. They splashed in much mushy mud on the way.

"We are three muddy, messy sheep," Fin, Fen, and Ben said.

Three Messy Sheep

Fin, Fen, and Ben are friends. Fin is fluffy. Fen is fuzzy. Ben is bushy.

One day, Fin opened the gate.
"I want to eat soft grass out
here," he said.

Out went Fin. Out went Fen
and Ben, too.

The three sheep went far to
look for nice grass. They did not
see the sky get cloudy. Then the
rain fell.

Two Places, Two Animals

DECODABLE WORDS

Target Skill: open syllables (CV)

even	humid	over	spider
female	lazy	rodents	

Previously Taught Skills

and	eggs	ice	lot	seals
as	fish	in	makes	such
bear	for	insects	not	that
bears	food	is	on	these
big	he	it	packs	things
cub	her	just	place	this
damp	his	like	places	warm
eat	how	little	rains	wet
eats	hunt	lives	seabirds	

SKILLS APPLIED IN WORDS IN STORY: consonants *m, s, t, c*; short *a*; consonant *n*; consonant *d*; consonant *p*; consonant *f*; short *i*; consonant *r*; consonant *h*; /z/ spelled *s*; consonant *b*; consonant *g* (hard); short *o*; consonant *l*; inflection *-s*; short *e*; consonant *w*; consonant *k*; consonant *v*; consonant *j*; short *u*; consonant *z*; consonants *-ck*; blends with *l*; blends with *s*; final blend *mp*; final blend *nt*; final blend *nd*; final blend *st*; digraph *th*; ending *-s*; ending *-es*; digraph *ch*; digraph *sh*; long *a* (CVCe); soft *c* /s/; long *i* (CVCe); long *o* (CV); long *e* (e); long *e* (CVCe, ea); final consonants *ng*; long *a* (ai); compound words; short *e* (ea); *r*-controlled *ar*; *r*-controlled *or*; *r*-controlled *er, ir*; /o͞o/ spelled *oo*; closed syllables (CVC); /ou/ spelled *ow*; long *e* spelled *y*; syllable *_le*; open syllables (CV)

HIGH-FREQUENCY WORDS

a	earth	mother	two	where
animal(s)	even	the	very	
are	learn(s)	they	watch(es)	
cold	live(s)	to	water	

© Houghton Mifflin Harcourt Publishing Company

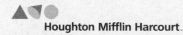
Houghton Mifflin Harcourt.

Two Places, Two Animals

High-Frequency Words Taught to Date

Grade 1

a	bring	every	have	loved	over	sorry	use
about	brothers	eyes	he	make	own	starts	very
above	brown	fall	head	many	paper	stories	walk
across	buy	family	hear	maybe	party	story	warms
after	by	far	heard	me	people	studied	was
again	call	father	help	minute	pictures	sure	wash
all	car	few	her	more	play	surprised	watch
almost	carry	field	here	most	please	take	water
along	caught	find	high	mother	pull	talk	we
always	city	first	hold	my	pushed	teacher	were
and	cold	five	house	myself	put	the	what
animal	come	fly	how	near	read	their	where
are	could	follow	I	never	ready	there	who
around	country	food	idea	new	right	these	why
away	covers	for	into	night	said	they	window
baby	cried	four	is	no	school	think	with
ball	different	friend	kinds	noise	second	those	work
be	do	friendship	know	nothing	see	thought	world
bear	does	full	large	now	seven	three	would
beautiful	done	funny	laugh	of	shall	to	write
because	don't	give	learning	off	she	today	years
been	door	go	light	old	should	together	yellow
before	down	goes	like	once	show	too	you
began	draw	good	listen	one	sing	took	young
begins	earth	great	little	only	small	toward	your
bird	eat	green	live	open	soil	try	
blue	eight	ground	long	or	some	two	
both	enough	grow	look	our	sometimes	under	
boy	even	happy	loudly	out	soon	until	

Decoding skills taught to date: consonants *m, s, t,* c; short *a*; consonant *n*; consonant *d*; consonant *p*; consonant *f*; short *i*; consonant *r*; consonant *h*; /z/ spelled *s*; consonant *b*; consonant *g* (hard); short *o*; consonant *l*; consonant *x*; inflection *-s*; short *e*; consonant *y*; consonant *w*; consonant *k*; consonant *v*; consonant *j*; short *u*; /kw/ spelled *qu*; consonant *z*; final consonants *ll*; final consonants *ss*; consonants *-ck*; final consonants *ff*; final consonants *zz*; blends with *r*, blends with *l*, blends with *s*; final blend *mp*; final blend *nt*; final blend *nd*; final blend *st*; digraph *th*; ending *-s*; ending *-es*; ending *-ed* /ed/; ending *-ed* /d/; ending *-ed* /t/; ending *-ing*; digraphs *ch, tch*; possessives with *'s*; digraph *sh*; digraph *wh*; digraph *ph*; contractions *'s, n't*; long *a* (CVC*e*); soft *c* /s/; /j/ spelled *g, dge*; long *i* (CVC*e*); digraph *wr*; digraph *mb*; long *o* (CV, CVC*e*); long *u* (CVC*e*); long *e* (*e, ee*); final consonants *ng*; final consonants *nk*; long *a* (*ai, ay*); contractions *'ll, 'd*; long *o* (*ow, oa*); contractions *'ve, 're*; compound words; short *e* (*ea*); *r*-controlled *ar*; *r*-controlled (*or, ore*); *r*-controlled *er, ir, ur*; /o͞o/ spelled *oo*; closed syllables (CVC); /o͞o/ spelled *ou, ew*; /o͞o/ spelled *oo*; /o͞o/ spelled *u, ue*; /o͞o/ spelled *u_e* (CVC*e*); /ou/ spelled *ou, ow*; /oi/ spelled *oy, oi*; /aw/ spelled *aw, au*; ending *–ing*: drop *e*, double consonant; ending *-ed*: drop *e*, double consonant; long *e* spelled *y, ie*; endings *–ing, -ed*: change *y* to *i*; ending *–er*; ending *–est*; ending *–er*: drop *e*, double consonant; ending *–est*: drop *e*, double consonant; endings *-er, -est*: change *y* to *i*; syllable *_le*; long *i* spelled *ie, igh*; long *i* spelled *y*; long *i* spelled *y*: change to *i*, add *–es, -ed*; suffix *–ful*; suffix *–ly*; suffix *–y*; open syllables (CV)

Spiders are not lazy. They hunt for food. They eat insects. This big spider even eats little rodents —just like bears!

4

Two Places, Two Animals

Some bears live in very cold places. This female bear watches over her cub. The cub watches his mother. That is how he learns to hunt.

1

These bears hunt for food on ice packs. They eat such things as seals, fish, seabirds, eggs, and little rodents.

Big spiders live in warm, wet places on earth. This spider lives where it rains a lot. The rain makes this a damp, humid place.

Making Music

DECODABLE WORDS

Target Skill: **open syllables (CV)**

banjo	program	Toby	trophy
music	student	Toby's	

Previously Taught Skills

afternoon	glad	Miss	this	we
at	go	on	tiny	win
best	had	played	took	with
big	handed	playing	trumpet	
Brown	his	she	turn	
day	last	shocked	us	
each	making	then	waited	

SKILLS APPLIED IN WORDS IN STORY: consonants *m, s, t, c*; short *a*; consonant *n*; consonant *d*; consonant *p*; consonant *f*; short *i*; consonant *h*; /z/ spelled *s*; consonant *b*; consonant *g* (hard); short *o*; consonant *l*; short *e*; consonant *w*; consonant *k*; consonant *j*; short *u*; final consonant *ss*; consonants *ck*; blends with *r*; blends with *l*; blends with *s*; final blend *nt*; final blend *nd*; final blend *st*; digraph *th*; ending *-s*; ending *-ed* /ed/; ending *-ed* /d/; ending *-ing*; digraphs *ch*; possessives with '*s*; digraph *th*; digraph *sh*; digraph *ph*; long *a* (CVCe); long *o* (CV); long *e* (ea); final consonants *ng*; final consonants *nk*; long *a* (*ai, ay*); compound words; *r*-controlled *er*; *r*-controlled *ur*; /o͞o/ spelled *oo*; closed syllables (CVC); /o͞o/ spelled *oo*; /ou/ spelled *ow*; ending *-ing*: drop *e*; long *e* spelled *y*; open syllables (CV)

HIGH-FREQUENCY WORDS

a	every	school	was
all	friend	some(thing)	who
come	one	the	would

Houghton Mifflin Harcourt.

Making Music

Music Program Today

High-Frequency Words Taught to Date

Grade 1

a	brothers	fall	hear	me	pictures	surprised	water
about	brown	family	heard	minute	play	take	we
above	buy	far	help	more	please	talk	were
across	by	father	her	most	pull	teacher	what
after	call	few	here	mother	pushed	the	where
again	car	field	high	my	put	their	who
all	carry	find	hold	myself	read	there	why
almost	caught	first	house	near	ready	these	window
along	city	five	how	never	right	they	with
always	cold	fly	I	new	said	think	work
and	come	follow	idea	night	school	those	world
animal	could	food	into	no	second	thought	would
are	country	for	is	noise	see	three	write
around	covers	four	kinds	nothing	seven	to	years
away	cried	friend	know	now	shall	today	yellow
baby	different	friendship	large	of	she	together	you
ball	do	full	laugh	off	should	too	young
be	does	funny	learning	old	show	took	your
bear	done	give	light	once	sing	toward	
beautiful	don't	go	like	one	small	try	
because	door	goes	listen	only	soil	two	
been	down	good	little	open	some	under	
before	draw	great	live	or	sometimes	until	
began	earth	green	long	our	soon	use	
begins	eat	ground	look	out	sorry	very	
bird	eight	grow	loudly	over	starts	walk	
blue	enough	happy	loved	own	stories	warms	
both	even	have	make	paper	story	was	
boy	every	he	many	party	studied	wash	
bring	eyes	head	maybe	people	sure	watch	

Decoding skills taught to date: consonants *m, s, t,* c; short *a*; consonant *n*; consonant *d*; consonant *p*; consonant *f*; short *i*; consonant *r*; consonant *h*; /z/ spelled *s*; consonant *b*; consonant *g* (hard); short *o*; consonant *l*; consonant *x*; inflection *-s*; short *e*; consonant *y*, consonant *w*, consonant *k*; consonant *v*, consonant *j*; short *u*; /kw/ spelled *qu*, consonant *z*; final consonants *ll*; final consonants *ss*; consonants *-ck*; final consonants *ff*; final consonants *zz*; blends with *r*, blends with *l*, blends with *s*; final blend *mp*; final blend *nt*; final blend *nd*; final blend *st*; digraph *th*; ending *-s*; ending *-es*; ending *-ed* /ed/; ending *-ed* /d/; ending *-ed* /t/; ending *-ing*; digraphs *ch, tch*; possessives with *'s*; digraph *sh*; digraph *wh*; digraph *ph*; contractions *'s, n't*; long *a* (CVC*e*); soft *c* /s/; /j/ spelled *g, dge*; long *i* (CVC*e*); digraph *wr*, digraph *mb*; long *o* (CV, CVC*e*); long *u* (CVC*e*); long *e* (*e, ee*); final consonants *ng*; final consonants *nk*; long *a* (*ai, ay*); contractions *'ll, 'd*; long *o* (*ow, oa*); contractions *'ve, 're*; compound words; short *e* (*ea*); *r*-controlled *ar*; *r*-controlled (*or, ore*); *r*-controlled *er, ir, ur*; /o͞o/ spelled *oo*; closed syllables (CVC); /o͞o/ spelled *ou, ew*; /o͝o/ spelled *oo*; /o͞o/ spelled *u, ue*; /o͞o/ spelled *u_e* (CVC*e*); /ou/ spelled *ou, ow*; /oi/ spelled *oy, oi*; /aw/ spelled *aw, au*; ending *-ing*: drop *e*, double consonant; ending *-ed*: drop *e*, double consonant; long *e* spelled *y, ie*; endings *-ing, -ed*: change *y* to *i*; ending *-er*; ending *-est*; ending *-er*: drop *e*, double consonant; ending *-est*: drop *e*, double consonant; endings *-er, -est*: change *y* to *i*; syllable *_le*; long *i* spelled *ie, igh*; long *i* spelled *y*, long *i* spelled *y*: change to *i*, add *-es, -ed*; suffix *-ful*; suffix *-ly*; suffix *-y*; open syllables (CV)

Music Program

Miss Brown shocked us. She handed each student a tiny trophy. We all win with music!

4

Making Music

Music Program Today

Toby was glad the big day had come at last. The music program at his school would go on this afternoon. The student who played the best would win a trophy.

1

Music Program Today

Toby's best friend played
the trumpet. Toby played
the banjo.

Each student took a turn
playing something. Then we
waited.

Decodable Words

DECODABLE WORDS

Target Skill: **prefix** *un-*

unhappy	unpacked	unwrapped

Previously Taught Skills

and	Gramps	make	saw	this
boy	happier	Mom	say	van
can	home	new	spotted	waving
day	in	no	still	we
felt	Jude	now	them	Wendy
girl	lifted	place	then	when
goodby	looked	rode	things	with

SKILLS APPLIED IN WORDS IN STORY: consonants *m, s, c*; short *a*; consonant *n*; consonant *d*; consonant *p*; consonant *f*; short *i*; consonant *r*; consonant *h*; /z/ spelled *s*; consonant *b*; consonant *g* (hard); short *o*; consonant *l*; short *e*; consonant *w*; consonant *k*; consonant *v*; consonant *j*; final consonants *ll*; consonants *ck*; blends with *r*; blends with *s*; final blends *mp, nd*; digraph *th*; ending *-ed* /ed/; ending *-ed*/t/; ending *-s*; ending *-ing*; digraph *wh*; long *a* (CVCe); soft *c* /s/; digraph *wr*; long *o* (CV; CVCe); long *e* (*e*); final consonants *ng*; long *a* (*ai*); compound words; *r*-controlled *ir*; /oo/ spelled *oo*; closed syllables (CVC); /oo/ spelled *ew*; /oo/ spelled *u_e* (CVCe); /ou/ spelled *ow*; /oi/ spelled *oy*; /au/ spelled *aw*; ending *–ing*: drop *e*; ending *–ed*; double consonant; long *e* spelled *y*; long *i* spelled *y*; endings *-er, -est*: change *y* to *i*; open syllables (CV); prefix *un-*

HIGH-FREQUENCY WORDS

a	every	one	they	was
all	family	the	thought	watch
carry	friend(s)	their	to	were

Houghton Mifflin Harcourt

A New Home

High-Frequency Words Taught to Date

Grade 1

a	bring	every	have	loved	over	sorry	use
about	brothers	eyes	he	make	own	starts	very
above	brown	fall	head	many	paper	stories	walk
across	buy	family	hear	maybe	party	story	want
after	by	far	heard	me	people	studied	warms
again	call	father	help	minute	pictures	sure	was
all	car	few	her	more	play	surprised	wash
almost	carry	field	here	most	please	take	watch
along	caught	find	high	mother	pull	talk	water
always	city	first	hold	my	pushed	teacher	we
and	cold	five	house	myself	put	the	were
animal	come	fly	how	near	read	their	what
are	could	follow	I	never	ready	there	where
around	country	food	idea	new	right	these	who
away	covers	for	into	night	said	they	why
baby	cried	four	is	no	school	think	window
ball	different	friend	kinds	noise	second	those	with
be	do	friendship	know	nothing	see	thought	work
bear	does	full	large	now	seven	three	world
beautiful	done	funny	laugh	of	shall	to	would
because	don't	give	learning	off	she	today	write
been	door	go	light	old	should	together	years
before	down	goes	like	once	show	too	yellow
began	draw	good	listen	one	sing	took	you
begins	earth	great	little	only	small	toward	young
bird	eat	green	live	open	soil	try	your
blue	eight	ground	long	or	some	two	
both	enough	grow	look	our	sometimes	under	
boy	even	happy	loudly	out	soon	until	

Decoding skills taught to date: consonants *m, s, t, c*; short *a*; consonant *n*; consonant *d*; consonant *p*; consonant *f*; short *i*; consonant *r*; consonant *h*; /z/ spelled *s*; consonant *b*; consonant *g* (hard); short *o*; consonant *l*; consonant *x*; inflection *-s*; short *e*; consonant *y*; consonant *w*; consonant *k*; consonant *v*; consonant *j*; short *u*; /kw/ spelled *qu*; consonant *z*; final consonants *ll*; final consonants *ss*; consonants *-ck*; final consonants *ff*; final consonants *zz*; blends with *r*, blends with *l*, blends with *s*; final blend *mp*; final blend *nt*; final blend *nd*; final blend *st*; digraph *th*; ending *-s*; ending *-es*; ending *-ed* /ed/; ending *-ed* /d/; ending *-ed* /t/; ending *-ing*; digraphs *ch, tch*; possessives with *'s*; digraph *sh*; digraph *wh*; digraph *ph*; contractions *'s, n't*; long *a* (CVC*e*); soft *c* /s/; /j/ spelled *g, dge*; long *i* (CVC*e*); digraph *wr*, digraph *mb*; long *o* (CV, CVC*e*); long *u* (CVC*e*); long *e* (*e, ee*); final consonants *ng*; final consonants *nk*; long *a* (*ai, ay*); contractions *'ll, 'd*; long *o* (*ow, oa*); contractions *'ve, 're*; compound words; short *e* (*ea*); *r*-controlled *ar*, *r*-controlled (*or, ore*); *r*-controlled *er, ir*, *r*-controlled *ur*; /ŏŏ/ spelled *oo*; closed syllables (CVC); /ŏŏ/ spelled *ou, ew*, /ōō/ spelled *oo*, /ōō/ spelled *u, ue*; /ōō/ spelled *u_e* (CVC*e*); /ou/ spelled *ou, ow*; /oi/ spelled *oy, oi*; /aw/ spelled *aw, au*; ending *–ing*: drop *e*, double consonant; ending *-ed*: drop *e*, double consonant; long *e* spelled *y, ie*; endings *–ing, -ed*: change *y* to *i*; ending *–er*; ending *-est*; ending *–er*: drop *e*, double consonant; ending *–est*: drop *e*, double consonant; endings *-er, -est*: change *y* to *i*; syllable *_le*; long *i* spelled *ie, igh*; long *i* spelled *y*; long *i* spelled *y*: change to *i*, add *-es, -ed*; suffix *–ful*; suffix *–ly*; suffix *–y*; open syllables (CV); prefix *un-*

Then Jude and Wendy saw
a boy and girl waving to them.
"We can make new friends,"
they thought. Now no one
was unhappy.

A New Home

Jude and Wendy rode in the
van with Mom and Gramps.
Everyone felt unhappy to say
good-by to this place.

Mom and Gramps looked happier when they spotted their new home. Jude and Wendy were still unhappy.

All day the family unpacked, unwrapped, and lifted things. Jude and Wendy were still unhappy.

Decodable Words

DECODABLE WORDS

Target Skill: **prefix** *un-*

unable	uncover	unsafe	unwilling

Previously Taught Skills

and	down	is	out	track
at	explore	it	park	under
be	for	like	pick	up
bite	from	look	plants	will
boys	get	may	rocks	willing
bugs	girls	no	still	you
but	hard	not	sting	
can	if	on	them	
city	in	or	too	

SKILLS APPLIED IN WORDS IN STORY: consonants *m, s, t,* c; short *a*; consonant *n*; consonant *d*; consonant *p*; consonant *f*; short *i*; consonant *r*; consonant *h*; /z/ spelled *s*; consonant *b*; consonant *g* (hard); short *o*; consonant *l*; consonant *x*; short *e*; consonant *y*; consonant *w*; consonant *k*; short *u*; final consonants *ll*; consonants *-ck*; blends with *r*; blends with *l*; blends with *s*; final blends *nt, nd*; digraph *th*; ending *-s*; ending *-ing*; digraph *tch*; long *a* (CVCe); soft *c* /s/; long *i* (CVCe); long *o* (CV); long *e* (e); final consonants *ng*; long *a* (ay); compound words; *r*-controlled *ar*; *r*-controlled (*or, ore*); *r*-controlled *er, ir*; *r*-controlled *ur*; /o͞o/ spelled *oo*; closed syllables (CVC); /o͞o/ spelled *ou, ew*; /o͞o/ spelled *oo*; /ou/ spelled *ou, ow*; /oi/ spelled *oy*; long e spelled *y*; syllable *_le*; open syllables (CV); prefix *un-*

HIGH-FREQUENCY WORDS

a	country	find	some	to
are	everywhere	live	the	watch

Houghton Mifflin Harcourt.

Explore!

High-Frequency Words Taught to Date

Grade 1

a	bring	every	have	loved	over	sorry	use
about	brothers	eyes	he	make	own	starts	very
above	brown	fall	head	many	paper	stories	walk
across	buy	family	hear	maybe	party	story	want
after	by	far	heard	me	people	studied	warms
again	call	father	help	minute	pictures	sure	was
all	car	few	her	more	play	surprised	wash
almost	carry	field	here	most	please	take	watch
along	caught	find	high	mother	pull	talk	water
always	city	first	hold	my	pushed	teacher	we
and	cold	five	house	myself	put	the	were
animal	come	fly	how	near	read	their	what
are	could	follow	I	never	ready	there	where
around	country	food	idea	new	right	these	who
away	covers	for	into	night	said	they	why
baby	cried	four	is	no	school	think	window
ball	different	friend	kinds	noise	second	those	with
be	do	friendship	know	nothing	see	thought	work
bear	does	full	large	now	seven	three	world
beautiful	done	funny	laugh	of	shall	to	would
because	don't	give	learning	off	she	today	write
been	door	go	light	old	should	together	years
before	down	goes	like	once	show	too	yellow
began	draw	good	listen	one	sing	took	you
begins	earth	great	little	only	small	toward	young
bird	eat	green	live	open	soil	try	your
blue	eight	ground	long	or	some	two	
both	enough	grow	look	our	sometimes	under	
boy	even	happy	loudly	out	soon	until	

Decoding skills taught to date: consonants *m, s, t,* c; short *a*; consonant *n*; consonant *d*; consonant *p*; consonant *f*; short *i*; consonant *r*; consonant *h*; /z/ spelled *s*; consonant *b*; consonant *g* (hard); short *o*; consonant *l*; consonant *x*; inflection *-s*; short *e*; consonant *y*; consonant *w*; consonant *k*; consonant *v*; consonant *j*; short *u*; /kw/ spelled *qu*; consonant *z*; final consonants *ll*; final consonants *ss*; consonants *-ck*; final consonants *ff*; final consonants *zz*; blends with *r*; blends with *l*; blends with *s*; final blend *mp*; final blend *nt*; final blend *nd*; final blend *st*; digraph *th*; ending *-s*; ending *-es*; ending *-ed* /ed/; ending *-ed* /d/; ending *-ed* /t/; ending *-ing*; digraphs *ch, tch*; possessives with *'s*; digraph *sh*; digraph *wh*; digraph *ph*; contractions *'s, n't*; long *a* (CVC*e*); soft *c* /s/; /j/ spelled *g, dge*; long *i* (CVC*e*); digraph *wr*; digraph *mb*; long *o* (CV, CVC*e*); long *u* (CVC*e*); long *e* (*e, ee*); final consonants *ng*; final consonants *nk*; long *a* (*ai, ay*); contractions *'ll, 'd*; long *o* (*ow, oa*); contractions *'ve, 're*; compound words; short *e* (*ea*); r-controlled *ar*; r-controlled (*or, ore*); r-controlled *er, ir*; r-controlled *ur*; /o͝o/ spelled *oo*; closed syllables (CVC); /o͞o/ spelled *ou, ew*; /o͞o/ spelled *oo*; /o͞o/ spelled *u, ue*; /o͞o/ spelled *u_e* (CVC*e*); /ou/ spelled *ou, ow*; /oi/ spelled *oy, oi*; /aw/ spelled *aw, au*; ending *–ing*: drop *e*, double consonant; ending *-ed*: drop *e*, double consonant; long *e* spelled *y, ie*; endings *–ing, -ed*: change *y* to *i*; ending *–er*; ending *–est*; ending *–er*: drop *e*, double consonant; ending *–est*: drop *e*, double consonant; endings *-er, -est*: change *y* to *i*; syllable *_le*; long *i* spelled *ie, igh*; long *i* spelled *y*; long *i* spelled *y*: change to *i*, add *–es, -ed*; suffix *–ful*; suffix *–ly*; suffix *–y*; open syllables (CV); prefix *un-*

You may be unwilling to pick up bugs. But if you are willing, watch out! It may be unsafe to pick them up. Some bugs bite or sting.

Explore

Boys and girls everywhere like to look at bugs. To track down bugs, get out and explore!

If you live in the country, it is not hard to find bugs. If you live in the city, will you be unable to find bugs? No! You can still explore for bugs in a park.

Look for bugs on plants. You can uncover bugs from under rocks, too.

Our Stories

DECODABLE WORDS

Target Skill: **prefix re-**

recheck	reread	rethink	rewrite

Previously Taught Skills

asked	explained	next	story	with
Blake	first	not	stories	write
can	happy	now	that	wrote
checked	her	our	them	you
class	is	own	then	
complete	it	part	until	
don't	like	read	us	
drafts	Miss	she	will	

SKILLS APPLIED IN WORDS IN STORY: consonants *m, s, t, c*; short *a*; consonant *n*; consonant *d*; consonant *p*; consonant *f*; short *i*; consonant *r*; consonant *h*; /z/ spelled *s*; short *o*; consonant *l*; consonant *x*; short *e*; consonant *y*; consonant *w*; consonant *k*; short *u*; final consonants *ll*; final consonants *ss*; consonants *-ck*; blends with *r, l, s*; final blend *st*; digraph *th*; ending *-s*; ending *-ed* /d/; ending *-ed* /t/; digraph *ch*; digraph *sh*; contraction *n't*; long *a* (CVCe); long *i* (CVCe); digraph *wr*; long *o* (CVCe); long *e* (*e, e_e*); long *e* (*ea*); final consonants *nk*; long *a* (*ai*); long *o* (*ow*); compound words; *r*-controlled *ar*; *r*-controlled *or*; *r*-controlled *er, ir*; closed syllables (CVC); /o͞o/ spelled *ou, ew*; /ou/ spelled *ou, ow*; long *e* spelled *y*; open syllables (CV); prefixe *re-*

HIGH-FREQUENCY WORDS

a	are	their	thought	your
about	everyone	there	to	
all	said	they	what	

Our Stories

High-Frequency Words Taught to Date

Grade 1

a	bring	every	have	loved	over	sorry	use
about	brothers	eyes	he	make	own	starts	very
above	brown	fall	head	many	paper	stories	walk
across	buy	family	hear	maybe	party	story	warms
after	by	far	heard	me	people	studied	was
again	call	father	help	minute	pictures	sure	wash
all	car	few	her	more	play	surprised	watch
almost	carry	field	here	most	please	take	water
along	caught	find	high	mother	pull	talk	we
always	city	first	hold	my	pushed	teacher	were
and	cold	five	house	myself	put	the	what
animal	come	fly	how	near	read	their	where
are	could	follow	I	never	ready	there	who
around	country	food	idea	new	right	these	why
away	covers	for	into	night	said	they	window
baby	cried	four	is	no	school	think	with
ball	different	friend	kinds	noise	second	those	work
be	do	friendship	know	nothing	see	thought	world
bear	does	full	large	now	seven	three	would
beautiful	done	funny	laugh	of	shall	to	write
because	don't	give	learning	off	she	today	years
been	door	go	light	old	should	together	yellow
before	down	goes	like	once	show	too	you
began	draw	good	listen	one	sing	took	young
begins	earth	great	little	only	small	toward	your
bird	eat	green	live	open	soil	try	
blue	eight	ground	long	or	some	two	
both	enough	grow	look	our	sometimes	under	
boy	even	happy	loudly	out	soon	until	

Decoding skills taught to date: consonants *m, s, t, c;* short *a;* consonant *n;* consonant *d;* consonant *p;* consonant *f;* short *i;* consonant *r;* consonant *h;* /z/ spelled *s;* consonant *b;* consonant *g* (hard); short *o;* consonant *l;* consonant *x;* inflection *-s;* short *e;* consonants *y;* consonants *w;* consonants *k;* consonant *v;* consonant *j;* short *u;* /kw/ spelled *qu;* consonant *z;* final consonants *ll;* final consonants *ss;* consonants *-ck;* final consonants *ff;* final consonants *zz;* blends with *r;* blends with *l;* blends with *s;* final blend *mp;* final blend *nt;* final blend *nd;* final blend *st;* digraph *th;* ending *-s;* ending *-es;* ending *-ed;* ending *-ed* /ĕd/; ending *-ed* /d/; ending *-ed* /t/; ending *-ing;* digraphs *ch, tch;* possessives *'s;* digraph *sh;* digraph *wh;* digraph *ph;* contractions *'s, n't;* long *a* (CVC*e*); soft *c* /s/; /j/ spelled *g, dge;* long *i* (CVC*e*); digraph *wr;* digraph *mb;* long *o* (CV, CVC*e*); long *u* (CVC*e*); long *e* (*e, ee*); final consonants *ng;* final consonants *nk;* long *a* (*ai, ay*); contractions *'ll, 'd;* long *o* (*ow, oa*); contractions *'ve, 're;* compound words; short *e* (*ea*); *r*-controlled *ar;* *r*-controlled (*or, ore*); *r*-controlled *er, ir;* *r*-controlled *ur;* /o͞o/ spelled *oo;* closed syllables (CVC); /o͞o/ spelled *ou, ew;* /o͞o/ spelled *oo;* /o͞o/ spelled *u, ue;* /o͞o/ spelled *u_e* (CVC*e*); /ou/ spelled *ou, ow;* /oi/ spelled *oy, oi;* /aw/ spelled *aw, au;* ending *–ing:* drop *e,* double consonant; ending *-ed:* drop *e,* double consonant; long *e* spelled *y, ie;* endings *–ing, -ed:* change *y* to *i;* ending *-er;* ending *-est;* ending *–er:* drop *e,* double consonant; ending *–est:* drop *e,* double consonant; endings *-er, -est:* change *y* to *i;* syllable *–le;* long *i* spelled *ie, igh;* long *i* spelled *y;* long *i* spelled *y:* change to *i,* add *–es, -ed;* suffix *–ful;* suffix *-ly;* suffix *-y;* open syllables (CV); prefix *un-,* prefix *re-*

"Now recheck your stories,"
Miss Blake said. "Then you will
all read them to us!"

4

Our Stories

Miss Blake asked her class to
write their own stories. Everyone
thought about what to write.
Then they wrote their first drafts.

1

Miss Blake explained that a story is not complete until it is checked. "First, reread your story," she said.

Next Miss Blake asked, "Are you happy with your story? Is there a part you don't like? You can rethink what you wrote. Then you can rewrite that part."

Waste Less

DECODABLE WORDS

Target Skill: **prefix** *re-*

recycle	recycled	refill	refilling	reuse

Previously Taught Skills

and	cans	less	that	we
at	can't	look	them	you
be	don't	make	things	
bin	how	more	this	
bottle	in	over	trash	
bottles	instead	paper	use	
by	is	plastic	waste	
can	it	same	way	

SKILLS APPLIED IN WORDS IN STORY: consonants *m, s, t, c*; short *a*; consonant *n*; consonant *d*; consonant *p*; consonant *f*; short *i*; consonant *h*; /z/ spelled *s*; consonant *b*; short *o*; consonant *l*; short *e*; consonant *y*; consonant *w*; consonant *k*; consonant *v*; final consonants *ll*; final consonants *ss*; blends with *r*; blends with *l*; blends with *s*; final blend *nd*; digraph *th*; ending *-s*; ending *-ed* /d/; ending *-ing*; digraph *sh*; contractions *n't*; long *a* (CVCe); soft *c* /s/; long *o* (CV); long *u* (CVCe); long *e* (e); final consonants *ng*; long *a* (ay); compound words; short *e* (ea); r-controlled *ore*; r-controlled *er*; /o͞o/ spelled *oo*; closed syllables (CVC); /o͞o/ spelled *ou*; syllable *_le*; long *i* spelled *y*; /ou/ spelled *ow*; open syllables (CV); prefix *re-*

HIGH-FREQUENCY WORDS

a	buy	one	the	water
all	everyone	put	to	

Waste Less

High-Frequency Words Taught to Date

Grade 1

a	bring	every	have	loved	over	sorry	use
about	brothers	eyes	he	make	own	starts	very
above	brown	fall	head	many	paper	stories	walk
across	buy	family	hear	maybe	party	story	warms
after	by	far	heard	me	people	studied	was
again	call	father	help	minute	pictures	sure	wash
all	car	few	her	more	play	surprised	watch
almost	carry	field	here	most	please	take	water
along	caught	find	high	mother	pull	talk	we
always	city	first	hold	my	pushed	teacher	were
and	cold	five	house	myself	put	the	what
animal	come	fly	how	near	read	their	where
are	could	follow	I	never	ready	there	who
around	country	food	idea	new	right	these	why
away	covers	for	into	night	said	they	window
baby	cried	four	is	no	school	think	with
ball	different	friend	kinds	noise	second	those	work
be	do	friendship	know	nothing	see	thought	world
bear	does	full	large	now	seven	three	would
beautiful	done	funny	laugh	of	shall	to	write
because	don't	give	learning	off	she	today	years
been	door	go	light	old	should	together	yellow
before	down	goes	like	once	show	too	you
began	draw	good	listen	one	sing	took	young
begins	earth	great	little	only	small	toward	your
bird	eat	green	live	open	soil	try	
blue	eight	ground	long	or	some	two	
both	enough	grow	look	our	sometimes	under	
boy	even	happy	loudly	out	soon	until	

Decoding skills taught to date: consonants *m, s, t, c*; short *a*; consonant *n*; consonant *d*; consonant *p*; consonant *f*; short *i*; consonant *r*; consonants *h*; /z/ spelled *s*; consonant *b*; consonant *g* (hard); short *o*; consonant *l*; consonant *x*; inflection *-s*; short *e*; consonant *y*; consonant *w*; consonant *k*; consonant *v*; consonant *j*; short *u*; /kw/ spelled *qu*; consonant *z*; final consonants *ll*; final consonants *ss*; consonants *-ck*; final consonants *ff*; final consonants *zz*; blends with *r*; blends with *l*; blends with *s*; final blend *mp*; final blend *nt*; final blend *nd*; final blend *st*; digraph *th*; ending *-s*; ending *-es*; ending *-ed* /ed/; ending *-ed* /d/; ending *-ed* /t/; ending *-ing*; digraphs *ch, tch*; possessives with *'s*; digraph *sh*; digraph *wh*; digraph *ph*; contractions *'s, n't*; long *a* (CVCe); soft *c* /s/; /j/ spelled *g, dge*; long *i* (CVCe); digraph *wr*; digraph *mb*; long *o* (CV, CVCe); long *u* (CVCe); long *e* (*e, ee*); final consonants *ng*; final consonants *nk*; long *a* (*ai, ay*); contractions *'ll, 'd*; long *o* (*ow, oa*); contractions *'ve, 're*; compound words; short *e* (*ea*); r-controlled *ar*; r-controlled (*or, ore*); r-controlled *er, ir*; r-controlled *ur*; /o͞o/ spelled *oo*; closed syllables (CVC); /o͞o/ spelled *ou, ew*; /o͞o/ spelled *oo*; /o͞o/ spelled *u, ue*; /o͞o/ spelled *u_e* (CVCe); /ou/ spelled *ou, ow*; /oi/ spelled *oi*; /aw/ spelled *aw, au*; ending *–ing*: drop *e*, double consonant; ending *-ed*: drop *e*, double consonant; long *e* spelled *y, ie*; endings *–ing, -ed*: change *y* to *i*; ending *-er*; ending *-est*; ending *-er*: drop *e*, double consonant; ending *-est*: drop *e*, double consonant; endings *-er, -est*: change *y* to *i*; syllable *_le*; long *i* spelled *ie, igh*; long *i* spelled *y*; long *i* spelled *y*: change to *i*, add *-es, -ed*; suffix *-ful*; suffix *-ly*; suffix *-y*; open syllables (CV); prefix *un-*; prefix *re-*

Waste Less

Everyone can waste less.
Recycle and reuse, don't waste.

Look at all this trash! How can we make less waste?

4

1

One way to waste less is to recycle. Don't put bottles, paper, plastic, and cans in the trash. Put them in a bin to be recycled instead.

One more way to make less waste is to reuse things. Don't buy water in plastic bottles that you can't refill. Use the same bottle over and over by refilling it.